ᔡ The Poetics of Impudence and Intimacy in the
Age of Pushkin

To Pavel
Samoilovich,
with great respect
and much
gratitude,
    Joe

D1738813

Publications of the Wisconsin Center for Pushkin Studies

David M. Bethea and Alexander Dolinin
Series Editors

The Poetics of Impudence and Intimacy in the Age of Pushkin

Joe Peschio

THE UNIVERSITY OF WISCONSIN PRESS

Publication of this volume has been made possible, in part, through support from the Andrew W. Mellon Foundation and from the Wisconsin Center for Pushkin Studies in the Department of Slavic Languages of the University of Wisconsin – Madison.

The University of Wisconsin Press
1930 Monroe Street, 3rd Floor
Madison, Wisconsin 53711-2059
uwpress.wisc.edu

3 Henrietta Street
London WC2E 8LU, England
eurospanbookstore.com

Printed in the United States of America

Library of Congress Cataloging-in-Publication Data

Peschio, Joe.
    The poetics of impudence and intimacy in the age of Pushkin / Joe Peschio.
        p.   cm. — (Publications of the Wisconsin Center for Pushkin Studies)
    Includes bibliographical references and index.
    ISBN 978-0-299-29044-3 (pbk. : alk. paper) — ISBN 978-0-299-29043-6 (e-book)
        1. Russian literature—19th century—History and criticism. 2. Russian wit and humor—19th century—History and criticism. 3. Pushkin, Aleksandr Sergeevich, 1799–1837—Criticism and interpretation. 4. Arzamas (Literary circle) I. Title. II. Series: Publications of the Wisconsin Center for Pushkin Studies.
PG3012.P47   2012
891.709'003—dc23
                                                                                    2012010173

For Richard Daly (1914–99)
and Daniel Peschio (1910–2009)

Contents

Acknowledgments

This book has been in the works for a long time, and I owe a debt of gratitude to more family, friends, colleagues, administrators, and students than I can possibly list here. However, I would first like to thank the Milwaukee thieves who spirited away the computers and all the backup DVDs containing the first, almost complete draft of this book when they burglarized our home in June 2009. There is no doubt in my mind that it is better for having once been lost irrevocably and rewritten from memory and moldy printouts (though I wish they hadn't stolen my great grandmother's engagement ring). Aside from these kind souls, none of the individuals and institutions named here bear responsibility for this book's shortcomings and failures, and the views expressed in it do not necessarily represent their own.

My wife, Elena Zakharova, has lived with this book almost as long as I have, and I could not have finished it without her patience and good humor. My friend, collaborator, and mentor Igor Pil'shchikov, who broke much of the ground tread here, has been incredibly generous with comments, advice, corrections, instruction, and pep talks over the years. Alyssa Gillespie read a draft of the manuscript and provided invaluable feedback as well as a great deal of moral support. My teachers at the University of Wyoming and the University of Michigan – Lewis Bagby, Deborah Keller-Cohen, Michael Makin, John Mersereau, David Porter, Omry Ronen, Andreas Schönle, Serge Shishkoff, Pavel Sigalov, and Andrei Zorin – inspired, nurtured and guided the project at its very earliest stages.

Many librarians and archivists here and abroad showed me exceptional kindness while I was conducting the research for this book. Among them, I would like to single out for special thanks the staff at the Institute for Russian Literature (Pushkin House) in Saint Petersburg, and particularly Tatiana Krasnoborodko, the head Pushkin archivist, whom I have to thank for making possible all my work on the Green Lamp.

My colleagues at the University of Wisconsin–Milwaukee are also due my sincerest thanks. Without their unflagging support for the nascent Russian program here and without their scholarly counsel, I would not have been able to see this project through. The UWM Classics Program faculty, with whom I am privileged to share a corridor, were regular and enthusiastic guides to my classical subtexts. Lorena Terando of the UWM Translation Program assisted me with translations from the French. I would especially like to thank Ruth Schwertfeger of the UWM German Program, who commented on early drafts and guided me through the publication process. It was her constant encouragement that gave me the gumption to try to get this book published and the fortitude to overcome all manner of setbacks.

I am eternally indebted to my heroic copyeditor, Marlyn Miller, and the wonderful collective at the University of Wisconsin Press. Series Editor David Bethea has been remarkably supportive of the project throughout. I am also grateful to Gwen Walker, Sheila McMahon, and their associates at the press for all their kindness and help.

The research and writing of this book were supported by grants and fellowships from the American Council of Teachers of Russian, the Fulbright-Hays Program, and the National Endowment for the Humanities, as well as the Rackham School of Graduate Studies and the Center for Russian and East European Studies at the University of Michigan. I also received generous support in the form of travel funding and teaching releases from the Department of Foreign Languages and Literature, the College of Letters and Science, and the Graduate School at the University of Wisconsin–Milwaukee.

This book is dedicated to my grandfathers. I have in my possession two artifacts that were always near to hand as I wrote it. First is Dr. Daniel Peschio's stethoscope, which he used to listen to many a human heart. Second is a silver cup that belonged to Richard Daly. It is inscribed with a cryptic graphic that reads "SBC," as well as the words "Dick Daly, President." My discovery that "SBC" stands for "Stupid Bastards Club," a familiar society that he founded in the 1960s, was my first bit of research on such societies. I am grateful to my grandfathers for a great many things and can only hope that, were they still alive, they would not hesitate to nominate me to the ranks of Stupid Bastards for having written such a book.

Note on Transliteration and Translation

Russian words and names in this book have been transliterated using a simplified version (without ligatures and diacritics) of the Library of Congress Romanization table. All translations are my own except where otherwise indicated.

∾ *The Poetics of Impudence and Intimacy in the Age of Pushkin*

Introduction

According to legend, it was around three in the morning when the knock came at the door.[1] Outside, in the Russian expression, June of 1826 was standing in the yard. These were tough times. Six months had passed since the Decembrist Uprising, and over three thousand people had already been arrested on suspicion of sedition.[2] The new tsar, Nicholas I, had created an Investigatory Commission, and his gendarmerie was single-mindedly focused on rounding up all the conspirators and their sympathizers, friends, and relatives for detention, interrogation, and torture all over the empire and abroad. The bureaucratic apparatus created for this purpose was later institutionalized as the now infamous "Third Section" (*Tret'e otdelenie*), a secret police organ of unprecedented scope and savvy.

The door at which the knock came was Aleksandr Polezhaev's door in a student boarding house near Moscow University. The tsar was in town to prepare for his coronation ceremony, a grim holiday for many. And he wanted to see Polezhaev personally.

Polezhaev had just finished university with some success and a degree in literature. The bastard son of a nobleman, he had been left to fend for himself without rank, means, or family – handed over to his aunt, who was a cattle herd, at the age of six. Somewhat miraculously, when his father fetched him from the barn and sent him to the university some years later, Polezhaev shined in the hard-scrabble student life of the 1820s, making a considerable name for himself as a gifted poet by the age of twenty-two and testing into a rank that granted him status as a "personal" (i.e., non-hereditary) nobleman. Polezhaev's muse was a free-wheeling one in keeping with the libertine bent of his student life. His poems were not fettered by the stylistic and moral constraints of literary propriety. As one school textbook anthologizer very aptly puts it, "his poetic thumbing-of-the-nose – at both stylistic and thematic convention – was perceived by the student milieu of the time as something equivalent to a bold social-political statement, a 'slap in the face to public taste' in its own right."[3] This free-wheeling muse found its apotheosis in Polezhaev's burlesque "Sashka" ("Sashka," 1825) – a comic *poema* drawn from student life, which most scholars agree is a parody of *Eugene Onegin*. And it was "Sashka" that the tsar held in his hand when Polezhaev entered his Kremlin *kabinet* that night in June 1826.

But back to the knock. When he opened the door, a blowsy Polezhaev was ordered to report to the rector's office immediately. When he got there, he was met by the rector and his boss, the head warden of the Moscow Educational District, who whisked him off to the residence of the minister of popular education,

3

Admiral Aleksandr Shishkov. Shishkov, in turn, took Polezhaev to the Kremlin for an audience with the tsar. Once there, the tsar ordered him to read aloud a copy of "Sashka" prepared by Imperial scribes – so that Shishkov could hear for himself "what they're teaching at the university." Polezhaev attempted to demur, but was again ordered to read. He later recalled: "Never had I seen "Sashka" so beautifully copied and on such fine paper!"[4] When he finished, the tsar turned to his minister and vowed to put an end to such immorality, saying that these were "the last remnants" (apparently of the dissent that had precipitated the Decembrist Uprising) to be uprooted. He asked Shishkov about Polezhaev's behavior, and Shishkov, who likely had no idea, said it was good. "That report saved you, my friend," said the tsar. He then granted Polezhaev the opportunity to put things right by serving in the military and sent him off with a kiss on the forehead.

Polezhaev, to put it mildly, found the soldier's life difficult, and after twelve years of repeated desertions, corporal punishment, imprisonment, sickness, and alcoholism, he died of tuberculosis in an army hospital. Over the years, the tsar never forgot him and personally saw to it that Polezhaev should continue to suffer in the worst conditions. When he died, Herzen reports, his corpse was to be sold for use as a cadaver, but was rescued by a friend from the bottom of a rat-infested pile of bodies waiting for their buyers to pick them up.

And so, "Sashka," a poem that can in no way be read as overtly political, brought ruin upon its author. While many instigators of the Decembrist Uprising – true revolutionaries who really did try to kill the tsar in their quest for a constitution – whiled away their sentences pleasantly enough in the company of their wives and children, Polezhaev, the hapless student-poet, was hounded to death in the ranks. He was, clearly, perceived as the greater danger. Perhaps these serious-minded and often ascetic aristocratic revolutionaries were something the tsar could understand and bring under control, but déclassé jokers like Polezhaev were dangerous and unpredictable.

This fear of the "unserious" was endemic not only to Nicholas I's reign, as is illustrated by the subsequent fate of Polezhaev's works. A century and a half later, Polezhaev had gained a place at the table of Russian canonical writers, and many of his poems were widely anthologized throughout the Soviet period. This was largely due to the fact that he was appropriated by the radical intelligentsia as a martyr in the 1850s, and his story later served Soviet literary history well as an example of Imperial despotism. Long after his death, though, he remained a dangerous figure. According to his memoirs, Aleksandr Herzen got the story of that night in summer 1826 directly from Polezhaev in 1833, at which point the latter was already quite mentally ill and suffering from the physical maladies common to the inhabitants of Russian military barracks. But since Herzen himself was of course no favorite of the regime and lived in self-imposed exile from 1848 on, the story was suppressed in Russia. "Sashka" itself was first published in an abridged, heavily censored form only in 1881. It was accompanied by the story of Polezhaev's fall, quoted almost entirely from Herzen, though the source, naturally, could not be revealed.[5] The first proper edition of Polezhaev's poetry was published in 1888 to mark the fiftieth anniversary of his death. That same year, the scholar-editor-publisher Petr Efremov published a brochure on Polezhaev's biography in which he tells his story, naming the source as "the author of *Byloe i dumy*."[6] Though he figured prominently in the Soviet canon, only one monograph on Polezhaev was published in the Soviet

Union, and it is careful to treat his light verse, especially "Sashka," with moralistic disdain – even though, by all indications, "Sashka" was by far the most "revolutionary" of all his works.[7]

The story of Polezhaev and "Sashka" gives the lie to the entrenched literary-historical notion that strident civic verse was the *real* voice of social change and that this makes it somehow more significant than the "light" verse of the period. In fact, the more trenchant challenge to the legitimacy of the regime and of the social order it created and oversaw is to be found in the formal innovations forged in the lightest genres: the friendly epistle, the burlesque, the familiar letter, the comic narrative poem, the epigram, the prose parody. This is the curious and mostly unacknowledged fact to which this book is devoted.

My purpose is, in no small part, to recover a few important texts from the literary-historical oblivion into which they have fallen as a result of censorship, ideologized scholarship, and, disturbingly often, sheer prudishness.[8] In US obscenity law there is a curious concept of "redeeming social value." In many states, a book, film, audio recording, or other work cannot be banned under obscenity law if such value is demonstrable. This Western legal concept is naturally of little use in understanding other cultures (Russian, for example, calqued "obscene" [*obtsennyi*] and "obscenity" [*obtsennost'*] only in the late twentieth century). In the Russian cultural-historical context, redeeming social value in the form of literary-historical value can, however, rescue certain texts from what is perhaps an even more damning label: insignificance.

My case for the significance of the insignificant, so to speak, relies heavily on a concept for which I have been forced to borrow a term from the formalists that has long since fallen into disuse: "domesticity." This is a rough calque from Boris Eikhenbaum, who describes the role of "literary domesticity" (*literaturnaia domashnost'*) in the early nineteenth century as part of the shift of authorial ethos from the court to high society.[9] A fairly rare word, *domashnost'* is used by the formalists in a sense peculiar to the early twentieth century. Only Ushakov's dictionary defines this usage: "A familial, unofficial attitude toward something. *Domesticity cannot be allowed in public work.*"[10] Domesticity is distinct and isolated from larger structures of social power. It is that private reserve, that exclusive and insular social space in which one is much freer to do as he pleases and be who he wants. Later, I make the case that the contexts of Russian literary discourse in the early nineteenth century can be described typologically as "domesticity," "society," and "state" – a triad that is much more conceptually effective when applied to the Russian Golden Age than the Anglo-American binary opposition "public versus private."

As Eikhenbaum notes, domesticity became an increasingly important social context for Russian poetry of the early nineteenth century, and it was, in many respects, the period's most important "laboratory" for the creation of new forms. In particular, domesticity served as the pragmatic setting for the development of the light genres, from which the new Russian poetry of the 1820s and 1830s, in large part, emerged. These were all, in one way or another, intensely personal genres, and much of this poetry was produced not for public consumption but, as Zhukovskii liked to put it, *für wenige* (for the few). This is especially true of a little-known genre called the *shalost'*, which has been all but ignored in Russian literary history, and which lies at the conceptual heart of this book. With Igor Pil'shchikov, I have described *shalosti* as a peculiar but stable verse genre practiced by the poets of the Lyceum Circle, the Green Lamp, and Arzamas.[11] The word *shalost'* is usually translated into English as "prank," "caper," "mischief," or "naughtiness." In the early nineteenth century, as I discuss at length in chapter 1, an even broader range of behaviors was associated with the word, including deception, practical jokes, assault, mutiny, vandalism, rape, and kidnapping. Lacking a single English equivalent, I am compelled to use the Russian throughout. As a verse genre, the *shalost'* is defined not by formal characteristics but by behavioral ones. In other words, it was called thus because it was defined by what it *did* rather than what it *was*: whether a long poem or just a couple of lines in the context of a larger work, a *shalost'* in one respect or another flaunts the prescriptions of literary propriety, adhering instead to the behavioral codes and semantics of domesticity. When published – or even distributed in manuscript form or declaimed in a semi-public setting – a *shalost'* effects the projection of the private, personal relationships of domesticity (especially the author's relationships with fellow writers) onto the author's interaction with larger readerships. It thus simultaneously asserts domesticity as part of literature proper and brings the broader readership into this inner sanctum, providing readers a peek – though, as we shall see, often no more than a tempting and frustrating glimpse – behind the curtains.

The popularity of the *shalost'* is part of a larger trend. Many scholars have remarked and few would deny that a strain of prankish iconoclasm became increasingly prominent in Russian literature over the late 1810s and early 1820s and then steadily declined after the Decembrist Uprising of 1825. Indeed, a certain cynical spirit of play – a devotion to all manner of jokes, impertinence, erotica, impenetrably obscure allusions, intimate and inconsequential genres, and Epicureanism – came to characterize the period 1810–37. Pushkin was this trend's main proponent, and it ended more or less with his death. A thumbnail sketch of this literary and cultural trend – "prankishness," as I call it – would look something like this: In the 1810s two literary societies, Arzamas and the Green Lamp, adopted prankishness as their behavioral lingua franca. Seminal literary works that emerged from these societies, particularly Pushkin's "Ruslan i Liudmila" ("Ruslan and Liudmila," 1820), introduced prankishness to a broader readership around 1820, and it enjoyed wide popularity during the relative liberalism of the early 1820s as both an iconoclastic literary-aesthetic ethos and a behavioral paradigm. After the Decembrist Uprising of 1825, in which many famous pranksters were implicated, the state began to take prankishness even more seriously, subjecting perpetrators of the most innocent pranks (e.g., writing bawdy poetry) to exile and worse. In the late 1820s political opposition became the hallmark of the Russian literary sphere, and prankishness was still associated with writers and writing well into the 1830s, when it became an embattled political discourse. By the late 1830s, prankishness was on the wane. In the early 1840s it was supplanted by a new "serious" political activism in literature that arose in reaction to what was perceived as the aristocratic frivolity of prankishness. It continued to exist on the margins of Russian literature, producing some of the nineteenth century's humorous masterpieces, such as Aleksei Tolstoi's and Aleksei, Aleksandr, and Vladimir Zhemchuzhnikovs's Koz'ma Prutkov and Ivan Miatlev's Madame Kurdiukova, before undergoing a metamorphosis and a revival in the early twentieth century.

The social consciousness for which Russian literature is famous was, in some respects, a reaction to prankishness. For example, the striking earnestness of the Russian "social prose" that came to the fore at midcentury and subsequently gave world literature Lev Tolstoi and Fedor Dostoevskii can be understood in historical perspective partly as a counterpoint to the "frivolity" and "cynicism" of their forebears. A comparison might be made to the recent "death of irony" in American culture: after a decade of amused detachment in the 1990s, the earnest brusquely staked a claim to cultural authenticity in the early years of the twenty-first century, often piggybacking on tragedy and fear.[12] This *bien-pensant* "new sobriety" can be understood only in terms of its precursor. In much the same way, the writers of the "post-Pushkin" era homed in on the angst of a nation built on slavery.

Perhaps not surprisingly, prankishness was more often than not connected to all sorts of unauthorized behavior both on and off the page, especially liberalism and libertinage. The celebrated social critics of midcentury, including Vissarion Belinskii, Dmitrii Pisarev, Aleksandr Herzen, Nikolai Dobroliubov, and Nikolai Chernyshevskii, explicitly denounced prankishness as the aristocratic foibles of days gone by, or as the trappings of despotism and slavery. They found the liberalism dilettantish, the libertinage depraved, and the neglect of serious social issues unforgivably callous. By and large, the literary scholars who followed have tended to avoid the most prankish texts for essentially the same reasons.

Indeed, there was an institutional prejudice in the Soviet Union against studying anything deemed "frivolous," and many important texts were left unpublished due to their "frivolity." Soviet literary scholarship had a certain, shall we say, humorlessness from on high. This was an attitude inherited, in large part, from late-Imperial literary scholarship, which also sought to purge literature, that all-holy realm, of any and all peccadilloes which might compromise the moral integrity of the national canon. As a result, by the 1880s, the large corpus of saucy, unpublishable literary texts which had been accumulating for several decades came to be known as the "hidden literature" (*potaennaia literatura*) – a whole tradition that had not the slightest chance of being published (or republished) in Russia. The echoes of both Imperial and Soviet "decorum" in such matters are felt to this day. Clearly, these so-called frivolous texts presented some sort of challenge to the Russian state of all modern periods – the Imperial, the Soviet, and the post-Soviet alike.

Meanwhile, the situation in American Russian-literature scholarship was little better until recently. Founded as it was on a wave of highly conservative anticommunism, the discipline was, with notable exceptions, unreceptive to work on anything "unserious." At the same time, most Western scholars had very little contact with their Russian colleagues and knew Russian literature, by and large, only through the prism of Soviet editorial practice. One might say, "At least the Soviet scholars *knew* about the material that couldn't be published." In any case, a whole dimension of Russian literature has been sorely neglected. True, many great Soviet scholars remarked in passing on prankishness, and I build on their scattered observations throughout this book. But most of them could ill afford to dwell at any length on anything to do with libertinage.

Of course, things have changed in both Russia and the West over the last twenty years, though not as quickly as one might hope. There is now a growing body of work on the obscene, the lighthearted, the playful, the prankish side of Russian literature. Work in this direction has already yielded some profoundly significant findings. Maksim Shapir's study of the obscene burlesque as a source of

Derzhavin's style is a prime example: no one (not any specialist, at least) will ever read Derzhavin in the same way.[13] Publications by Vadim Vatsuro, Igor Pil'shchikov, Andrei Zorin, Marcus Levitt, Oleg Proskurin, Martin Schruba, and others have also enabled great strides since the collapse of the Soviet Union.

Yet, we still lack any working hypothesis as to where Golden Age prankishness came from, what it actually meant in the context of the period, how writers and readers used it, to what ends, and with what impact on literary evolution. In seeking to answer these questions, my conceptual point of departure is the thesis that radical formal innovation was, at root, an expression of disregard for the rules and conventions of literary discourse. Further, because these aesthetic rules and conventions embodied and propagated real-life social rules and conventions, innovation was in and of itself an antisocial act. A pattern of literary misbehavior was cultivated in the insular domesticity of unofficial literary societies, where it both served as the social glue binding together the membership and allowed them to assert the social and literary autonomy of the groups. Such cohesion and autonomy were a necessity in the highly charged polemical atmosphere of the literary language debates, which were then at the center of intellectual life. Later, central members of these groups – most importantly, Pushkin – brought this mode of domestic behavior to the broad stage of literature. This emergence was, at root, a brusque and sometimes pointedly rude intrusion of the personal and fraternal into the spheres of officialdom and the *Grande Monde*. This was not the genteel, gradual, inevitable shift of subject from the collective to the individual that serves as the clichéd centerpiece of so many textbook histories of Russian literature. Rather, it was a raging war of hard-won victories and bruising defeats with many casualties – and it was fought not in the grand arena of the bellicose civic ode, but in the hidden backwaters of what has been traditionally disregarded as the light, frivolous, and inconsequential.

∾1

Roots and Contexts

In 1825, soon before her marriage to the poet Anton Del'vig, Sofia Mikhailovna Saltykova wrote to one of her girlfriends: "A propos, le cher Pouchkin a été renvoyé au village chez son père pour de nouvelles folies." If we cut off Saltykova's letter here, it would be unclear in early nineteenth-century usage what kind of behavior had warranted Pushkin's latest bout of trouble with the authorities. He could have been insubordinate, written a dirty poem, hit on his superior's wife, spilled wine on his boots, beaten somebody up, verbally abused someone, and so on. The truly puzzling thing for a twenty-first-century Westerner is that, in this particular historical and cultural context, there was relatively little difference between these behaviors. Saltykova continues, "Tu sais qu'il était près de [Mikhail] Vorontsoff, eh bien, celui-ci lui a donné une soumission pour laquelle il devait absolument partir; il n'en a rien fait, et a composé une Satyre sur Vorontsoff. Каковъ мальчикъ? Je suis persuadée qu'il fera de nouveaux vers dans sa retraite, qui seront plus piquants encore."[1]

She has three distinct behaviors in mind, all of which she describes with the word "folies": insubordination, ridicule of one's superior, and writing a trifling lampoon. Moreover, these are just Pushkin's "nouvelles folies," the most recent in a series of such behaviors that got Pushkin exiled in the first place: insubordination; demonstrative sloth; writing epigrams that ridiculed important officials, as well as politically charged odes; incitement to regicide; debauchery, and more. When writing in Russian, Pushkin's contemporaries used the word *shalost'* to describe this broad range of behaviors. Aleksandr Strudza, for example, wrote that Pushkin was exiled "for the *shalost'* of his muse."[2] This was the same Pushkin who was wont to do things like dress down a senior official in the coarsest language in the middle of a crowded theater.[3] Or attend a gathering at a regional governor's house wearing see-through pantaloons and no underwear.[4] Or pass an engraving of the regicidal killer Louis Pierre Louvel around another crowded theater after inscribing it with the phrase "A Lesson to Tsars."[5] And all these behaviors came under the single heading of *shalosti*.

Pushkin was not the last man Mikhail Vorontsov ejected from Odessa for *shalosti*. A few months later, Pushkin's distant relative Mikhail Dmitrievich Buturlin (1807–76) was similarly punished. Buturlin came into Vorontsov's service in 1824, soon after returning to Russia from Florence, where he lived seven years from the age of ten. When he began his military service, Buturlin was still unused to Russian behavioral norms and felt more at home in Florence, where he returned after Vorontsov turned him out in 1825. In his memoir, he complains, "I make no excuses for my frivolous behavior in Odessa; but I still think that Count Vorontsov was excessively severe with regard to my childish *shalosti*."[6] Buturlin's Odessa *shalosti* are no less heterogeneous than Pushkin's. He describes three of them in his memoir.

First, when a vaudeville artiste by the name of Madame D'Angeville came on tour to Odessa, her show included the performance of Italian arias in vaudeville contexts. Buturlin, who spent his adolescence in Italy and considered himself a master musician, took great affront at such a travesty of Italian opera. He chose a rather odd means of asserting his authority as a moderator of imported cultural practice, though. Eschewing more civil options, he instead urged a group of friends in the audience to catcall poor Madame D'Angeville when she came to the arias. He fancied that the rest of the audience would find this funny, and that the laughter would turn into general derision of Madame D'Angeville. Instead, her admirers in the audience became so annoyed that a fistfight ensued.

Second, Buturlin got so carried away with a boar hunt that he ran one of Vorontsov's prized Limousine geldings to death. Buturlin admits to some willfulness in this act, as he despised Vorontsov for his chilly condescension despite the fact that the latter gave him free use of his stable of superb horses. Mostly, though, this is a loss of control: Buturlin, drunk with the pursuit, simply got carried away.

The third episode was the last straw for Vorontsov. One night, Buturlin got into an argument with a certain Schwarz about the singing abilities of two local society matrons. In the course of the dispute, Schwarz said something nasty about Buturlin's favorite, to which Buturlin replied that Schwarz would not dare say such a thing to her face, whereupon Schwarz "authorized me to convey his words to her husband. Who would believe that I was such a novice that I thought it my duty to literally carry out Mr. Schwarz's instructions!"[7] An immense scandal broke out, of course. A duel was narrowly avoided, and Vorontsov locked Buturlin up in the stockade for a few days before firing him and expelling him from Odessa.

That Buturlin uses this single word, *shalosti*, to describe such a broad range of behaviors is typical of nineteenth-century usage. And beyond the simple homonymy of the wide-ranging meanings of the word *shalost'*, there was also a peculiar kind of polysemy at the level of the morpheme. The Russian language boasts a remarkably productive lexical cluster centered on the root *shal-*. For example: *shalit'* (to misbehave or caper), *shalovlivost'* (mischievousness or prankishness), *shal'noi* (stray or wild), *oshalet'* (to be overwhelmed or go mad). This root is a descendant of the Common Slavic roots **shal-* and **khal-*. In other Slavic languages these roots have shed all but one or two meanings, trending toward monosemy.[8] The Russian root *shal-*, however, had yielded an exceedingly cohesive polysemous cluster by 1800. This often resulted in the conflation of behaviors as disparate as childish misbehavior (*Deti shaliat*) and highway robbery (*Shaliat po bol'shim dorogam*). Thus, in Golden Age Russia, play could be perceived as an act of defiance because the most fearful violence could be perceived as a kind of play. And a combination and conflation of play, violence, and rebellion was exceedingly common.

Consider this example from the childhood recollections of the memoirist and chronicler of everyday life Petr Mart'ianov. At a funeral repast, the eternally inebriated millionaire merchant Aleksandr Petrovich Kvasnikov "took the *klobuk* from the head of a bishop or an archimandrite (I don't remember which) and put a watermelon rind in its place. There was a terrible scandal."[9] The tsar became personally involved in this scandal, and the perpetrator was spared only after Count Aleksandr Benkendorff, the chief of the gendarmes, received a considerable bribe. There is a concatenation here of play, a loss of self-control, and a disregard for authority that was provocative enough to turn a drunken caper into a matter of state security.

This semantic association between play and violence makes for what would appear to be a paradox: "harmless" fooling around was often taken as a serious threat to social and political institutions (and punished accordingly), while genuine violence was often viewed as a kind of play. For example, during Paul's reign, a couplet was found scrawled on some building materials at the construction site of Saint Isaac's Cathedral, which was then being finished on the cheap: "This is the comely monument of two reigns / The bottom is marble, but the top is brick." Ekaterina Raevskaia, the daughter of a major secret police official of the 1830s, later recalled: "The real author of this couplet was never found out, but a gentleman whose name I have forgotten was suspected. His tongue was cut off and he was exiled to Siberia, whence he was returned when Alexander I ascended the throne. My father often used to see this unfortunate man in Moscow, at the English Club. Around his neck hung a slate and a bit of chalk. He would write his replies on this slate during conversation."[10] Such cruelty (mutilation and exile for graffiti!) was of course a hallmark of Paul's regime, but his sons were little more tolerant of jokesters. Recall that Nicholas, for example, sentenced the poet Polezhaev to madness and death in the ranks for writing a slightly prurient poem called "Sashka." At the same time, truly brutal behavior was often condoned as mere "fooling around." For example, when an officer kidnapped and raped a merchant's wife in the early 1830s, the governor-general of Moscow at the time, Prince Dmitrii Golitsyn, persuaded the merchant to refrain from filing a report because he took pity on the officer, saying that he himself had "capered plenty [*nashalil*] as a young man."[11]

The Semantics and Etymology of Misbehavior

To say that the root "*shal-*" is productive in Russian would be an understatement. In the pages of this book alone, I quote dozens of usages of words from this cluster. Just in this small sample, we observe a tremendously broad array of meanings and associations. To name a few: practical jokes, mutiny, unauthorized sex, deception, a verse genre, insubordination, insignificance, violent crime, ritual humiliation, inside jokes, mischievousness, a blunder, vandalism, a faux pas ... the list goes on.

Despite such diversity, all these usages have in common a single concept, from which (in etymological thinking, at least) all their many, disparate connotations must have derived: *defying expectation* – not doing what is expected of one, or doing what is not expected of one. This single, core concept can be broken down into three useful semantic categories: play, dysfunction, and rebellion.

1. *Play.* This is a very specific kind of play that involves liberation from the restrictions of decorum. Engaging in this sort of play in the wrong context is regarded as a symptom of mental illness (see *Dysfunction*) or a thumbing-of-the-nose at authority (see *Rebellion*). A distinct act in the spirit of this kind of play – denoted by the noun *shalost'* – is best translated into English as a "caper." In contemporary usage, *shalost'* refers to the rambunctious play of young children

or to slightly deviant sex acts. One meaning of the verb *shalit'* is "to caper" or "to fool around." Another is "to joke by means of deception," as in: "You must be joking!" (*Nu shalish'!*).

2. *Dysfunction.* This category has to do with pathologies – when one's mind, one's body, or one's objects are not working as they should. The verb *shalit'* can, for example, also be translated as "acting up," as in, "my watch is acting up." The verb *shalet'* (in contemporary usage, "to go crazy") and its corresponding participial-adjectival forms *oshalelyi* and *oshalevshii* denote a dysfunction of one's mental capacities, generally due to overwhelming stimulus. These pathologies are also related to a loss of control. For example, the synonymous adjectives *shalyi* and *shal'noi* mean either "irrational, crazy" or "stray, accidental," as in, "a stray bullet." An adverb formed from the root *shal-*, *shaliaivaliai* ("haphazardly" or "incorrectly"), also falls into this category.

3. *Rebellion.* This class has to do with willful acting up. It is almost extinct in contemporary usage, but in early nineteenth-century usage it included insubordination, mutiny, assault, vandalism, kidnapping, brigandage, and reckless endangerment. For example, Nicholas I recalls that during the Decembrist Uprising he rallied loyal regiments, shouting, "The Moscow Regiment is fooling around [*moskovtsy shaliat*]. You mustn't follow them, but do your duty bravely!"[12]

In Count Buturlin's account of his youth, we see these three categories interact with particular vividness. Clearly, none of his three "Odessa *shalosti*" fits neatly into any single one of the three categories. Rather, each is a mixture of play, loss of control and/or pathological incompetence, and willful insubordination. In the first episode – the disruption of Madame D'Angeville's performance – Buturlin is rebellious: he flouts the rules governing comportment at the theater, where audience members may harass one another to their hearts' content (though not always with impunity, as we shall see), but harassing the performer was strictly taboo and could even get one in trouble with the authorities. There is also an element of play here, for, in Buturlin's telling, the scene was no more than a practical joke gone awry. In the second episode – the killing of Vorontsov's horse – he is rebellious in that he is reckless with his commanding officer's property. He also experiences a pathological loss of control, carried away with the hunt and oblivious to the property damage he was causing. Finally, the third episode – involving Mr. Schwarz's musical discernment – stems from dysfunction, an ignorance of social convention, and an inability to correctly read his interlocutor.

Buturlin complains that both his horsemanship and his familiarity with Russian culture were sorely lacking when he was repatriated at the age of seventeen. And these are indeed "childish" acts, as Buturlin says, in the sense that they reveal the full extent of his naiveté, his unfamiliarity with Russian culture. Once he learned the rules of horsemanship and social conduct, however, his behavior grew more, not less, scandalous. Subsequent turns in his biography are no less illustrative of our three categories.

Buturlin's rebellious proclivities were given shape by his milieux. He went back to Florence after Vorontsov expelled him from Odessa, but later returned to Russia and joined the Pavlograd Hussar Regiment, a military division fabled for its devotion to all manner of drunken debauchery. After serving with this unit in the

Turkish Campaign of 1829, he was transferred to the Hussar Regiment of the Life Guards stationed outside Saint Petersburg. In the summer of 1830, he fell in with two rich, young, Petersburg civil servants, Petr Golitsyn and Sergei Romanov, an association which soon brought an end to Buturlin's tenure in the prestigious Life Guards. Buturlin speaks of this period of his life with regret, for his "Petersburg *shalosti*," as he calls them, were to ruin his military career and his chances at following in the footsteps of his accomplished father. These *shalosti* included vandalism, practical jokes, assault, and offending the emperor.[13]

In the fall of 1830, Petersburg was subject to a rash of vandalism, something unheard of in the orderly Imperial capital. The perpetrators – who once made so bold as to break windows at the Rumiantsev palace – remain unknown, but Petersburg society widely suspected Golitsyn and Romanov, and perhaps rightly so. They were known for their drunken roughhousing. With Buturlin, they formed an infamous trio that terrorized Petersburg sidewalks for months. Buturlin reports that their favorite pastime was to imbibe liberally at one fashionable restaurant or another and then "walk along Nevskii Prospekt, knocking around any passersby that we came upon."[14] Once, they were nearly caught after Buturlin's cloak came open, revealing his Guard uniform while his comrades were pushing around Aleksandr Chernyshev, the war minister. Clearly, like window-breaking, this kind of escapade falls into the third semantic category of "rebellion" (aggressive insubordination and acting out against the social code), but there are elements of "play" and "dysfunction" to it as well. Buturlin describes these scenes as hilarious rather than vicious – that is, as play. At the same time, the hooligans were always drunk, which is a form of self-induced dysfunction.

Buturlin relates two other *shalosti* that demonstrate just how closely the three semantic categories described earlier were linked. He concludes his narration of these escapades with an expression of relief that the authorities did not find the banned volume of songs from the French Revolution stowed in his carriage.[15] As Iurii Lotman puts it, "This is no coincidence: 'wild feasts' and drunken carousing were inevitably colored in oppositional tones on the backdrop of [Aleksei] Arakcheev's (and later Nikolai's) capital."[16] The first of these episodes involves a pharmacy, the second – soup.

"One night I was walking along Gorokhovaia Street with Prince Golitsyn and Romanov," Buturlin recalls. "When we passed the pharmacy next to the Krasnyi Bridge, one of us three thought of climbing up on the awning over the front stoop of the pharmacy to rip the scepter and globe (the emblems of the state) from the pharmacy eagle, and with these trophies we set off to visit F. F. Pouteau, who then occupied, as I said, Manycharov's house on the corner of Malaia Morskaia Street. We woke him and handed over the regalia." Pouteau was of course horrified, but, fortunately for Buturlin, Romanov, and Golitsyn, he was also sober enough to immediately destroy the evidence, "this red-hot trophy, which, if the affair had come to light, would have brought us all under criminal prosecution for sedition in the view of the day's administration. For many years afterwards, Mr. Pouteau could never recall our nighttime visit without horror."[17]

The second episode, also involving sedition in the form of the abuse of state symbols, concluded less fortuitously for Buturlin and his comrades. It took place in a private room at Dubois's restaurant in the early evening, a common starting time and place for this trio's exploits.

Romanov arrived there already a little, as they say, *in his cups*, sat down on a divan, behind which stood a pedestal with a plaster bust of Emperor Nicholas I, and, accompanying his speech with gesticulations, produced a tremor which passed to the bust. I remarked that he should be more careful, and not break the bust, which would have added to our already considerable debt at the restaurant. To this he replied with a laugh: "Bah! Ce n'est qu'une tête de platres" (it's nothing but a plaster head), and then, with an indecent (of course) joke (but purely a schoolboy joke), he began to bring a few spoonfuls of soup up to the mouth of the bust. There was no one in the room besides us three; but it must be assumed that someone heard and saw everything from the next room because the whole episode was reported to the highest authorities in detail.[18]

Later that week, Buturlin was summoned by General Arps of the Life Guards. Arps informed him that reports of "certain incidents" had reached the tsar, and that Buturlin was under suspicion of involvement in them. He ordered Buturlin to write an account of his association with Romanov and Golitsyn. Buturlin was then arrested and spent six weeks in the stockade before being demoted and sent back to the Pavlograd Regiment. Golitsyn was transferred to a civil post in the Caucasus, and Romanov – to Arkhangel'sk.[19]

One can surmise from the structure of Buturlin's narrative that he felt the incident was in no way politically motivated. For him, it was more a matter of getting carried away, that is, a *shalost'* of the second category – a loss of control. Romanov's behavior builds from mere drunken incaution to a denouncement of the symbols of power, from a crude joke to a boisterous prank demonstrating his disrespect for the "plaster heads" keeping watch over their merry-making. All this happens in a split second, and a blowsy Romanov just cannot help himself. Buturlin, however, does not see this lack of willfulness as a justification. Rather, he sees the act as no less a crime than breaking windows and acknowledges that all three young men were perfectly well aware of the potential consequences. He does not suggest that the punishment was overly severe, but he does express amazement that the incident would attract the attention of the highest authority in the land. Buturlin characterizes the emperor's interest in such a trifle as paranoia brought on by recent events in European and Russian Imperial politics: "great significance was given [this episode], perhaps because they suspected in it an echo of the French and Belgian revolutions then underway, as well as the Polish rebellion, which had just flared up."[20] This speculation, of course, makes it clear that, though Buturlin refuses to acknowledge any political motivation for Romanov's act, he at least sees its political subtext in retrospect.

Contexts: Domesticity, Society, State

The preceding section's framework of play, dysfunction, and rebellion is, of course, wholly context-dependent. Behaviors that were received as play in one context might be perceived as seditious or deranged in another – this is the difference between reciting an obscene epigram at table with friends and during an audience with the emperor. But how to define these contexts? The binary opposition "public versus private" has been a scholarly mainstay for many years, but it is a troublesome one, and is increasingly viewed as a conceptual stumbling block rather than a useful distinction. For example, in a recent article, Andrei Zorin calls into question the line between the public and the private by looking at the ways in which Andrei Turgenev labored in his diaries to mold "public ways of feeling" (a la Geertz) into a usable form of private emoting.[21] "When we attempt to draw a clear border between 'the private' and 'the public,' individual emotional experience inevitably falls in the sphere of 'the private,'" Zorin writes.[22] Yet, as he shows, Turgenev's "private feeling" was derived from available forms of "public feeling." Other scholars rely heavily on the private-public opposition even as they question and complicate it. For example, it lies at the very heart of David Powelstock's literary biography of Lermontov.[23] Lermontov, Powelstock finds, was compelled by a nascent and swiftly growing culture market to fabricate closeness with his readers, which he effected by projecting them as intimates in the pragmatic structure of his poetry.[24] Thus, far from a quantifiable constant, Lermontov found the boundary between public and private malleable and subject to aesthetic manipulation.

But if the public-private opposition does not work particularly well for Golden Age Russia, how then are we to situate the period's texts in social context? The concept of privacy itself provides a useful opening on these issues. By privacy, I mean a social space in which one can, to a greater or lesser degree, count on certain freedoms. Privacy is typically understood as the freedom to be left alone, to avoid intrusion, imposition, and interrogation. But it is also a positive freedom: the freedom to do as one pleases according to one's own moral code rather than behavioral codes imposed from outside the private space.[25] These two freedoms of privacy, the negative and the positive, are loosely analogous to the concept of "face," which was introduced by the sociologist Erving Goffman in the 1960s. Face is the construction of self that people project in any interaction in order to regulate and modulate the shape that interaction will take. Face, Goffman says, is "the positive social value a person effectively claims for himself by the line others assume he has taken during a particular contact."[26] Face is "something that is diffusely located in the flow of events in the encounter and becomes manifest only when these events are read and interpreted for the appraisals expressed in them." And "the maintenance of face is a condition of interaction, not its objective."[27] Interactants must attend to two kinds of face – negative face and positive face. One preserves her interactants' *negative* face by not imposing on them and by not impeding or interfering with their projected self-image, the "line" they have taken. And one preserves the *positive* face of interactants by supporting, ratifying, and enabling them to maintain their "line" in a given interaction. Preserving the privacy of a group is about shielding members from outside threats to their negative face: being left alone. But it is also about allowing members to claim a certain personality or set of characteristics – positive face – which they might not be able to claim in other contexts.

In its usual sense, however, privacy is not a concept that can be applied to Russian culture without some qualification. To this day, there is no Russian equivalent for the word "privacy," and there is no calque.[28] Russian culture and jurisprudence have not appropriated this thoroughly Anglo-American concept. There was little inkling of it in the early nineteenth century, either, when no single "public" existed.[29] As Andreas Schönle notes, privacy is always problematic, and has always to fend off a number of potential intruders: "Privacy is the result of a complex negotiation between various private and public parties and ... is fated to remain in a state of precarious flux. Privacy rights result from a complex and contradictory triangular relationship that pitches a private individual or collective entity against another private individual or collective entity and against the state. Privacy cannot be thought of simply as that which emerges in opposition to the state."[30] In Russian culture of the early nineteenth century this state of flux was further complicated by the absence of the rule of law. According to Schönle, this instability engendered a highly ritualized and theatrical form of social interaction in public contexts, as well as a wariness of privacy: "Since the law and social institutions failed to enforce objectified, binding rules of behavior, the need was felt to propagate a particular discourse, an ideology of sorts, that would discourage individuals from fashioning themselves in too idiosyncratic a fashion. This discourse spread what I call a scare of the self, a strong reluctance to heed the desire for psychological and moral autonomy and to explore the interiority and subjectivity of one's self."[31] The volatility and instability Schönle describes also allowed for and, to some extent, fueled a kind of social creativity among the nobility. Torn as they were between various social institutions – the court, high society, family, branches of service – noblemen were somewhat adrift in the social landscape. In order to root themselves amid all this flux, many of them formed elective, but relatively formalized social groups, such as literary societies, circles, salons, and so on. Many, though not all, such self-created social formations sought to overcome the "scare of the self" by asserting autonomy as a group, and this often necessitated a sealing-off from the rest of polite society. As we shall see, *shalosti* were often used as a way to achieve such insularity.

In his *Fiction and Society in the Age of Pushkin*, William Todd describes the period's literary institutions using the framework of Roman Jakobson's famous model of communication.[32] For example, Todd defines polite society as a literary institution in Jakobsonian terms: the addresser = "gentle (wo)man amateur," the addressee = "interlocutor," context = "society," message = "bouts-rimes, letters," contact = "familiar group," code = "the conversational language of polite society." Taking Todd's lead, I would like to proceed by homing in on just one component of Jakobson's model – namely, context. As Todd writes, "Polite society, although it cherished a self-image of harmony and homogeneity, did weave itself from many strands (individuals, groups, institutions, cultures), and different viewpoints addressed different strands of this intricate fabric."[33] My intention is to delve into the internal contradictions of polite society in the period as they bear on literary-institutional practice.

I propose three basic descriptors of the communicative contexts in which Schönle's "complex and contradictory triangular relationship" played out in the literary *byt* (praxis) of early nineteenth-century Russia: domesticity, society, and state. These are the contexts, each with its own distinct set of behavioral and linguistic norms, in which most of the Westernized nobility had to function on a daily basis. Naturally, these are purely heuristic categories; they are the poles between which social entities and individuals trafficked; they are also settings – and, of course, the concrete social, temporal, and spatial context of any given behavior can be a mixture of all three.

The first of these is *domesticity*. This is a rude calque from the Russian *domashnost'*. The term is borrowed from the formalists, primarily Eikhenbaum, who argues that domesticity was the main engine of Golden Age literary innovation, and from Tynianov, who describes literary *shalosti* as a transplantation of "the domestic, intimate semantics of the friendly circle" into literature at large.[34] A fairly rare word, *domashnost'* is used by the formalists in a sense peculiar to the early twentieth century, and it is in this meaning that I use it. Only Ushakov's dictionary defines this usage: "A familial, unofficial attitude toward something. Domesticity cannot be allowed in public work." Domesticity is distinct and isolated from larger structures of social power. It is that exclusive and insular social space in which one is much freer to do as he pleases and be who he wants.

The second context is that of *society*, meaning "high" or "polite" society – the corporate social entity of the noble elites. This small but powerful segment of the population had a well-formed ideology, and its own behavioral, linguistic, and political rules.[35] Drawing the boundaries of this context is of course nearly impossible (and in any case, hardly necessary). For our purposes here, society is, loosely speaking, the context of what Sam Driver calls "the aristocratic party": "Like the English one, the Russian aristocratic party was scarcely even conscious of itself (except perhaps as 'exclusive,' the *obshchestvo* or *svet*), but its aims were clear: assertion of its own privilege (which meant opposition to the autocracy) and self-protection (which meant exclusiveness vis-à-vis the lower orders)."[36]

The third context is that of *state* – where the autocracy is most in evidence; the context of service, the church, and the court. Driver's take on society should be moderated in one important respect: though it certainly struggled for it, Russian society had practically no independence from the state in the early nineteenth century. True, society's power waxed and waned over the years, but it was afforded only as much independence as the autocracy wanted to grant it at any given moment. This independence could be taken away with a single ukase, and in reaction to the flare-ups of aristocratic dissent of the late Alexandrine period that culminated in the Decembrist Uprising, society was kept firmly under the emperor's heel for over a decade.

The balance of power between state and society was constantly shifting in the early nineteenth century. This is evident, for example, in dress codes of the period. Tsar Paul's state-imposed dress codes constituted an imposition on basic bodily privacy. They also infringed upon one of society's key mechanisms of self-regulation – fashion – which, though merely a dress code dictated by a different, more diffuse authority, could also be interpreted for purposes of individual self-expression. Soon after Alexander I came to power, the urban gentry began to appear on the streets in long pants, round hats, topcoats, and vests, all of which were forbidden during Paul's reign. When the wearers of round hats were not molested by the police, society took this in with a sigh of relief. It was perceived as an indication that Alexander would afford some respect to the bodily privacy of his subjects and to one of society's internal means for regulating behavior.[37] As in the first decades of Catherine's reign, fashion again became a more or less free mode of expression for those who could afford it. Twenty-five years later, though, the dress codes of the state again came into force, and they were regulated at the very highest levels. Stern punishments were meted out for violations, and even the tsar concerned himself with such matters. For example, Nicholas I wrote in 1830 to the chief gendarme, Count Benkendorff, on the matter of Pushkin's coat: "Apropos that ball. You might tell Pushkin that it is improper for him *alone* to be dressed in a tailcoat when we are all in uniform, and that he could at least acquire a nobleman's uniform."[38]

The tensions between these three poles – domesticity, society, and state – reflect the continual struggle between individual autonomy, the nobility's attempts to build its corporate strength, and the autocracy's need to keep both of these subjugated to its interests. A passage from the writer Vladimir Sollogub's memoirs provides an amusing illustration of these tensions. Sollogub recounts three exploits of the famous "prankster" (*shalun*), Dmitrii Mikhailovich Kologrivov, each in a different context. These episodes cannot be dated exactly, but they appear to have taken place in the late 1810s. Kologrivov was the half-brother of Prince Aleksandr Nikolaevich Golitsyn, a childhood friend of the tsar and one of the most powerful courtiers in the country. As such, the punishments Kologrivov received for his pranks are perhaps not characteristic. Nonetheless, the very structure of Sollogub's narrative demonstrates both the degree to which these contexts functioned independently, as well as the interconnections between the three.

First, there is domesticity: "Once, two nuns seeking donations for their convent were announced at the home of Tatiana Borisovna Potemkina, so well known for her piety and charity. The nuns were immediately given an audience. Once inside, they threw themselves to the floor, began to bow and scrape and wail, begging for a donation. Touched, Tatiana Borisovna went to her bedroom to get money, but when she returned, she froze in horror. The nuns were wildly dancing the Trepak. It was Kologrivov and another prankster [*shalun*]."[39] The domestic setting was one in which Kologrivov could get away with this masquerade. When he pulled a similar stunt on the street – this time costumed as a female beggar and accosting people on the sidewalk, sometimes even waving a broom at them – he was arrested.[40] In the domestic context, though, the prank was not grounds for a severe rebuke – or, in this case at least, the rebuke is not significant enough to merit mention.

In Sollogub's rendering, this prank centers on a very particular kind of masquerade. There is, first of all, a hint of anti-clericalism. The solicitation Kologrivov and his comrade parody here was exceedingly common. Even as the Holy Synod gained power throughout the early nineteenth century, many smaller, more local institutions of the Church survived on donations, from the village priests who regularly fleeced the peasants for grain and fowl to urban nuns who made the rounds of noble families in search of hard currency.[41] Though such local institutions were, for the most part, financially self-reliant, they were nonetheless an arm of state. As such, we might think of the parodic "nuns" as an incursion, even in the physical sense, of the state sphere into the domestic sphere, an incursion which becomes the focus of a slapstick "sight gag." At the same time, noblemen who wished to cultivate an image of piety and uprightness were obliged to donate money to clerics and church institutions with some regularity. In a sense, they paid for the prerogative to project themselves as righteous – and the more they gave, the more often the solicitors came around. Thus, Potemkina, "famous for her piety and charity," is also the butt of the joke.

The whole iconoclastic exercise of masquerading as nuns was of course designed to shock. According to Sollogub, Kologrivov took particular delight in shocking the most proper of Saint Petersburg matrons. Even when Kologrivov was an old man, Sollogub writes, "I often … noticed that when he was in the company of hostesses who were extremely strict with regard to propriety, his grey eyes would spark with mischief, and he would recall anecdotes so bawdy that the women listening to him did not know whether to get angry or laugh."[42]

Another of Sollogub's anecdotes that features Kologrivov is set on a parade ground. Obviously, one could hardly find a context more closely associated with the state and its regimentation of behavior and social standing. "The Tsar was getting ready to inspect a cavalry regiment at the Gatchinskaia Esplanade. All of a sudden an unexpected cavalcade flew by in front of the open ranks at a gallop. In front, an unusually fat lady in a green riding-habit and a hat with feathers galloped full speed. Next to her, at a canter, a desperate fop showered her with flattery. And behind them was a small retinue. This unfitting masquerade was immediately brought to halt. The portly Prince Fedor Sergeevich Golitsyn was dressed as the lady. Her chivalrous cavalier turned out to be Kologrivov. I don't remember the others. The pranksters were officially reprimanded, but their careers did not suffer."[43] Here, the response is cut-and-dried: an official reprimand. As Sollogub implies, such a reprimand could potentially damage one's career; and Kologrivov's cavalcade suffered no serious consequences perhaps only because they had family in the very highest places. Nonetheless, Sollogub says, Kologrivov's career was, in fact, stunted by such shenanigans: "He had a brilliant mind, and, had it not been for his passion for jesting, he could have had an enviable career."[44]

Just as in the first anecdote, there is both a masquerade and an incursion of one context into the physical space of another. Flirtation and courtship, the province of society, are transplanted onto the parade ground, the province of state. This prank challenges not only the regimentation of the parade ground, but also the internal social regimentation of the audience. The officers lined up on the parade ground were, in that setting, supposed to behave (and even think) not as noblemen, not as husbands, sons, or brothers, but as guardsmen single-mindedly devoted to the service of the tsar. Introducing colorful transvestitism and a courtship farce into this setting appealed to a different side of their social being: it was not guardsmen guffawing into their mustaches, but members of society. By drawing its viewers out of the role they were forced into on the parade ground, Kologrivov's cavalcade, in a sense, impugned that role and asserted the primacy of society over state.

Sollogub's third anecdote takes place in the theater – a combination of society and state:

At the French [language] Theater, Kologrivov took note of a spectator who, he thought, could not understand the production at all. He had found his victim. Kologrivov descended to the stalls and started a conversation with him.
"Do you understand French?"
The stranger glanced at him and answered curtly: "No."
"Well, would you like me to explain what's happening on the stage?"
"Be so kind."
Kologrivov began to explain, rattling off some terrible galimatias. Their neighbors were listening in and guffawing. People were laughing in the loges. All of a sudden, the man who did not know French asked in French:
"Now explain: why you are telling me such nonsense?"
Kologrivov was chastened:

"I didn't think, I didn't know!"

"You didn't know that with one hand I can pick you up by your nape and toss you up in the loge to those ladies you were trading winks with?"

"I apologize!"

"Do you know who I am?"

"No, I don't!"

"I am Lukin!"

Kologrivov froze.

Lukin was a legendary strongman. His bogatyr feats were legendary, and they still tell stories about him at the Naval Department, where he served. That is the kind of man Kologrivov had run up against.

Lukin stood up.

"Stand up," he said.

Kologrivov stood up.

"Follow me!"

Kologrivov followed.

They went to the buffet. Lukin ordered two glasses of rum punch. The punch was served. Lukin gave Kologrivov a glass:

"Drink!"

"I can't, I don't drink."

"That's not my problem. Drink!"

... In vain Kologrivov tried to refuse and begged for mercy – both glasses were drunk, and then more and more. In the end, they drank eight glasses apiece. But Lukin, as though nothing had happened, returned to his seat, while Kologrivov, dead drunk, was driven home.[45]

Thus, in the context of the theater, almost as much a society setting as the ballroom, the response is self-contained because society maintained its own mechanisms for regulating behavior: forced alcohol poisoning, the duel, ostracism, cuckolding, and the like.[46] At the same time, the theater was also a state institution with an appointed bureaucracy and carefully regulated "literature departments," and behavior at the theater was often regulated by state organs. Therefore, an offended party could choose to exact punishment on the perpetrator via two different power structures: by keeping the prank a society matter, or by complaining to the authorities, and bringing it into the state context. The manner in which Lukin chose to deal with Kologrivov falls in the first category; he preferred to maintain autonomy from the state rather than run to the authorities.

This was certainly not always the case, and many confrontations in the theater were brought to the attention of the state authorities. The poet Pavel Katenin, for example, was exiled from the capitals for misbehaving at the theater in 1822; he was stripped of his guard commission (colonel) and kept under house arrest in his village for three full years. And Pushkin was reprimanded in 1819 by his superiors at the College of Foreign Affairs after they received a complaint from the police chief, Ivan Gorgoli. In the distinctly non-society language of state officialdom, the complaint details a run-in Pushkin had with Collegiate Counselor G. Perevoshchik at the Kamennyi Theater. During an intermission, Perevoshchik asked Pushkin not to loiter between the rows in front of him and his wife, whereupon, "taking affront at this, Pushkin made coarse remarks and berated him with indecent words." Pushkin's boss wrote back to assure Gorgoli that he had reprimanded Pushkin and had extracted a promise from him to behave.[47]

In Sollogub's story, the punishment Lukin exacted on Kologrivov was rather more immediate and centers on both self-control and physical prepossession. In the society context, Lukin could hardly let Kologrivov get away with trying to make a fool of him. He devised a punishment that would make a fool of Kologrivov, thus canceling out the offense. He makes a fool of Kologrivov first by allowing him to continue on with a joke that hinges on a mistaken perception (that Lukin was a yokel with no French) and, second, by forcing him to lose self-control. At the same time, he demonstrates that he can maintain his self-control (i.e., hold his liquor) better than the impudent joker who saw fit to take him for a fool.

For obvious reasons, *shalosti* were linked most closely to one communicative context – domesticity. By placing them in the domestic context, I do not mean to say that *shalosti* were not committed in the contexts of society or state. To the contrary, as we have seen, they could be potent public demonstrations. Carrying such domestic behavior into the realms of society and state – that is, executing a *shalost'* in a non-domestic context – constituted a transposition of domesticity into the spheres of society and state. And asserting the domestic was a way of challenging both. All the same, such contextual transpositions are significant only when a behavior or set of behaviors is associated most closely with a particular context. And *shalosti* were associated most closely with domesticity.

Returning to the exploits of Count Buturlin, it is significant that the episode in Dubois' restaurant involving soup and a bust of the emperor took place out of earshot and sight – or at least Buturlin, Romanov, and Golitsyn thought so. Buturlin says that the room was empty, but someone must have been eavesdropping, and when they got caught, they were quite surprised. By and large, *shalosti* were things that people did when they knew the audience well – that is, under the assumption that they were being observed only by certain people. This is primarily because, as Buturlin and his comrades discovered, one could get in a lot of trouble for engaging in this sort of behavior without control over one's audience. In that episode, Romanov thought that his audience consisted solely of Golitsyn and Buturlin. His exile to Arkhangel'sk came as a result of the fact that he was wrong. Recall likewise Kologrivov's transvestite/beggar routine: when performed in the confines of Potemkina's house, it brought no trouble upon him; but when he performed it on a public street, he was arrested.

Even if one's audience consisted only of one intimate friend or family member, an obscene joke at the expense of, say, Arakcheev was still seditious. And, like the use of taboo words, such behavior could serve as a means to create and maintain particular kinds of social bonds – personal, unofficial bonds not governed by the behavioral prescriptions of society and state. Disregarding propriety was a way to project upon interactants a certain intimacy partly because it entailed some risk.

A description of a domestic scene from the memoirs of the actress Aleksandra Karatygina (née Kolosova) illustrates the connection between the domestic and *shalosti*. It comes from a brief memoir of her friendship with Pushkin, which was published just after her death in 1880. Like many of Pushkin's contemporaries, she was anxious to portray herself as a close friend of Pushkin, but only long after he died. As the Pushkin cult began to pick up momentum in the 1860s, it turned out that the long-dead poet had a huge number of very close friends, confidantes, and admirers whom he never suspected of being so well-disposed toward him. In her memoir, she emphasizes the domestic in order to underscore the intimacy of her relationship with Pushkin, now a hero of the fatherland.[48] One element of the domestic scenes she portrays is the *shalost'* – Pushkin, she implies, felt so at home with her that he carried on like a child.

> He was gloomy and taciturn in a crowd, but when Sasha Pushkin was at our house, he would make us laugh with his playfulness and childish prank-ishness [*shalovlivost'*]. Sometimes, he could not sit still for a moment, and would fidget, leap, change places, make a mess of mama's sewing box, tangle up a ball of yarn in my embroidery, scatter the cards my mother had laid out for a game of solitaire. Sometimes my Evgeniia Ivanovna would yell, "Will you knock it off, flighty? Stop it!" Sasha would settle down for about two minutes and then he would commence fooling around again. Once mama threatened to punish the irrepressible Sasha: to trim his "claws" (as she called his enormous fingernails, which he had let grow long on his hands).[49] "Hold his hand," she told me, taking up the scissors, "and I'll trim them!" I took Pushkin by the hand; he raised a shriek loud enough to be heard through the whole house and whimpered, moaned, complained that we were hurting him, and brought us to tears with laughter.[50]

There are a number of other interesting moments in this passage. It relates to evenings between January and November of 1819, when Pushkin was a frequent guest at the Kolosovs'.[51] This was also the period in his biography characterized by wild debauchery, constant bouts of venereal disease, radical civic poetry, participation in at least one secret society, the first taste of celebrity, frequent rebukes from his supervisors for misbehavior, and a penchant for unbridled public demonstrations of free-thinking and even regicidal fantasies. In short, this was the period during which he created his reputation as "a dangerous man." In the spring of 1820, the tsar had finally had enough and sent him to the south. To the modern-day observer, all this seems to be in stark contrast to the childish playfulness Karatygina depicts. However, the childish and the threatening behaviors are of a piece, and their combination presented no paradox to Pushkin's contemporaries. For example, when Nikolai Karamzin wrote his brother-in-law and former ward, Petr Andree-vich Viazemskii, about the circumstances of Pushkin's exile to the south, he uses the same word as Evgeniia Ivanovna Kolosova – *uniat'sia* ("to knock it off") – in relation to Pushkin's literary and political activities: "For several days, A. Pushkin was in entirely unpoetic fear because of his poem on Freedom and some epigrams. He gave me his word to knock it off [*uniat'sia*] and left without a hitch for about five months in the Crimea."[52]

Karatygina focuses on the permissiveness of her mother's drawing room: "Gloomy and taciturn in a crowd, Sasha Pushkin, at our house, made us laugh with his friskiness and childish prankishness [*shalovlivost'*]." The implication is of course that Pushkin's behavior was made possible by this very specific social context. She gives us a number of clues about it. First, it is distinctly female. No males are mentioned, and all the trappings – knitting, solitaire, embroidery boxes –

mark it as the feminine inner sanctum of a Russian noblewoman's home. None of the paraphernalia of society ritual are in view. Second, these same trappings mark it as a family setting. Karatygina mentions only her mother, Evgeniia Ivanovna (once a famous dancer). No outsiders but Pushkin, a family friend, are present. The very fact that Pushkin was admitted to this domestic sphere underscores the fact that he was "a member of the family" [*svoi*], a male who was neither a suitor nor an outsider.[53] Most importantly here, though, this context is presented as a dim and homey retreat very distinct from the public stage of Petersburg society with its glaring footlights. According to Karatygina, it is primarily this setting that enabled Pushkin to engage in the sort of behavior he did – and not only Pushkin, for Karatygina's mother is also drawn in to the play: the women's reaction to Pushkin's tomfoolery was to join in. Not only is it permitted, but it is encouraged by laughter. And it is sustained by the active participation of Karatygina and her mother in Pushkin's play. Ultimately, the domesticity Karatygina describes both makes possible these *shalosti* and is defined by them.

One usage of the word *shalost'* – as a reference to sex acts – further underscores the connection with domesticity. In this usage, the word seems to have referred to various kinds of illicit sex rather than sex in general. It could not be used, for example, to refer to sanctioned sex with one's wife. In his poem "Opravdanie" ("An Exoneration," 1825), Evgenii Boratynskii makes a distinction between betraying his beloved and having a little fun with the prostitutes around the corner:

Приветливых, послушных без ужимок,
Улыбчивых для шалости младой,
Из-за угла Пафосских пилигримок
Я сторожил вечернею порой;
На миг один их своевольный пленник,
Я только был шалун, а не изменник.[54]

[I sometimes guarded of an evening the [girl] pilgrims to Pathos from around the corner, who were welcoming and obedient, smiling for a young *shalost'*; for one moment their voluntary prisoner, I was only a *shalun*, and not a betrayer.]

In other words, sexual *shalosti* were not "serious sex," so to speak, with all the attendant emotional and social bonds, but a purely sensuous pleasure. For Boratynskii, this kind of sexual behavior is linked to the intemperance, freedom, and energy of youth. In his poetry, the word *shalost'* usually occurs in collocation with the word *mladaia* (young). For example, his poem "Moia zhizn'" ("My Life," composed 1818–19), reads:

Люблю с красоткой записной
На ложе неги и забвенья
По воле шалости младой
Разнообразить наслажденья.[55]

[On the whim of a young *shalost'* I like to vary the pleasures on the berth of languor and oblivion with an inveterate floozy.]

This usage was not exclusive to verse, and it did not refer only to sex with sex workers from the lower classes. In his diary, the famous Lovelace A. N. Vul'f – who was purportedly trained in his art by his neighbor, Pushkin – describes a phase in a fairly unhappy love affair that he carried on for years with one of the noblewomen of Trigorskoe, Aleksandra Ivanovna Osipova. "At Malinniki," he writes, "I devoted my time exclusively to *shalosti* with Sasha. She and I have long ago grown out of declarations of love and other such romantic foolishness: knowing one another, we took our pleasure as often as our strength, time, and the place allowed."[56] Note that Vul'f mentions "place" – this was highly secretive behavior because it was patently against the rules. And *shalosti* are here, again, sex for sex's sake.

Not all illicit sexual behavior, of course, was so private. Visits to the bordello were in fact often society occasions, usually undertaken at the end of a night of drinking and gambling. But here, too, the sex itself was concealed, taking place in some hidden back room. The "waiting room," however, was often the scene of various practical jokes and scandals. One contemporary, for example, reports that the famous madame, Sofia Evstaf'evna, lodged complaints with the police against Pushkin, one of her regular clients. "Sometimes Aleksandr Sergeevich would pick an interesting subject [i.e. one of the prostitutes] and start to ask her about her childhood and about all her previous life, and then he would counsel her and try to persuade her to have done with this brilliant company, to occupy herself with honest labor – work, to go to work as a servant, and he would give her money to get out of prostitution, and he thus saved more than one victim from ruin. But the best part is that the upright Sofia Evstaf'evna filed complaints with the police on Pushkin, [describing him as] an immoral man who was debauching her flock."[57] The domestic permissiveness of the elite bordello sitting room, which was very much a society institution regulated with help from the Imperial administration, derives from its proximity to the *shalosti* going on in the back rooms.

In general, not only were *shalosti* of all three categories – play, rebellion, and dysfunction – naturally associated with domesticity, but they were, in fact, one of its defining characteristics. And when members of the urban Westernized gentry sought to manufacture domesticity, to construct it in settings and situations in which it was not "naturally occurring," they often used *shalosti* in order to do so.

The Verse *Shalost'*

Poetry written for a close, intimate circle of friends and loved ones was central to Russian literary evolution in the early nineteenth century. In his essay "Literaturnaia domashnost'" ("Literary Domesticity," 1929), Boris Eikhenbaum argues that this was a natural result of the diminishing court patronage of literature. Poets increasingly asserted domesticity as the legitimate social context for poetry: "In the early nineteenth century these 'domestic' forms of poetry, in connection with the departure from the court ode, are employed as literary innovation, as a new genre.... The central verse genre of this epoch was lyric poetry 'for albums,' and the most common type of litterateur was the dilettante poet who did not strive for the position of a court 'bard' and who, as yet, had no need of a public 'stage.'"[58] Literary domesticity, he continues, was a laboratory for new forms, the orogen of the Golden Age's tectonic shifts. In his version, literature rejected the state context in favor of the domestic one, with little consideration of their role in society. Writers found themselves in a rather more unstable position than Eikhenbaum lets on, however. It is not the case that writers simply moved from the state to domesticity. In fact, the writer's role in society was a point of contention and debate for nearly three decades around the turn of the nineteenth century. Eikhenbaum places great emphasis on literary societies, but many of these groups were not of a domestic character at all. As I discuss at length in chapter 2, the literary society Beseda, for example, derived its ethos from the pomp and paraphernalia of officialdom.

But the "domestication" of literature Eikhenbaum describes is certainly characteristic of Karamzin and his followers, who saw the writer's role as fundamentally antisocial. For them, the writer's avocation forces him to forego participation in society or state, mostly because writing is a solitary activity that takes place in one's *kabinet* (the room in a Russian nobles home that served the combined functions of a study, a reception room, an office, a bedroom, and a library). At most, one can strive to be an *observer* of the outside world, not a participant. Still under the spell of Jean-Jacques Rousseau, Karamzin himself became keenly interested around the turn of the century in social isolation and its implications for writing. In his essay "Mysli ob uedinenii" ("Thoughts on Solitude," 1802), he writes that observers must exclude themselves from society in order to see it better and therefore portray it better, but only from time to time. He concludes, "Solitude is like those people whom it is good and pleasant to see now and again, but with whom to live always is onerous to the mind and heart!"[59] But a month later, in his essay "Otchego v Rossii malo avtorskikh talantov?" ("Why are There Few Literary Talents in Russia?," 1802), Karamzin offers a different portrait of the writer's social existence. By way of answering the question posed in the title, he runs down the list of social-institutional catch-22s that Russian literature faced. Authors must turn to the literary tradition in order to learn the language of "pleasant" literary style. But there is no such tradition in Russia, so authors must instead listen to the cultivated speech of high society. Unfortunately, Russian is not spoken in society, and learned people are not accepted or valued in such circles. To overcome these obstacles, authors-in-training must spend their days in solitary study in order to acquire "taste." In fact, he writes, society is dangerous to the writer. The writer's task is to become so learned in languages that he can invent or translate new phrases and turns of expression in such an artful way that his readers will not be able to discern their artificiality, so that no well-bred lady will think, "Oh, that's so coarse!" or, "People don't speak that way!" So, in the end, according to Karamzin, the writer's place is among his books: "One should look in on society – without fail, at least at a certain age – but live in the *kabinet*."[60]

Six years later, Vasilii Andreevich Zhukovskii revisits Karamzin's subject in his essay "Pisatel' v obshchestve" ("The Writer in Society," 1808). In it, he argues that writers cannot truly participate in society for three reasons: (1) the writer's dedication to his art causes him to remain always in the lofty sphere of his ideas and prevents him from interacting for the sake of interaction, (2) writers are prone to a peculiar variety of pride and vanity that makes their company unpleasant, and (3) poverty, which is the lot of any writer, prevents him from savoring to the fullest all the pleasures of society. Nonetheless, like Karamzin, Zhukovskii insists that writers must *observe* society. As a result, the writer's social life is divided.

For him, human society is divided into two circles: one is the broad circle, which he enters occasionally with the firm determination to be only a calm, cold spectator ... who wishes only to acquire some new ideas, a new education, which is indispensible for his talent.... The other circle – a close-knit one – is the one in which he is happy, he is loved, and loves, where he is successful without any effort, without resorting to refined and treacherous artistry; his solitude is in this circle, where he takes pleasure in life, in his serene and munificent labors, where he converses with himself, where he perfects his soul with high feelings and thoughts, where he entrusts to paper the treasures of his own thoughts and feeling for the good of his contemporaries, and perhaps for posterity; his friends are there, united with him by the same work and the same lot, predilections, gifts; their strict discernment trains him, their benign devotion to their work brings alive the creative flame in him, his recompense and his glory is in their sincere praise; and there, lastly, is his family.... Family ties are more indispensible to the writer than anyone else; tied as he is to one place by his occupation, he must find around himself those pleasures which nature has made indispensible to the human soul.[61]

It is Zhukovskii's portrait of domesticity – this second, parallel social existence – that most interests me. This privacy, where a writer can be at peace among his family and friends, protected from intrusion, and is free to do as he pleases, becomes a locus of both social and aesthetic authenticity in the early nineteenth century.

In his essay "Nechto o poete i poezii" ("On the Poet and Poetry," 1816), Konstantin Nikolaevich Batiushkov takes a rather different approach. He argues that the poet has no need for social interaction at all to create "purely." Instead of Zhukovskii's domestic circle, he advocates nature as the proper venue for the labors of an aspiring author: "Withdraw, then, from society, surround yourself with nature."[62] But without this domestic circle, for Zhukovskii, it is simply impossible to be a poet. He develops Karamzin's considerations of the necessary conditions for the development of craft into a consideration of the necessary conditions for the development of the artist. One of these conditions is that the artist must have a domestic milieu (preferably, close at hand) in order to have any of the authenticity without which, for Zhukovskii, true art cannot be wrought.

But what, exactly, does this "authenticity" consist of? More than anything, authenticity, for Zhukovskii and his contemporaries, had to do with the connection between morals and social conduct (including literary conduct). In large part, it was impossible for, say, abolitionists to conduct themselves in society in accordance with their beliefs. And this separation of moral conviction from social conduct in non-domestic contexts is one of the most important themes of nineteenth-century Russian literature. An episode from the history of the notion of "etiquette" is very instructive here.

Jorge Arditi describes the emergence of the concept of "etiquette" in eighteenth-century Britain, where, he argues, it originated with Lord Chesterfield's *Letters* (1774). This book inspired a vitriolic response from critics who saw in Chesterfield's prescriptions about "manners" a self-contained ethical system, a "little ethics" (*une ethique petite*) or, in Chesterfield's coinage, an "etiquette." This "little ethics" caused outrage among Chesterfield's critics because in it, "the criteria guiding manners were no longer connected to morals."[63] "Etiquette" in Chesterfield also refers to the rules of ceremonial, ritualistic behavior at court: when to kiss the pontiff's slipper, for example. According to Arditi, what most incensed Chesterfield's critics was that he advocated the expansion of such rules of ceremonial behavior (which were in their eyes empty conventions that were not rooted in a moral system) beyond ceremonial contexts, to all social interaction. Chesterfield's critics cursed him in vain, for this new "etiquette" subsequently eclipsed the regnant notion of "civility," which was "a practical expression of ethics: good behavior was understood as the embodiment of an ethical concept."[64]

It seemed to many Russian litterateurs that such a dissociation of behavior from morality resulted in behavior that was fundamentally inauthentic. Though a talent for what Chesterfield terms "the lesser virtues" (*lentiores virtutes*) of agreeable conduct was prized in Russian society, it was nonetheless considered an *art*, something one could be skillful at as one is skillful at, say, watercolor. This "art," this "talent" for executing the dictates of etiquette with aplomb was viewed, therefore, as being without any moral content and any genuine feeling. It is of a piece with the *comme il faut* (Russian *komil'fo*) that Tolstoi would later excoriate in nearly all his novels. If I may transplant the terms of eighteenth-century British culture to early-nineteenth-century Russian culture, the behavioral ethics most prized in Russian domesticity, and the one that was its most fundamental defining characteristic, was the Russian equivalent of "civility," while "etiquette" was the favored mode of society and state.

For Batiushkov, who believed that the poet ought to withdraw from all social interaction and take his inspiration from nature, the isolation of the poet is more tragic than it is for Zhukovskii and Karamzin. One "resorts to art" in order to share one's feelings and thoughts because he is isolated and has nobody to share them with in real life. At the same time, Batiushkov has a more optimistic view than Zhukovskii of the role that the writer can play in society. He writes that the gift of expression is the greatest human achievement, "for by means of it [the writer] leaves the surest traces in society and has a strong influence on it."[65] Still, for Batiushkov, as for Karamzin and Zhukovskii, writing is a fundamentally solitary, antisocial vocation that centers on study and reflection. While, as Schönle argues, Russian culture at large may well have been in the grips of a "scare of the self" during the age of sentimentalism, the opposite is certainly true of these, the most important writers of the 1810s. In the work of their ideological descendants, such as Pushkin and Nikolai Iazykov, palpable contempt for the outside social world is invariably couched in terms of protecting this inner sanctum of the writer's self from outside influence, of exercising writerly freedom and asserting a right to privacy. This, in turn, goes back to Karamzin, who thought that the truly virtuous dilettante has no need of the public stage. For example, in his essay "Na grob moego Agatona" ("For the Grave of My Agathon," 1793), he extols the virtue of his friend, the Mason A. A. Petrov, who declined to publish his literary labors. "He liked better a quiet circle of readers than the harrying condition of the Author, whose peace of mind often depends on people's opinion. He had the great paragons before his eyes. *One must compare to them* (he thought) *or not go out on the stage.*"[66]

Literary *shalosti* were an important means of expanding the ethos of domesticity into the fabric of the discourses of society and state. Let me explain what I mean by borrowing a metaphor from Zhukovskii. A true writer, he says, cannot truly participate in society because "he is always absent from society: he brings into a noisy crowd the solitude of his *kabinet.*"[67] In other words, in society, the writer is still at work, absorbed in his thoughts and his self-reflection. It is only among his intimates that he can truly enjoy the pleasures of human interaction. This fits to a tee, for example, the image of the young Pushkin's behavior that we find in the recollections of his contemporaries: gloomy and taciturn in the ballroom, but joyful, warm, and prankish at home. Most importantly, it is in his immediate milieu, among his extended family of close friends, that the writer finds his true audience, for it is only here that he is truly understood and loved. As a result, for the Karamzinians and their followers, the literary domesticity Eikhenbaum describes was a mark of authenticity throughout the first three decades of the nineteenth century.

The bounds of this domestic context are very limited, however, and if one wants, like Batiushkov, to influence society and, ultimately, state, one has to reach new readers. There were several options available to the Karamzinians, but chief among them were two. First, one can attempt to address a broader audience, writing about things of interest to people outside one's domestic circle in a way that might appeal to readers without the shared social and aesthetic values and experiences of that domestic circle. But according to Zhukovskii, this would constitute an abandonment of authenticity. The second option they had was to expand the boundaries of the domestic sphere by projecting ever-broader sections of the readership as part of the writer's intimate circle. By and large, Karamzinians like Zhukovskii, Batiushkov, Viazemskii, and Pushkin chose the latter route. They made their readers into domestic intimates, in part, by bringing domestic genres and themes into the fold of public literature. For example, they made their personal correspondence into a literary artifact and used this incursion onto the literary scene to assert their views and values. In his study of the Arzamasian letters, William Todd notes a key feature of the Karamzinian pathos: "Civility and literacy cannot be imposed by governmental or authorial ukase but must be communicated to the reader by example, by the illustration of their pleasures and benefits."[68] The Arzamasian letters were designed as exempla, not only of how a true writer writes, but also of how he conducts himself with his friends. Significantly, the Arzamasians consistently referred to their literary activities as "literary *shalosti*": these were acts of domestic speech destined for exposure in society and state.[69]

As Igor Pil'shchikov writes, "It is precisely to this domestic sphere that [literary] *shalosti* belong."[70] *Shalosti* were viewed as a domestic form, but one that writers brought onto the broad stage of literature – that is, into the state and society contexts – with increasing frequency during the first two decades of the nineteenth century. Returning to Zhukovskii's metaphor, the writer carried not only the solitude of his *kabinet* with him into society, but sometimes also the fun and liberties of the adjacent parlor. It is, after all, in comparison to the pleasures of genuine interaction that the hypocrisy and callowness of society become apparent. And therefore, Zhukovskii would have it, the writer ought to feel himself fortunate for being excluded from society: "A writer with true talent is generously rewarded by nature for all the slights of fickle fortune."[71] Inasmuch as literary *shalosti* were a representation of the authentic, legitimate, intimate social life of the writer, performing them on the public stage of literature constituted an implicit critique of society and state.

In its simplest form, a literary *shalost'* was a frivolous trifle presented in the aesthetic context of "serious" literature; in other words, presented in such a way as to excite the same aesthetic expectations the reader would have for a piece crafted with due sobriety and self-importance. The basic "prank" here is the impudence implied in the act of seeking an audience for the trifles one would typically share only with his intimates. It is primarily in this sense that Aleksandr Griboedov, for example, referred to literary *shalosti*. In his memoirs of Griboedov, Aleksandr Bestuzhev-Marlinskii recalls their first conversation:

> Before me lay a tome of Byron, and I said that it is comforting to live in our age, if for no other reason than the fact that our age is able to value the ingenious works of Byron.
>
> "Indeed, sometimes they are valued more than they merit," said Griboedov.
>
> "I think that accusation cannot be leveled with regard to authors the like of Goethe or Byron," I objected.
>
> "And why not? Perhaps both. Do not the admirers of the former proclaim to high heaven every one of his poetic *shalosti*? Do they not attribute to every phrase he drops a thousand contradictory meanings?"[72]

A *shalost'* here is something unworthy of praise. It is neither the product of lofty inspiration nor the fruit of true poetic labors. Yet, it is something that poets do, even "The Great Thinker" Goethe. And it is something that Griboedov himself did with some regularity.

At the same time, though, Griboedov seemed to view *shalosti*, in some sense, as serious business. In the closing couplets of his "Proba intermedii" ("A Sample Interlude," 1818), Griboedov facetiously prescribes the manner in which a *shalost'* should be received by the audience:

> Довольно всѣ плясали, пѣли!
> Покуда вамъ не надоѣли,
> Всего умнѣе разойтись.
> Кто хочетъ, тотъ пускай сердись,
> Надъ нашей шалостью острись.
> А мы не съ авторскимъ умишкомъ –
> Хоть пошалили, да не слишкомъ.
> Притомъ, кто осуждать насъ станетъ,
> Не худо, ежели вспомянетъ,
> Что позабавиться насчетъ
> Кто интермедіи идетъ,
> Не много умнаго онъ ждетъ.[73]

[Everyone has sung and danced enough! It would be wisest to part before we tire you. Let he who wishes be angry and ridicule our *shalost'*. But we did it without authorial wit [*umishko*] – though we pranked [*poshalili*], we didn't get carried away. Anyway, it would be well for him who takes to condemning us to remember that whoever goes to be entertained at an interlude does not expect much wit.]

A jesting Griboedov excuses the frivolity of his *shalost'* by claiming "we did it without writerly wit" (*My ne s avtorskim umishkom*). This concept of *um* (wit, mind, reason), the source of woe in Griboedov's *Gore ot uma* (*Woe from Wit*, 1825), requires some decoding here: when he writes that his *shalost'* is without authorial *umishko*, Griboedov means that he intended no harm, that his *shalost'* does not hide any seditious impulse. Slonimskii notes that "the term '*um*' acquired a conventional meaning, denoting the new free thinking and the new, independent spirit of criticism. It was in this positive sense that Pushkin used it – for example, in his epistle to Kaverin of 1817: 'that a *lofty um* can be hidden beneath the light cover of a wild *shalost'*.' "[74]

An episode from Griboedov's career as a playwright provides an illustration of how a *shalost'* could be used to redraw the lines of social alliance and affiliation. In 1817, Mikhailo Zagoskin published a taunting, negative review of Griboedov's play *Molodye suprugi* (*The Young Spouses*, 1815) in his journal *Severnyi nabliudatel'* (*The Northern Observer*).[75] Griboedov was so enraged by the review that he wrote what he terms "a *shalost'*," the satirical poem, "Lubochnyi teatr" ("The Lubok Theater," 1817). As soon as he finished it, he put it into active circulation. On October 19, 1817, he sent the poem to his friend Pavel Katenin, along with a letter in which he describes the writing and dissemination of the poem as an intemperate act, a loss of his cool. He writes, "That fool Zagoskin scrawled a bunch of nonsense about me in his journal.... Finally, I could not take it any more and I wrote my own facetia and put it out, and, can you believe it? It's been three days since I wrote it, and yesterday it was being read in all corners of the theater, thanks to my friends, who are eagerly circulating copies of this *shalost'*."[76] He also asks Katenin to find a publisher for the poem and suggests a possible nom de clef for Zagoskin: Mikhailo Mos'kin.

Griboedov's image of the theatergoing public clustered in the corners reading his *shalost'* aloud underscores, in almost physical terms, the domesticity of this text – bypassing the stage, Griboedov connects directly with the public. Collective reading was a thoroughly domestic activity, something that people did at home to pass the time.[77] The theater is thus turned into a giant parlor, and the audience before which Griboedov is compelled to defend himself is recast as his own, intimate, domestic circle. In this way, he makes a claim to the audience's allegiance, and his *shalost'* becomes the focus of a concerted campaign of insult designed to discredit Zagoskin's authority as a critic.

For Griboedov, a literary *shalost'* was a domestic text purely by virtue of its general insignificance. For other writers, however, the poetics of domesticity were more complex. Igor Pil'shchikov describes *shalosti* as a kind of stable verse genre practiced by Batiushkov, Zhukovskii, Boratynskii, Del'vig, Pushkin, and many others. Its main characteristic is behavioral rather than formal: whether a long poem or just a couple of lines, a *shalost'* brings the intimate, local semantics of a domestic setting, an "inside joke," to the broader stage of literature. The main thrust of Pil'shchikov's argument is that domestic semantics are based in allusions and references accessible only to a limited few: "The literary sources which constitute the associative horizon of 'domestic texts' can acquire for certain addressees (and only for them) a special meaning, and sometimes they can be known only to them. A reader who does not belong to this small group of people risks taking a comic, playful text as being more or less 'serious.' "[78] In a word, there is a curious kind of polysemy at work here that divides the readership into groups: those who "get it," and those who don't. For those who get it, the text takes on an entirely different meaning. In many respects, the same is true of any obscure literary allusion. The few erudite souls, for example, who get all of Nabokov's allusions feel themselves part of an elite club.[79] *Shalosti* are different in that a concrete social connection is necessary for one to perceive their purely domestic subtexts. In other words, the readership is divided not by factors like education and erudition, but by social proximity to the author and his immediate milieu. It is not the clever who "get it," but those who are privy to the domestic discourse of the author's immediate circle – in a word, his friends, the friends of his friends, and so on.[80]

The notion that particular texts can *acquire* special meanings in an intimate circle of friends – and that these meanings are often available only to those who belong to this circle – is key here. Given its almost conspiratorial nature, this phenomenon can of course but rarely be observed by literary historians. One of the best examples, oddly, is a widely known pun on a line from *Eugene Onegin* (3.1.1–4), as a result of which the word *blagonamerennyi* (well-intentioned) acquired an indecent meaning. It comes from a teasing digression on Tatiana's command of Russian.

Я знаю: дам хотят заставить
Читать по-русски. Право, страх!
Могу ли их себе представить
С Благонамеренным в руках!

[I know: they want to make ladies read in Russian. Frightful really! Can I picture them with the Blagonamerennyi in their hands!]

This pun is based on the word *Blagonamerennyi* (The Well-Intentioned), which was the title of a journal edited by Aleksandr Izmailov and an important outlet for Russian poetry in the 1810s and 1820s. Shortly after Pushkin published the third chapter of *Eugene Onegin*, Viazemskii reported that their mutual acquaintance Beketov "entend malice a votre vers: 'With *Blagonamerennyi* in their hands' and thinks that you are thrusting into ladies' hands that which is between our legs.... And the name *blagonamerennyi* is outstanding for it."[81] Pushkin takes up the pun with great verve. He writes Viazemskii in September 1828, "If it wasn't for Zakrevskaia, your bronze Venus, I would die from boredom. She is comfortingly funny and sweet. I write poetry for her. And she has promoted me to her pimp (to which I was brought by my perennial proclivities and by the present condition of my *Blagonamerennyi*, about which one might say the same as has been said of its print namesake: I swear the intentions are good, but the execution is bad)."[82] Viazemskii replies: "I've already heard that you have been messing around with my bronze Venus, but one must penetrate her with a bronze *blagonamerennyi*."[83] Pushkin's social milieu, in turn, also adopted the pun. It may be that the enthusiasm for this pun was in reaction to the political connotations of the word *blagonamerennyi*. In Faddei Bulgarin's reports and denunciations to the secret police (Third Division), for example, *blagonamerennyi* means "politically reliable" or "uncritical of the status quo," the opposite of "*mepris*" and "*litseiskii dukh*" (Lyceum spirit).[84] In any case, none of the people who knew the pun – all of them linked socially to Viazemskii and Pushkin – would ever again read those lines from *Eugene Onegin* with a straight face. The text acquired a specific meaning for a closed circle of friends, and this meaning was available only to people with a direct or indirect connection to that group.

The Arzamasians created a similarly obscure and prurient pun, which they so loved that they continued to revisit it for decades. That pun focuses on the court title *kammerger* (the last syllable can be pronounced "*kher*" – "prick") and the golden key that they were required to display on the rear tails of their uniform coats.[85] The prurience of these puns underscores an important point. Today, the phrase "*poeticheskaia shalost'*" means "an indecent license taken in verse."[86] The reason for this is that the *shalosti* of old very commonly employed the "low" discourses of sex, excrement, and so forth. The reason for this, in turn, is that such discourses were disallowed in society and state, and sneaking them into literature was, as we have seen, a *shalost'* in the sense of "prank" or "caper." Inasmuch as such transgressions across the lines of social contexts constituted a demonstrative break with the behavioral norms governing social conduct, such *shalosti* were acts of insubordination. Hence, *shalosti* like Polezhaev's "Sashka" could become dangerous or seditious. It is precisely this aspect of bawdy verse, for example, that prompted the radical N. Ogarev to compile his anthology of bawdy poetry, *Russkaia potaennaia literatura XIX stoletiia* (*The Hidden Russian Literature of the Nineteenth Century*, 1861), a very politically tendentious volume that could be published only in London. In a word, this nexus of rebelliousness, *pokhabshchina* (vulgarity, obscenity), and humor reflects larger sociopolitical dynamics.

The type of *shalost'* discussed earlier hinges on a collective action: an insular group attaches an inside joke to a literary work. It was also often the case that the referent of a domestic literary allusion was, from the start, known only to a small group of intimates. Again, we find perhaps the best example in *Eugene Onegin*. For nearly a century, Pushkin's readers were unable to identify the referent of an allusion in "Zhenshchiny" ("Women"), the first four stanzas of chapter 4:

Словами вещего поэта
Сказать и мне позволено:
Темира, Дафна и Лилета –
Как сон забыты мной давно.[87]

[I, too, can say, in the words of the prophet-poet: I long ago forgot Temira, Daphne, and Lileta like a dream.]

Meanwhile, this is a highly performative reference. The line breaks and the colon are performative markers (called in speech act theory "illocutionary force indicating devices") like the word "hereby," as in: "I hereby quote a poem." The poem Pushkin quotes is Del'vig's "Fanni" (composed 1814–19), which was known in the 1820s only to their Lyceum classmates and fellow members of the Green Lamp.[88] "Fanni" was a text typical of the prankish aesthetic of the Green Lamp, and I will discuss it at length in chapter 3. For now, suffice it to say that "Fanni" centered on references that were very specific to the Green Lamp. One of the main intertextual referents of the poem is Diderot's *Les bijoux indiscrets*, in which one of the talking vaginas ("jewels") belongs to a courtesan named Fanni. Diderot's Fanni gained special significance in the context of the Green Lamp because one of their favorite entertainers/prostitutes also happened to be named Fanni.[89] "Zhenshchiny" was written in 1827, and it is perhaps a little surprising that Pushkin would return to the semantics of the Green Lamp seven years after he left it in 1820. It was not uncommon, however, for Pushkin to do this kind of thing. In 1830, for example, he dusted off the parodic lingua franca of Arzamas, by then twelve years gone, for his "Besy" ("The Devils"), a parody of Katenin that originally carried the subtitle "a *shalost'*."[90] In "Zhenshchiny," the return to the Green Lamp also serves to summon up a concrete poetic subtext for this "romantic autobiography."

By quoting Del'vig, Pushkin secretes an indecent domestic text inside his sprawling masterwork. Moreover, he impudently dangles this in front of his readers: "I hereby quote a poem that practically none of you can have read." Speech act theory and pragmatics provide a good framework for looking at what is going on here. John Searle makes the case that referring is a speech act governed by the same principles as other speech acts.[91] And other speech act theorists have proposed a cooperative model of referring whereby the identification of a referent is a collaborative outcome of semantic negotiation.[92] So this is a discrete speech act – and a highly performative one – that projects the (implied) reader in the text.

In terms of H. Paul Grice's pragmatics, Pushkin's reference to the unknowable is a peculiar kind of non-observance.[93] It is not, strictly speaking, a "violation" of a maxim, which is an *unostentatious* non-observance. At the same time, Pushkin does not flout any maxim either. In fact, Pushkin's very ostentatious reference to an unknowable referent evinces a deliberate refusal to observe the so-called cooperative principle: Pushkin does not *want* most of his readers to get it, to calculate an implicature. Rather, in J. L. Austin's terms, he *wants* the speech act to be infelicitous, or, rather, to be felicitous only for a small portion of his readership. This deliberate discursive dysfunction is a way of selecting from among one's readership. Pushkin snubs much of his readership while privileging the few members of his immediate milieu who will be able to identify the referent. The felicity of the speech act is determined exclusively by social proximity to Pushkin: only those close to him or to the Green Lamp could "get" the reference to Del'vig. The effect is to build an insulated domestic circle into the broader readership. As a result, those of his readers who were able to "get" the reference felt themselves part of a very exclusive club composed of the few individuals who knew to laugh at it.

This mechanism of privileging a small portion of the readership is, I believe, emblematic of how a literary *shalost'* works in general. As Lotman puts it, this is a poetics of making a text understandable only to those who are in the know, of conjuring up a closed social sphere within the boundaries of a published text: "The text must conceal (though, in reality, it recalls) a whole world of jokes, stories, and witticisms."[94] In a word, *shalosti* could be used to construct domesticity verbally. The author retains his seclusion from society even while interacting with it – as Zhukovskii says, "He carries the solitude of his *kabinet* into the noisy crowd."

∾2

Arzamas
Rudeness

The Arzamas Society of Obscure Men (1815–18), or simply "Arzamas," as it is usually called, has been the subject of so much excellent scholarship that it requires little introduction.[1] In short, though, Arzamas was a jocular, familiar literary society, which sprang out of the foreign policy and literary language debates of the early nineteenth century. It was conceived in large part as a polemical counterpoint to a stuffy, official literary society called the Colloquium of Amateurs of the Russian Word (Beseda liubitelei russkogo slova), commonly called "Beseda," and its membership included the day's leading literary lights – Zhukovskii, Batiushkov, Viazemskii – and other prominent defenders of Karamzin's literary and linguistic programs. Their meetings were flesh-and-blood parodies of Beseda and other learned societies and academies, as well as various religious rituals. From this parodic root grew a massively complex symbolic system, one still only partially described. Though Arzamas was short-lived (October 1815–April 1818), the social bonds forged and strengthened in Arzamas persisted for decades in a loose association of writers and statesmen known as "the Arzamasian brotherhood."[2] And, true to its origins as a vehicle for furthering the "modernization" of Russia, Arzamas had a massive impact on the evolution of Russian literature and culture.

In an 1826 denunciation, the publisher and author Faddei Bulgarin described Arzamas to the gendarmes as the product of "injured pride."[3] It arose, he said, because Zhukovskii and his friends were catching hell in the plays of the Beseda favorite, Aleksandr Shakhovskoi, and others. They had no recourse in the press because publishing articles on the productions of Imperial theaters was banned from 1815 until new censorship regulations came into force in 1828.[4] As such, they were forced to form an underground alliance to fend off the attacks, an alliance that Bulgarin viewed as insidious and, ultimately, detrimental. He went so far as to blame the Decembrist Uprising, in part, on the pernicious influence of Arzamas. His account is, of course, only partly correct. Theater was one of the peripheral concerns of Arzamas, not its raison d'être. But it is true that Arzamas formed for lack of a fitting forum in society and state. Yet, reading the voluminous scholarship on Arzamas, one often comes away with the impression that Arzamas took the shape it did because that is how the Arzamasians wanted it. In fact, though, Bulgarin was right: it was not whimsy but struggle that led to the formation of Arzamas. And the hilarity and levity of its proceedings and texts – so-called Arzamasian laughter (*arzamasskii smekh*) – were sufficiently mysterious as to arouse the suspicions of people like Bulgarin.

The *shalost'* was the lingua franca of Arzamas. All the Arzamasian protocols, speeches, and most of their letters rely on a strange conglomeration of subtexts, which could be known and decoded only by Arzamasians and which, as such, took on a special, domestic meaning for them alone. This Arzamasian code language was so impenetrably dense to their contemporaries, in fact, that Zhukovskii was sometimes at great pains to explain emphatically that it was harmless. At one point, he wrote to the authorities, "No one would believe it possible to gather once a week with the sole purpose of reciting galimatias. Phrases which have no meaning for an outsider might seem mysterious, having their own key, which was known only to the members."[5]

The poems of Zhukovskii and Batiushkov were perhaps the most important source for this strange language, particularly Zhukovskii's ballads, which supplied the nicknames and much of the original iconography of Arzamas. Vasilii Pushkin's poetry was also important. It was the source of many Arzamasian catch phrases, such as "real talent everywhere finds protectors!"[6] The Arzamasians, and Zhukovskii in particular, also developed a whole set of stylistic conventions, which appropriates and exaggerates all those features of Beseda's stiff officialese that they most loathed. Fittingly, they deemed this language "galimatias" – and all protocols or any other linguistic trappings of formality were to be written in it.[7] Arzamas also developed a whole code language based in a system of *noms de clef* and caricature of their own invention. In this language, critics of the language politics of Karamzin and Dmitrii Dashkov were designated "Chaldeans" (because they resided in Babylon) or "Schismatics" (because, like the Old Believers, they favored the archaic). Beseda members were given Arzamasian nicknames: Admiral Shishkov, for example, was known as "Meshkov" (Mr. Sack) or "Sedoi" (The Gray-headed One), and Shakhovskoi was "Shutovskoi" (Mr. Jester). And in their epigrams, protocols, and speeches, Khvostov became something of a comic-book hero with superhuman soporific powers. Arzamas even had its own calendar, which started from the so-called Lipetsk flood, the premiere of Shakhovskoi's play *Lipetskie vody* (*The Lipetsk Spa*, 1815), in which Zhukovskii is ridiculed. The Arzamasians also had a creation myth, and the membership openly worshipped the jellied goose (for which the town of Arzamas was famed) consumed at the end of every meeting. All this was combined with tropes and rituals from learned academies, parliaments, and Freemasonry. As in the French Academy, new initiates delivered eulogies, but – since all Arzamasians were immortal – for *living* Beseda members. (Dmitrii Bludov got the Arzamasian nickname "Cassandra" because he pronounced a eulogy for Ivan Zakharov, a Beseda member who died shortly thereafter.) Arzamas had an oath of allegiance, bylaws, and elections, all painstakingly documented in galimatias. Parliamentary procedure was also followed, but with a republican twist – the red cap of the Jacobins was donned by a given session's elected chairman. And the intricacy and saturated symbolism of Masonic ritual was lampooned at every step.

As the Arzamasian Filipp Vigel' later recalled, "Arzamas was simultaneously a parody of learned academies, Masonic lodges, and secret political societies."[8] They also employed other parodic subtexts, such as Orthodox Christian ritual and symbolism. Yet, though parody was certainly the central mode of Arzamas, the group perceived itself as tremendously important. Until the recent publication of Mariia Maiofis's book on the politics of Arzamas, however, scholars were, at best, a little unclear on what the Arzamasians were so serious about. As it turns out, Arzamas was, in part at least, a tool of the modernizing reform project of the Arzamasian Count Kapodistrias (then the foreign minister), Sergei Uvarov, Bludov, and their allies in the administration of Alexander I. In keeping with this mission, even while playing with the gravity of learned societies, Arzamas cultivated an intricate and highly refined symbological system: "To paraphrase the famous saying, there was a method to Arzamasian madness."[9] In this system, the New Arzamas was the New Jerusalem – the center of a new religion of taste and reason; it was the New Rome – the capital of a new republic; the New Arzamas was also the New Athens – a new center of enlightenment and learning.[10] While these grand narratives were parodically subverted by introducing them into the absurd context of Arzamasian clowning, the fact remains that Arzamas constructed itself as a microcosmic model society. It was the maquette for a new capital of the enlightened future Russia that the Arzamasians dreamed of: a polis with no plebeians, governed by the god-kings of taste, reason, and elegance. The New Arzamas could not be built high on a hill for all to admire, however. As we shall see, circumstances and the beliefs and values of the Arzamasians conspired to keep it underground. The fact of this withdrawal from society and state both derived from and shaped what Viazemskii calls "the moral fraternity" of the Arzamasians, which bound them together for decades.[11]

The Arzamasians scorned Beseda not only because they disagreed with the linguistic and literary politics espoused at their meetings but also because the form of the meetings itself was not to their liking. Beseda set itself up as an institution of state, not of literature. Here is Vigel''s description of a Beseda meeting:

> the venerable Derzhavin ... provided a magnificent hall in his beautiful home on the Fontanka Canal for the sessions of Beseda. In this hall, as brightly lit as a temple to the god of light, in wintertime (I do not recall how many times) there were held the ceremonial evening meetings of Beseda. The members sat at tables in the center of the room, where there were also chairs set up for the most honored guests, and along the walls there were three rows of nicely built seating for other visitors, who were admitted only with tickets. In order to imbue these meetings with more grandeur, the fair sex came in ball costumes, the ladies-in-waiting with their portraits of the Tsar, the grandees and generals were in their ribbons and stars, and everyone was wearing dress uniforms.... As in a Government Council made up of four departments, Beseda, too, was broken up into four sections.... In each were a few members and a few corresponding-members, who made up something like the chancellery of Beseda. Overall, it had more the appearance of a government office than of a learned society, and even in the seating arrangement, the table of ranks was observed more than the table of talent.[12]

In the last sentence of his description, Vigel' alludes to his fellow Arzamasian Aleksandr Voeikov's "Parnasskii Adres-kalendar'" ("The Address-Calendar of Parnassus," composed 1815–16?).[13] The Address-Calendar that Voeikov parodies here was a directory published by the state that listed the addresses, government posts, ranks, and titles of the most important government officials and the aristocratic elite. Voeikov's "Parnassus" reworking lists the *literary* titles, posts, and

ranks of various figures on the scene.[14] Viazemskii, for example, is listed as the
minister of the police and the head director of penal institutions for the envious,
liars, and the lazy. And Batiushkov is a *Deistvitel'nyi poet* (Actual Poet). In setting
up an opposition between the "Table of Talent" and the "Table of Ranks," Vigel'
hits upon the main reason that the Arzamasians were contemptuous of Beseda:
rather than compete in what Arzamasians often called "the arena" or "the battle-
field" of literature, Beseda members sought to derive literary authority and status
from their official posts. In one of his speeches before Arzamas, for example, Uvarov (a.k.a. *Starushka*) laments that the denizens of "Old Arzamas" (the provincial
town), "in deep ignorance have no news of our battles, of our glory and, stubbornly
referring to the Address-Calendar, affirm that *Meshkov* [i.e., Shishkov] is a ruler
both in the government and on Parnassus."[15]

In essence, this is a question of rhetorical ethos – "the image of self built by the
orator in his speech in order to exert an influence on his audience."[16] The rhetorical
ethos of Shishkov and his comrades was not literary, but derived from station in
state and society, and the pomp and regalia of the Beseda meetings were designed
to reinforce that ethos. From the Arzamasian point of view, this was fundamentally
dishonest, cowardly, and ignoble. It also made for excruciatingly boring proceedings. But perhaps most importantly, the Arzamasians viewed it as an impediment
to the development of Russian literature, their greatest passion, a deep commitment
to which brought them together: bringing about a national literature on a level with
the European traditions was a fundamental part of the Kapodistrias-Uvarov modernization program. While mediocre (or bad) writers of the Beseda camp such as
Sergei Shirinskii-Shikhmatov and Count Dmitrii Khvostov were getting more than
their due share of the limited opportunities for publication because they had Beseda
backing, truly talented writers languished in obscurity, and the reading public suffered a lack of anything good to read. And this was the vicious cycle that the Arzamasians so often complained of: because there was nothing good to read, nobody
read Russian authors, and there were few good Russian authors because nobody
read Russian authors. As Viazemskii wrote Aleksandr Turgenev in 1816, "There is
nothing in the journals, / nothing in prose nor verse."[17]

The formation of Arzamas was not its founders' first attempt at institutional-
izing opposition to Beseda and similar societies. Many other literary societies and
salons were no less stifling. Of Aleksei Olenin, for example, whose circle was a
very powerful anti-Beseda force in the mid-1810s, Zhukovskii wrote: "His house is
the meeting place of authors, of whom he wants to be the dictator."[18] An episode
from the prehistory of Arzamas involving another official society is a particularly
good illustration of how the Arzamasians struggled to form a collective and find
an institutional voice. In the early 1810s, several of the men who would later form
Arzamas – most notably Dashkov, Viazemskii, Batiushkov, and Bludov – belonged
to the Free Society of Amateurs of the Letters, Sciences, and Arts (VOLSNKh).[19]
VOLSNKh was very much an "official" literary society, which is to say it was
licensed, monitored, and supported by the state. In 1811, for example, VOLSNKh
was given meeting space in the Mikhailovskii palace. Perhaps most importantly for
Viazemskii and his comrades, VOLSNKh had print organs, including an official
journal, its *Periodicheskoe izdanie* (*Periodic Edition*), which had been published
only once.[20]

At the March 14, 1812, meeting of VOLSNKh, three years before the "Lip-etsk flood," Count Dmitrii Ivanovich Khvostov was inducted as an honorary member. Now remembered only as the butt of innumerable parodies and epigrams, Khvostov was a major figure in Russian literature and politics at the beginning of the nineteenth century. Besides serving in high government posts, he was an astoundingly prolific writer and translator – according to most, a graphomaniac – who wrote in the eighteenth-century classicist style he grew up with. For various reasons, he became allied with Admiral Shishkov and was one of the four founding chairmen of Beseda exactly one year prior to his VOLSNKh induction, on March 14, 1811. Honorary membership in VOLSNKh was a position with no official duties, and the society inducted such members largely in an effort to boost its status and gain powerful sponsors. According to Vasilii Pushkin, Beseda had accused VOLSNKh of being hostile in late 1811.[21] The tension between the two groups heightened when Dashkov, a long-time polemical foe of Admiral Shishkov, was named president of VOLSNKh for the first three months of 1812.[22] So, the decision to induct Khvostov was almost certainly a political one. This was a peace offering to Beseda.

At Khvostov's induction, Dashkov, as president, was charged with pronouncing an encomium for Khvostov, who was regarded by Dashkov's circle as perhaps the biggest hack in Russian letters.[23] As it happens, Dashkov worked in a department headed by Khvostov, so it was natural that he should give the induction speech despite his open opposition to Khvostov's friend and protector, Admiral Shishkov. One might speculate that the pro-Beseda faction in VOLSNKh thought career anxiety would keep even a man as outspoken as Dashkov from doing anything unseemly. But Dashkov could not resist: his encomium was an exercise in deadpan mockery, and it precipitated not only his expulsion from VOLSNKh, but also the loss of VOLSNKh as an institutional structure for opposition to Beseda in general.

In his speech, Dashkov proposed to publish a detailed survey of the works of Khvostov – in order to "demonstrate to us all their merit." He quotes some of Khvostov's worst verse, saying, "I will also show some of his mistakes, which are spread among immense beauties, and by doing so I hope to prove my passionate zealousness for his glory." That is, the speech was more of a threat than a panegyric. It played on every aspect of Khvostov's rather inglorious literary reputation. Khvostov was tremendously prolific – or graphomanic, depending on one's allegiances: "His works are boundless [in number and size]: merely glancing at them exhausts the mind and imagination, and the symbols of his victories are staggering and astounding." Khvostov was a terrible translator: "He superseded Pindar, disgraced Horace, shamed La Fontaine." Khvostov published his own quite unsellable works at his own expense: "The storehouses of all the Russian booksellers filled with his priceless works are the most enduring testament to his glory." In short, Dashkov's encomium was a piece of oratory mock-heroic. From the opening lines, every word takes on an aura of double entendre such that the audience is compelled to take each lofty compliment as a scathing insult.

Scholars have long regarded Dashkov's encomium for Khvostov as the first work in the Arzamasian galimatias style. As Gillel'son writes: "It is not for nothing that one of the copies of his speech was later inscribed by its keeper as 'an Arzamasian speech' [i.e., a speech pronounced at an Arzamas meeting]; almost four years before the official opening of Arzamas, Dashkov pronounced a speech that presaged the verbal arabesques of the Arzamas speeches."[24] Mariia Maiofis concurs, adding that Bludov and Dashkov, not Zhukovskii, invented Arzamasian galimatias. In fact, she reports, Dashkov's speech was to mark the inception of a parodic society that would parallel Beseda closely with the sole aim of ridiculing it – an embryonic Arzamas – hence the selection of the date, the first anniversary of Beseda's founding, for Dashkov's opening salvo.[25] As Vadim Vatsuro puts it, "A polemical device had been found, and it later fit organically into the critical arsenal of Arzamas."[26]

This episode was also an important lesson for the Arzamasians on the difficulties of fighting Beseda in the open. The anti-Beseda camp, especially Viazemskii, had hopes that VOLSNKh could be transformed into an institutional home for opposition to Beseda; VOLSNKh was all the more attractive because it already had permission to publish a journal.[27] These hopes were dashed, however, when it turned out that Beseda had more pull in VOLSNKh than their detractors. The March 18, 1812, minutes of VOLSNKh read: "At the last meeting, D. I. Khvostov reacted with displeasure to Mr. Dashkov's proposal and took his praises as reproaches; and, as a result, Mr. Dashkov – to the regret of the entire Society – but as an example to all members to refrain henceforth from such behavior, though not unanimously – but by majority vote, is stripped of the title of Member."[28]

By summer 1812, VOLSNKh had purged the rest of the anti-Beseda faction from its membership. Batiushkov, Bludov, Dmitrii Severin, and Stepan Zhikharev, all founding members of Arzamas, quit or were expelled, and of the future Arzamasians, only Vasilii Pushkin remained. Reporting the news to Viazemskii, Batiushkov waxed comically philosophical: "[The Free] Society will certainly collapse. So all passes, all disappears! On the ruins of literature will remain one column – Khvostov, and [Aleksandr] Izmailov will give birth from his womb to new writers, who will again write and publish. It reminds me of nature's system of destruction and regeneration."[29]

Despite the looming threat of Napoleon's invasion, the text of Dashkov's speech was in circulation in both capitals by late March of 1812. By and large, the future Arzamasians were delighted with it. Turgenev enthusiastically circulated the text, and according to Viazemskii, Vasilii Pushkin "was slapping his ass, rubbing his hands, laughing, spraying everyone with spit while reciting it, and in his heart he swore to worship Dashkov and delight in his every word."[30] As is obvious from his tone here, Viazemskii was not so pleased with Dashkov's performance as the others. He found it a needless "insolence and stupidity." Upon hearing that Batiushkov enthusiastically congratulated Dashkov on his success, Viazemskii wrote the former an angry letter, chastising him for "falling into that Petersburg stupidity." Khvostov, he says, did not merit such an attack because, "he has no influence on taste.... And a piece like this piece of Dashkov's, whom you all worship so, might have an effect on your minds, and not for the better. And then you'll all run out into the streets to flash your bare asses at the passersby. What's with the Page Corps jokes?"[31]

Viazemskii's reaction is puzzling for a number of reasons. Between 1810 and 1817 he himself wrote no less than twenty-two works ridiculing Khvostov, and he published many of them.[32] In fact, just a year previous to Dashkov's encomium, in 1810–11, he had twice published the following epigram – once in *Tsvetnik*, a VOLSNKh journal. The epigram's target is Khvostov:[33]

Ага, плутовка мышь, попалась, нет спасенья!
Умри! Ты грызть пришла здесь Дмитриева том,
Тогда как у меня валялись под столом
        Графова сочиненья![34]

[Aha, I've caught you, you rascally mouse, there's no escape! Die! You came to gnaw on a tome of Dmitriev when I've got Grafov's [i.e., Count Khvostov's] Works lying around under the table!]

This epigram is a typical example of Viazemskii's "Khvostoviana," which later became a central genre of Arzamasian play. Fittingly, Viazemskii published most of his parodies, fables, and epigrams written at the expense of Khvostov over fifty years later under the heading "Arzamasian literary *shalosti.*"[35] Viazemskii was a prolific and sometimes vicious epigramist. It certainly cannot be said that he was known for his delicacy in matters of polemic. In 1810, for example, he attacked the recently deceased Beseda poet, Semen Bobrov, just as a fundraising campaign was launched to support Bobrov's penniless widow and children. Having only just uncovered Bobrov's attacks on Karamzin, Viazemskii and Batiushkov published epigrams ridiculing Bobrov as a talentless drunkard while his grave was still very fresh.[36] So, Viazemskii's dismay at Dashkov's mock encomium is a little hard to understand. It seems likely that he had strategic and political factors in mind. From his point of view, Dashkov's stunt was a poor tactical move. With no representation in VOLSNKh, the opposition to Beseda found itself without an institutional cover and without a print organ in which to "correct public opinion." The loss of access to publication in *Tsvetnik* and other VOLSNKh journals was especially vexing. This would drive the opposition underground.

As it turned out, Viazemskii was correct. Mark Aronson rightly characterizes the subsequent strategy of Arzamas as "guerrilla warfare": they could not face Beseda in the open, so they were forced to snipe from heavy cover.[37] In any case, Arzamasian galimatias was a pointedly domestic style not meant for publication. The Arzamasians often remarked that they could not publish one or another Arzamasian *shalost'*. Anything created for that particular domestic sphere in the language they developed to define and sustain its integrity was off limits for publication. For example, the junior Arzamasian Zhikharev wrote Viazemskii in July 1816 about Vasilii Pushkin's epistle, "Poslanie k Arzamastsam" ("Epistle to the Arzamasians," composed 1816): "It's a pity that we can't publish it: Pushkin hasn't written any verse this good for a long time."[38] In large part, they were forced to rely on manuscript circulation, which could be difficult. But, given the tiny readership for literary polemic in those days, it often was not necessary to publish something in order to stage a polemical victory.

Vigel' wrote in his memoirs about one such instance of polemic conducted not in the press, but in samizdat. Of Bludov's short story "Videnie v kakoi-to ograde" ("A Vision in Some Wall," 1815), which was in many respects the creation myth and founding text of Arzamas, Vigel' recalls, "It was terribly funny, and rather damaging to Shakhovskoi and his comrades. It could not be published, and it is always difficult for a manuscript to pass from hand to hand and gain exposure to the public; the main thing was to get it to Shakhovskoi and pour a lot of bitterness into his cup of happiness."[39] This Bludov achieved: a copy made it to Shakhovskoi (and, presumably, just about everyone he knew). What Vigel' does not mention is that it was he himself who passed the manuscript to Shakhovskoi through a distant relative![40]

The Arzamasian speeches and protocols – the most stunning group achievement of Arzamas – were entirely "restricted to internal use," though. One cannot say whether this huge body of highly intricate texts was a peculiar kind of literary play never meant for public consumption or a kind of practical joke on posterity. Indeed, Russian philologists have only begun to unravel its mysteries. In any case, there was no major publication of the Arzamas protocols until more than a century had passed since the society's demise.

Under these circumstances, the Arzamasians turned almost entirely to domestic genres. Even here, though, their options were rather limited. Since there could be no women in the New Arzamas – and the homosociality of Arzamas cannot be overstated – heterosocial society genres like the album lyric, madrigal, or love epistle were off limits. And the premium on levity and wit precluded gloomy elegies and graveyard ballads. With these limitations, the Arzamasians directed their literary energies to protocols, speeches, letters, epigrams, familiar epistles, familiar letters, and in the case of Pushkin's *Ruslan i Liudmila*, the comic narrative poem.

Arzamas is often characterized as a group that operated wholly within the bounds of the ideology of society and that ultimately served that ideology. No doubt, the Arzamasians could leave this ideology at the door no more than they could leave, say, their femurs. Yet, Arzamas set itself up as a distinctly domestic formation, and strenuously sought to insulate itself from society as much as possible. This insularity was reinforced most strongly in two ways: first, by the exclusion of women and second, by the group's devotion to polemic.

Much like the Hellfire Clubs, the Dilletanti, or the No-Nose Club of eighteenth-century England, Russian familiar literary societies were entirely homosocial – women were excluded, paradoxically, in order to free up the proceedings.[41] For noblemen, the presence of ladies was the number one factor in differentiating between domestic and society contexts, and decorum took entirely different forms depending on the gender composition of a gathering. It was precisely for this reason that one does not find any heterosocial groups listed in the materials of Nicholas's 1826 Investigatory Commission: it was presumed that nothing conspiratorial would be undertaken in the presence of ladies. Even mild literary polemic in mixed company ran against the stylistic and ideological prescriptions of society "talk," and was considered exceedingly uncouth. Thus, the Arzamasians were incensed by polemical readings (such as Aleksandr Shakhovskoi's "Raskhishchennye shuby" ["The Plundered Fur Coats," 1811]) performed at Beseda meetings not only because they were ridiculed, but because there were women present. Moreover, the mixed company of society engendered competition, which could undermine the ideology of friendship. In groups like Arzamas, a spirit of cooperation was vital to the group's continued existence. In the salon, on the other hand, competition among the male guests for the attentions and approbation of the hostess or female guests was a defining characteristic.[42] For example, Sofia Dmitrievna Ponomareva's salon, which straddled the boundary between the salon and the familiar literary society (i.e., between society and domesticity), is famous for the devotion that the hostess inspired and demanded from her guests, as well as the hostilities this caused among the admiring poets vying for her favor.[43] In the end, the familiar literary society was based in the idea of friendship, an idea still being laboriously (and often tediously) developed in the poetry of the early nineteenth century. As evinced in the period's many meditations on the difference between "friendship" and "love" (i.e., between homosociality and heterosexuality), friendship and cross-gender fraternizing were, with rare exception, mutually exclusive patterns of social interaction. And these social norms bore on poetic discourse as well. For example, bringing *Ruslan i Liudmila*, a text composed in the framework of "friendship," to a heterosocial audience caused an unprecedented scandal, which I dissect in chapter 4.

If it is clear why Arzamas adopted domesticity as its discursive context – insufficient clout to confront Beseda in society and state contexts; the sentimentalist imperatives of the Arzamasian linguistic program; their insistence on the autonomy of literature; and the ideology of friendship – an important question remains. Namely, how did the Arzamasians go about constructing domesticity? In the scholarly literature, one often encounters the erroneous assertion that the Arzamasians were all old friends and that their insistence on "familiar directness" (*druzheskaia neposredstvennost'*) was a natural outgrowth of relationships that were already close and long-standing. This is incorrect: many Arzamasians hardly knew one another before 1815, and many never did become friends. They came from a range of social circles and circumstances and had relatively little in common outside of Arzamas. True, some members (e.g., Turgenev and Zhukovskii) were old and close friends, but most were not. Arzamas used a forced, false, and calculated variety of rudeness in their interaction in order to create social cohesion. Their letters to one another support this interpretation.

Like Talk

As we have seen, the Arzamasians were more or less forced by the polemical atmosphere of the 1810s to create an intimate domesticity and to adopt the literary genres associated with it, most notably, the familiar letter, of which they produced a huge number. These letters are both literary objects and artifacts of social interaction. Though a fair amount of scholarly attention has been paid their literary characteristics – their aesthetic function – the social function of the letters has received less attention.[44]

At the heart of this issue is Kantian "disinterestedness" (*Interesselosigkeit*), which expanded in formalism to become the idea that an object is not amenable to a judgment of taste (i.e., is not an aesthetic object) except in the absence of interest, purpose, or desire. From this comes the urge to demonstrate the *literariness* of familiar letters, which has led scholars to downplay the transactional and performative aspects of these texts (in other words, to put aside considerations of what writers were trying to get done with the letters) in order to focus on their aesthetic features. There can be no doubt that the Arzamasian letters are literary objects because the Arzamasians clearly conceived of them as such, and generations of readers have read them as such. Nonetheless, the most striking feature of the Arzamasian letters is the *combination* of aesthetic play and social interaction. In the Arzamasian let-

ters, the transactional and performative serve aesthetic functions, and vice versa –
the literariness of the letters serves practical communicative and social functions.

In *The Familiar Letter as a Literary Genre in the Age of Pushkin*, William Todd
addresses this social versus aesthetic dichotomy in explaining how he determined
which of the letters should be included in his analysis. As an example of a letter
that is a borderline case between the literary and the "business" letter, Todd cites
Pushkin's letter to his uncle, Vasilii Pushkin, from August 14–15, 1825.[45] The letter
is a request for payment of two hundred rubles pitched in a hilarious imitation of
chancellery style.

> In 1811 my Uncle Vasilii L'vovich, in accordance with his favorable inclina-
> tion toward me and all my family, during a trip from Moscow to Saint Peters-
> burg, borrowed from me 100 rubles in paper money which had been given to
> me for pocket money by my late grandmother Varvara Vasilievna Chicherina
> and my late aunt Anna L'vovna. The witness of this loan was a certain Ig-
> natii; but Vasilii L'vovich himself, in the nobility of his heart, will not deny
> the same. Since more than ten years have already passed without any exaction
> or presentation for the same, and since I have already lost my legal right to
> exact the repayment of the aforementioned 100 rubles (with interest for 14
> years, which makes more than 200 rubles), I humbly beg his High Nobility,
> Dear Sir, my uncle, to pay me the 200 rubles according to Christian duty – I
> name as my plenipotentiary to receive this same money Prince Petr Andreev-
> ich Viazemskii, a well-known man of letters.
>
> Collegiate Secretary
> Aleksandr son of Sergei Pushkin
> 15 August 1825.
> *The Village of Mikhailovskoe.*[46]

As an explanation for the "stylistic exuberance" that marks this text as an Arzamasian familiar letter, Todd offers, "Plato's theory that all young creatures need to
leap may be as good as any."[47] One might also take a more social-materialistic perspective, however. Simply put, did making an elaborate joke of a request for money
make it more or less likely that Vasilii Pushkin would give Aleksandr Pushkin two
hundred rubles? At least in part, Pushkin's objective here, after all, is to get some
money. In order to achieve this objective (the perlocutionary act), he had to choose
among a set of options for forming the request. Unfortunately, we do not know
whether his request was successful, but we do know that he thought Arzamasian
play the form most likely to be successful for the simple reason that this is the form
he chose to employ.

When we cast a social-scientific eye on Pushkin's request, it becomes clear
that the very features that make this letter a literary object (stylistic exuberance,
parodic play) are also its most salient features as an artifact of social interaction. In
other words, Pushkin's "set toward the message" is not entirely disinterested and
unmotivated, but serves a social-interactive purpose.[48] Erving Goffman's concept
of "face" is once again useful here. According to Goffman, the participants in any
interaction attend to one another's face, and he distinguishes between two kinds of
face: negative face and positive face. One threatens her interactants' *negative* face
by imposing on them or by impeding or interfering with their projected self-image,

the "line" they have taken. And one threatens the *positive* face of interactants by not supporting, not ratifying, and/or not enabling their "line" – or, simply, by challenging it. The behaviors we use when it becomes necessary for us to threaten someone's face without offending her or him are what we call "politeness." For example, requests always involve an imposition, however slight, and therefore threaten the addressee's "claim to freedom from imposition" – a key component of negative face.[49] To soften or ameliorate (the politeness theorists use the verb "redress") the threat to negative face that all requests entail, we can do something as simple as tacking on the word "please" to the tail end of the request. Thus, in certain contexts, the utterance "Stand aside, please" is polite, while the utterance "Stand aside" is impolite. Goffman's concept of face and the models of politeness it inspired, which I revisit in more detail later, are useful here. We find in Pushkin's letter to his uncle a number of devices aimed at bolstering Vasilii Pushkin's positive face in order to ameliorate the threat to his negative face that requesting two hundred rubles inevitably involves. In politeness theory, this is called "positive politeness."[50] As Todd notes, this letter is marked as an Arzamasian familiar letter – and writing the letter in, so to speak, an "Arzamasian key" is in and of itself a form of positive politeness. In so doing, Pushkin "claims 'common ground'" with his uncle.[51] To do this, he uses the "in-group identity markers" of Arzamas: parody, galimatias, and a disdain for officialdom.[52] The mechanism of parody here is a simple juxtaposition of "high" and "low": the "high" diction of the official document is deflated by the "low" details of childhood everyday life (money "for nuts"; the servant-minder, Ignatii), the personal (aunts and grandmothers), and, of course, the inherent irregularity of a loan from a child to his uncle. The "low" details are from everyday life and the domestic specifics shared by Pushkin and his uncle, thus drawing the latter into the semantics of parody in a very personal way. This kind of displacement of traditional aesthetic categories, in which the despised discourse of officialese is adopted as a "high diction" (rather than, say, the Pindaric ode), is typical of Arzamas. Indeed, this displacement is the very heart of Arzamasian galimatias. By engaging in this sort of play, and by doing it well, Pushkin projects his uncle not only as an Arzamasian, but as someone capable of understanding and enjoying such verbal play. Rather than "baldly" requesting two hundred rubles, Pushkin found it more effective to make a game – specifically, an Arzamasian *shalost'* – out of it. As such, the aesthetic and the transactional here are highly interdependent, not independent. Far from being disinterested or unmotivated, the verbal play of this letter is designed to effect the perlocutionary act, to get the spendthrift Vasilii L'vovich to give up two hundred rubles.

Considering more broadly the Arzamasians' motivation for writing letters as they did, and whether or not it was a purely disinterested exercise of aesthetic play, a couple of key questions arise: Were these texts written purely for the sake of writing them?[53] Or were the letters intended as a substitute, however inadequate, for face-to-face interaction? We might test a very simple hypothesis: if the Arzamasians wrote literary letters to each other even when they were located in the same city and face-to-face interaction was possible, then it would seem that they were, indeed, writing solely for the fun of it. They often wrote verse epistles to one another under such circumstances. The fact is, though, that they hardly ever wrote letters to fellow Arzamasians living in the same city at the same time. When they did send a note across town, it was invariably brief and businesslike. From this, we can surmise three things. First, this was not just writing for the sake of writing. Second, face-to-face interaction was preferred to letter-writing. Third, letter-writing served the same social function for the Arzamasians as it did (and does) for everybody else: to keep in touch and interact verbally via post. That the letters are also literary objects is not a contradiction, but part of the ritualization and aestheticization of everyday life so characteristic of the period.

Linguistic markers also underscore the "social reality" of the letters, that is, the fact that they really can be viewed as artifacts of genuine social interaction, which distinguishes them from other interactive literary genres such as the verse epistle. Second-person pronoun usage is perhaps the most clear-cut of these markers and is undoubtedly the simplest expression of social proximity and relationship in the Russian language. Though it has certainly changed over the centuries, the T/V opposition in Russian differs little from other languages in the T/V typological group. Languages in this group have both a formal and an informal second-person singular pronoun, like the French *tu* and *vous*. Russian has both the informal *ty* and the formal *Vy*. In nineteenth-century epistolary Russian, it carried the same social meaning as it does in spoken Russian today. One could even conduct the *Brüderschaft* by post. A particularly interesting example comes from the correspondence of Zhukovskii and Nikolai Gogol. Between 1842 and 1852, the two maintained a lively correspondence from various points around Russia and Europe.[54] For the first five years, they were *na Vy*. When their mutual friend, Nikolai Iazykov, died in February 1847, Gogol wrote to Zhukovskii, "Iazykov, too, has gone! ... My beautiful brother, we must henceforth be even closer to one another and, living on Earth, look upon one another as if we had met in the house of the Heavenly Father of our brethren."[55] Here and in the rest of the letter Gogol assiduously avoids using any second-person pronouns or verb forms (no mean feat!). Apparently, however, there was only one way to interpret Gogol's plea for closeness. Zhukovskii took the hint, and his next letter opens, "My dear Gogolek, I received your [*tvoe*] short little letter with the enclosed excerpt from [Stepan] Shevyrev's letter."[56] In his subsequent reply, Gogol addresses Zhukovskii *na ty*, and the epistolary *Brüderschaft* is complete with nary a drop having been drunk.[57] Though this shift takes place not in person but in letters, it is still a binding, real social action. The two remained *na ty* until Zhukovskii's death in 1852. In at least this respect, epistolary discourse was no less real than face-to-face interaction.

There are, however, a few historical peculiarities of T/V usage in literary Russian that bear noting here. The T/V system in Russian was heavily influenced by French in the mid-eighteenth century, when the V form became a convention of politeness in spoken Russian, and writers of that period gradually introduced *Vy* in their works. Thus, Vasilii Trediakovskii qualifies his use of the formal pronoun in a 1744 translation: "While translating, I changed the pompous Latin Thou [*Ty*] to our softer You [*Vy*] nowadays in general polite usage."[58] The T form, however, retained its place in Russian literature as a conventional honorific. As a rule, court poets of the eighteenth century addressed the emperor or empress using the informal pronoun. This tradition carried over into the early nineteenth century in both literary and official language. For example, Karamzin addresses Alexander I as *ty* in the ode he composed for the new tsar's coronation, and his subjects addressed him as *ty* in their petitions.[59] This follows liturgical language, which observes the same rule with respect to the "Tsar above." But not only tsars were addressed as *ty*. Indeed, the Russian equivalent of Old Church Slavic *ty* was adopted as a conventional honorific in the familiar verse epistle. Naturally, there is a big difference between what we might call the "conventional *ty*" and the "actual *ty*." In an epistle, when Viazemskii addresses Zhukovskii *na ty*, the pronoun is somehow "real" or "actual" because the two really were on T-form terms. But when Batiushkov addresses Turgenev (with whom he was *na Vy*) using the T form in an epistle, the pronoun is a conventional honorific.[60]

Tellingly, though they always used this "conventional *ty*" in their verse epistles, the pronoun use in the prose of their letters was strictly "real." Sometimes, one encounters both within a single letter. In 1823, while in exile in Odessa, Aleksandr Pushkin wrote a letter to the Arzamasian Vigel', who had taken up residence in Kishinev, where Pushkin spent most of 1820–23. Pushkin's letter is very much in the Arzamasian tradition, Arzamas being the only connection between the two. It contains a comic verse epistle which compares Kishinev to Sodom and ends with a promise to visit Vigel' as soon as possible. Pushkin offers his companionship on one condition:

> Тебе служить я буду рад
> Своей беседою шальною –
> Стихами, прозою, душою,
> Но, Вигель, – пощади мой зад!

[I shall be glad to serve you with my wandering conversation – with my verses, prose, and soul, but, Vigel', spare my butt!]

Immediately following this epistle is a small apology: "This is a poem, and therefore a joke – don't be angry [*ne serdites'* – a V form imperative], but have a laugh, dear Filipp Filippovich – you [*Vy*] are languishing in the same godforsaken hole I languished in for three years. I wished to divert you for but a moment …"[61] Thus, even within a single letter, Pushkin uses the T form in verse, but reverts to the "real" V form in prose.[62] The same is true of Pushkin's 1817 epistle "Odin lish' ty s glubokoi len'iu …" ("Only you with deep laziness …") addressed to Turgenev, with whom he was *na Vy* in their correspondence. Such a pronoun disconnect is common in Arzamasian verse and letters. Batiushkov, for example, addresses both Dashkov and Turgenev as *ty* in his verse epistles to them, but in their correspondence, he was *na Vy* with both of them.[63] This was an established norm of Arzamasian discourse. The Arzamasians meant for their letters, though literary works, to be (or to seem like) genuine social transactions nonetheless. And this criterion of "social real-ness" distinguished the genre of the familiar letter from other, "purely literary" genres such as the verse epistle.

The letters are so "socially real" that we can even use second-person pronoun usage to map relative social proximity within Arzamas. Not all the Arzamasian correspondence was preserved, and not all the members corresponded with one another, so we have records of only sixty-three correspondences (of 380 possible).[64] At the center of this map would be Zhukovskii, who was *na ty* with nine out of his ten Arzamasian correspondents. Close by is Viazemskii – with nine of eleven. Other, more peripheral Arzamasians, were less likely to be *na ty* in the correspondence; Bludov, for example, was so familiar with only one out of seven correspondents.[65]

The Arzamasian letters beg treatment as both social and aesthetic constructs in no small part because their authors cast them as textual interactions. And the Arzamasians' efforts to make their familiar letters be and seem like interaction on paper has proven an analytical stumbling block to understanding the Arzamasian letters. The main difficulty here is precisely the concatenation of literary convention and social transaction in the letters. William Todd points to this difficulty when taking the Soviet scholar N. L. Stepanov to task for his use of the idea of "set" (*ustanovka*) to link the discourse of letters to the "grammar" of conversation.[66] "As we shall see, the idea that familiar correspondence is conversational in nature has been a cliché since Greek and Roman antiquity; Cicero and Demetrius used it, as did the Humanists for their Latin letters. This cliché and his oversimplification of Tynianov's theory led Stepanov to contradict his own empirical observation that familiar letters could be rather 'ornamental' in style."[67] Implicit here – both in Stepanov, and in Todd's critique of him – are notions about the nature of ornamentation and conversation that require further consideration. In important respects, Arzamasian epistolary discourse is fundamentally different from conversation. At the same time, it also relies on some of the key features of conversation, most importantly, turn-taking.

So-called conversational style in literary works is often characterized as a mimicking of actual conversational speech. The argument runs that an illusion of conversation between author and reader is maintained by borrowing certain conventions and features of real spoken discourse and representing them textually. The main obstacle here is laughably obvious: lacking recordings, we have no idea how people talked two centuries ago, and a priori definitions of conversational style are therefore an analytical dead end. Conversational style in familiar letters, as it is defined by some literary scholars, is plain, straightforward, and non-ornamental.[68] This definition harks back to the generic prescriptions of early modern practitioners of the genre, such as Thomas Sprat, who remarked in 1668 that "the Letters that pass between Friends ... should have a Native clearness and shortness, a Domesticall plainness." They should not "consist of ... elaborate Elegancies, or general Fancies."[69] Meanwhile, the actual language of Russian polite conversation was not at all plain in Pushkin's day. Consider, for example, one contemporary's description of Vigel''s conversational style: "His speech was generously spiced with felicitous turns of phrase, light verse, anecdotes, and all this together with a refinement of expression and a linguistic showiness imbued his conversation with an inexpressible appeal."[70] This hardly sounds like the conversational style described by literary scholars. In fact, the art of conversation was highly valued in Russia's salon culture, and it may well be that speaking plainly was the exception rather than the rule even in everyday life.

This difficulty is connected to another highly problematic literary-historical cliché: that Karamzin directed writers to write as they speak. Actually, Karamzin's take on the connection between oral speech and written language is far more complex. In "Otchego v Rossii malo avtorskikh talantov," he argues, in fact, not that writers should write as people speak in polite society, but that writers should write as they *do not yet speak* – the whole point being that Russian did not yet have its own version of polite discourse, and writers were obliged to invent it. As Batiushkov said in his famous "Rech' o vliianii legkoi poezii na iazyk" ("Speech about the Influence of Light Poetry on Language," 1816), "the Russian language has preserved a certain severity and obstinacy."[71] To remedy what he perceives as the bombastic coarseness of the national language, Batiushkov recommends the development of *all* types of poetry, including light poetry.

As Boris Uspenskii observes, there is a tension here between real and ideal language and between literary language and the language of society talk.

> [T]he Karamzinians focused not on real, but on, so to speak, ideal conversational speech approbated according the criterion of taste. "... Russians are still obliged to speak on many subjects in the same way a talented man would write about them," acknowledges Karamzin, and his follower P. I. Makarov – one the most prominent theoreticians of Karamzinism – notes in his review of a translation of Genlis: "... Sometimes one must write as people should talk, and not how they really talk." This position, clearly, allows for a certain incongruence between literary language and conversational speech, which, however, is in no way dictated by their fundamental opposition. They are talking about modifying and perfecting conversational speech as a way to create a literary language.[72]

It follows that in the familiar letter of the early nineteenth century, the "illusion of conversational style" is not about *representing* an existing set of linguistic norms, but about *inventing* new literary convention – literary convention that could serve as a model for the development of conversational speech. The aim of the Arzamasians was not to imitate the cadences, syntax, and lexicon of spoken language, but to observe (or bend and break) the standard conventions of letter-writing, and one of these conventions was "conversational style." As Cynthia Lowenthal notes, "Letters seem 'like talk' in part because the overall structures of the best familiar letters are much freer than the strict rhetorical patterns long established for excellence in formal and informal discourse. Moreover, letter writers and readers learn to interpret certain written conventions as spontaneity."[73] In the Arzamasian letters, Todd found that the main features of conversational style include ellipses, coordinate conjunctions, interjections and particles, short phrases in subject-verb order, the avoidance of relative clauses, a focus on everyday detail, colloquial vocabulary, controlled macaronicism, and so on. Like Lowenthal, he also notes features meant to evoke the rapid intonational patterns of talk, such as a preponderance of exclamation marks and question marks, as well as underscoring words for emphasis.[74] But it would be a mistake to conflate literary-stylistic convention with semblance. Letters are a fundamentally different kind of interaction than talk. They can "seem like talk" only to readers who know how to interpret these conventional stylistic features, all the more so in the Russian context because, according to Karamzin and his allies, real conversation did not yet have any defined stylistic norms.

Though letters and talk are different kinds of verbal interaction, there are a couple of important similarities. According to Austin's famous proposition about speech acts in verbal art, "a performative utterance will, for example, be *in a peculiar way* hollow or void if said by an actor on the stage, or if introduced in a poem, or spoken in soliloquy.... Language in such circumstances is in special ways – intelligibly – used not seriously, but in ways *parasitic* upon its normal use – ways which fall under the doctrine of the *etiolations* of language."[75] As we have already seen, this is certainly not true of the Arzamasian letters. To the contrary, speech acts in Arzamasian letters often had concrete results in the "real world" and are not in the least "hollow." The assertives, commissives, expressives, directives, and declarations (to use Searle's classification[76]) of the letters are very real, live illocutions. For this reason, we can glean from them clues about how the Arzamasians constructed and maintained their social relationships in much the same way linguists analyze any other kind of verbal interaction. Secondly, epistolary discourse shares with talk one central feature: turn-taking. The phenomenon of turn-taking is a key difficulty in Mary Louise Pratt's attempt to devise an interactive model of literature. In her *Toward a Speech Act Theory of Literary Discourse*, she argues convincingly that the formalist idea of "poetic language" is a fallacy.[77] She then proceeds to argue that literary discourse is merely one variety of language in general, and that literary texts are in fact part of a "conversation" – they are, so to speak, long turns in a one-sided interchange. Much as "hearers" grant "speakers" a disproportionate amount of time in conversation to relate a narrative, the reader grants the writer a long turn with the expectation that the writer's contribution will be sufficiently interesting and well-crafted to merit his/her holding the floor for a long time. Needless to say, Pratt's approach is fraught with difficulties when applied to, say, novels, but far less so when applied to correspondence.

In the Arzamasians' familiar correspondence, turn-taking is overtly moderated and negotiated – lacking as they did the resources of body language or, indeed, the ability to interrupt. Replies to letters were expected, and the Arzamasians invariably either acknowledge receipt of letters or berate one another for not writing. Not replying to a letter was an offense. Their awareness of turn-taking is particularly pronounced in the endings they gave their letters. As Todd notes, "The nature of familiar correspondence as an ongoing activity prevented strong closure in any single letter."[78] Common "end games" in Arzamasian letters include apologies for going on for so long, professions of weariness, and excuses for not writing more – all of which are geared toward moderating the writer's contribution to a cooperative discourse. For example: "I'm tired of scribbling. Farewell. I expect a reply on a whole quire."[79] Or: "That's enough for this time. There's no time to write more."[80] Or: "But I've worn you out. Excuse me and pardon."[81] So, turn-taking was part of the structure of the Arzamasian familiar letter. The apologies, especially, are telling: "I have overstayed my welcome, taken too long a turn."

In the end, the point I want to make is that Arzamasian letters are not a *representation* of "real" interaction or conversation, but a mode of real interaction in their own right. That is, these letters are not "like talk," but a distinct kind of social-linguistic behavior carried out in literary form. Letter-writers do not seek to represent conversation, but to write letters. Nonetheless, given the behavioral similarities to conversation, tools developed for the analysis of face-to-face interaction can be used to analyze the interaction that takes place in letters.

Rudeness and Domesticity in the Arzamasian Letters

In November 1818, just seven months after the last meeting of Arzamas, Zhukovskii wrote a long and impassioned letter to Viazemskii. "I should not be a buffoon for you; let's leave that for Arzamas," he implores.[82] Zhukovskii was upset about jokes which Viazemskii had made at his expense in a couple of communal Arzamasian letters. In his letter of August 27, 1817, Viazemskii writes that he had taken two incongruous books to his Kostroma estate: Zhukovskii and Henri Joseph Dulaurens's scabrous anti-clerical novel *Le compère Matthieu*. "You might more easily mate a good verse with one of Khvostov's verses, or Glinka with common sense," he jokes, continuing, "I can say of myself honestly: 'I erected a marvelous and eternal monument to myself.' Ask Zhukovskii if he got the hiccups. No doubt he wasn't spared nightmares. Poor thing!"[83] These jokes are entirely in an Arzamasian key and, as such, require some decoding. As his Arzamas name, Svetlana (the heroine of his eponymous ballad), suggests, Zhukovskii's sometimes extreme chasteness was the butt of many Arzamasian jokes. Viazemskii's quotation of the opening line of Derzhavin's famous adaptation of Horace is, of course, an indecent pun. And hiccuping, like burning ears, was a sign that someone was saying or thinking bad or improper things about the hiccuper. Adding insult to injury, in another letter, from October 18, 1818, Viazemskii asks Turgenev to pass on various messages to individual Arzamasians, and Zhukovskii again comes in for some ribbing: "Tell Zhukovskii on Sunday that he's a drunk; it will start a quarrel for the ages because Saturday will still be on his shoulders and in his head, and in his glassy eyes, and on his white tongue."[84]

Zhukovskii was incensed by these jokes, not so much because they were offensive to him personally, but because Turgenev was showing them around to non-Arzamasians. "And don't forget that you're writing to Turgenev! In this respect, he is much too careless. He wants for a witty letter that he can carry under his shirt and read to everyone he meets." Zhukovskii is offended that Turgenev saw fit to read such letters to outsiders, yet he casts his reproach in terms of personal fealty. "I am not concerned by what opinion one or another outsider might have of me from these letters; but I cannot say that it is pleasant for me to be playing the role I play in your letters in front of other people for even a minute; most importantly, it is unpleasant that Turgenev is *reading* these letters [to people] and, and that nothing stops him from reading them: in this case, he is more vexing to me than you are!" It was all well and good to abandon notions of propriety and honor within Arzamas, he says. "There was much indecency in our Arzamas, but we had resolved that everything was allowed there under the aegis of galimatias." Crossing the boundary of domestic Arzamas and bringing these jokes into society, though, changes their character entirely. They are no longer the amusing byproducts of camaraderie, but offensive and cruel. He continues, "We are all mistaken when we view as friendly unconstraint many things that we would not allow ourselves in the presence of outsiders. In this unconstraint there is often much that is insulting; sometimes you allow yourself with a certain careless ease to say in front of everyone that which should be spoken only when alone: can this really be called frankness [*otkrovennost'*]?"[85]

This dispute and especially Zhukovskii's language ("we had resolved," "outsiders") underscore the fact that Arzamasian domesticity was constructed, and not a "naturally-occurring" network of social connections. Its borders had to be policed because the meanings and social significance of Arzamasian *shalosti* became distorted when removed from this controlled domestic context. It is important to come to an understanding of how the Arzamasians went about constructing their relationships in the writing they addressed to one another, because in other, non-domestic works that were intended for external readerships they used similar techniques in

constructing new kinds of familiar relationships with the reader at large. As Zhukovskii's letter suggests, one of the main techniques they used in order to create
their insular social cohesion was, paradoxically enough, a calculated variety of
rudeness. By behaving with one another in ways impermissible outside the clois-
tered Arzamasian underground, the membership reified at every opportunity both
the insularity and the cohesion of the group. This rudeness plays out most clearly in
the Arzamas brotherhood's huge corpus of familiar letters.

Linguists working on politeness have often addressed the connection between
intimacy and rudeness. Geoffrey Leech, for example, argues that since rudeness
is associated with intimacy, some forms of rudeness can be used to foster and
build intimacy.[86] He terms this "the Banter Principle": "surface" impoliteness (that
is, impolite language that is patently not intended to insult or offend) is used to
strengthen social bonds. Jonathan Culpepper, who calls this variety of impoliteness "mock impoliteness," points out that Leech's Banter Principle "only works
in contexts in which the impoliteness is understood to be untrue."[87] Recall in this
regard that one of Zhukovskii's complaints is precisely that Turgenev and Viazemskii had been insufficiently mindful of context – an outsider might not understand
that Viazemskii is joking and think that Zhukovskii really was a drunk. Culpepper
warns that Leech's model is overly simplistic, as it does not specify these contexts
and does not consider the differences between genuine and mock impoliteness.
"The factors influencing the occurrence of impoliteness in equal relationships [i.e.,
relationships between social equals] are complex.... In a familiar relationship one
has more scope for impoliteness: one may know which aspects of face are particularly sensitive to attack, and one may be able to better predict and/or cope with
retaliation that may ensue."[88] One important resultant factor in Culpepper's model
of mock impoliteness is thus affect: whether and how much interactants like one
another. "The more people like each other, the more concern they are likely to have
for each other's face. Thus insults are more likely to be interpreted as banter when
directed at targets liked by the speaker."[89] The Arzamasian context was predicated
on mutual admiration (or at least the semblance of it), and a mutual admiration that
was not a given in non-domestic contexts. Thus, an Arzamasian insult delivered
in another context, per Culpepper, is more likely to offend. Indeed, Zhukovskii's
entreaty that Viazemskii not think of him as a buffoon except in the context of
Arzamas betrays genuinely hurt feelings and a fear that Viazemskii no longer loves
and respects him: "I would like you to treat your feelings toward me as a *touch-me-
not* [*nedotroga*] and preserve them for yourself in a certain purity."[90]

Renate Rathmayr's work on contemporary Russian politeness finds that projected intimacy is one of its central features. Her Russian informants stressed
warmth and genuineness in their descriptions of what makes a person polite.[91]
Commenting on Rathmayr, Richard J. Watts notes a peculiarity of Russian politeness: "Russians frequently maintain that a polite person should not use vulgar or
coarse language. There is, in other words, a link between language and politeness
in Russian metapragmatic politeness."[92] This makes Russian linguistic artifacts – in
our case, texts – especially well-suited to politeness analysis.

For my analysis of politeness and intimacy in the Arzamasian letters, I have
found a now-classic model of politeness most useful: Penelope Brown and Stephen Levinson's *Politeness: Some Universals in Language Usage* (Cambridge: Cambridge University Press, 1987). This book, though it still serves as the theoretical

foundation for most empirical work on politeness, has been much maligned.[93] Yet, of the available models, it provides the best conceptual framework for looking at politeness in the Arzamasian letters because it hinges on the idea that the social relationships between interactants predict the verbal form of speech acts, and we can observe such speech acts in textual artifacts.

Politeness is dedicated to the memory of Erving Goffman, and Goffman's concept of "face" is the central conceptual figure of Brown and Levinson's model. Here is how they describe their use of it:

(i) "face," the public self-image that every member wants to claim for himself, consisting in two related aspects:

    (a) negative face: the basic claim to territories, personal preserves, rights to non-distraction – i.e. to freedom of action and freedom from imposition.

    (b) positive face: the positive consistent self-image or "personality" (crucially including the desire that this self-image be appreciated and approved of) claimed by interactants.

    .... In general, people cooperate (and assume each other's cooperation) in maintaining face in interaction, such cooperation being based on the mutual vulnerability of face. That is, normally everyone's face depends on everyone else's being maintained, and since people can be expected to defend their faces if threatened, and in defending their own to threaten others' faces, it is in general in every participant's best interest to maintain each others' face, that is to act in ways that assure the other participants that the agent is heedful of the assumptions concerning face given under (i) above. (Just what this heedfulness consists in is the subject of this paper.)[94]

The "heedfulness" Brown and Levinson describe – that is, politeness – is the face-maintenance work that takes place when someone performs what they call a "face-threatening act" (FTA). FTAs include: requests, orders, suggestions, advice, remindings, threats, warnings, dares, expressions of disapproval, criticism, contempt, or ridicule, complaints and reprimands, irreverence, mention of taboo topics, blatant non-cooperation, and so on.[95] Here, I will confine myself to requests because they are relatively easy to identify and because it is possible to gauge the success or, in the terminology of speech act theory, the "felicity" of the act of requesting. For example, I can say that a request for a cigarette was felicitous if the requestee gives the requester a cigarette.

Brown and Levinson describe three factors people take into consideration when performing a FTA, three "sociological variables" that differ from culture to culture.[96] There is, first of all, one's social proximity to the person whose face she is about to threaten. In most cultures, people's social proximity is determined by how frequently they interact and by the kinds of things (material and non-material) they get from one another. I am "socially closer" to my wife or to the person I buy a newspaper from every morning than to the person I passed once on the street last week, and I take that into account when performing FTAs with them. Second, when performing an FTA, one must consider the measure of power that her interactant has over her and vice versa: is it her commanding officer or her maid? Third, one must consider how much of an imposition the FTA is. In most cultures, asking for the keys to someone's Cadillac is more of an imposition than asking him to shut the window.

In the politeness equation these three factors are equal to what Brown and Levinson call the "weightiness" of an FTA:

social distance + relative power + imposition = weightiness.

This weightiness, in turn, predicts the "politeness strategy" one will employ when performing the FTA. The more weighty the FTA, the more effort one must put into remediating it. Brown and Levinson describe five "superstrategies" for such remediation (do not do the FTA, do the FTA baldly, with positive politeness, with negative politeness, or off record) and twenty-four politeness strategies.[97] In fact, there are probably many, many more. The important thing here is that one can and often does project the weightiness of the FTA in the *form* of the FTA, the "politeness strategies" employed. Brown and Levinson point out that this is a universal cognitive process in interaction.

> Hence the choice of strategy will in general "encode" the estimated danger of the FTA; this is why one receives with considerable apprehension phrases like:
> (7) I'm awfully sorry to bother you, and I wouldn't but I'm in an awful fix, so I wondered if by any chance ...[98]

More to the point, the verbal form of FTAs can be manipulated in such a way as to project or "re-rank" social distance, relative power, or imposition.[99] In an attempt to be chummy with someone I do not know, I might, for example, wink, smile, and form a very bald FTA: "Gimme a smoke!" This is rather commonsensical, for, "in intimate relations there may be presumed to be minimal danger of face threats. This gives rise to the use ... of insults or jokes as a way of asserting such intimacy. Hence we get conventionalized (ritualized) insults as a mechanism for stressing solidarity."[100] And this is where we come back to the Arzamasians. In their letters, they often employ politeness strategies that encode a very low weightiness – which is to say, very little social distance and very little power asymmetry. Arzamasian impoliteness projects intimacy, solidarity, and equality that may or may not have actually existed. This is part of how they constructed domesticity.

There is a particularly striking example of such exploitation of (im)politeness strategies in a letter Zhukovskii wrote to Sergei Uvarov, a.k.a. *Starushka*, in April 1837. In the letter, Zhukovskii makes a request of Uvarov. Gauging the actual weightiness of this request requires some background. To put it mildly, Zhukovskii and Uvarov were not close in 1837, and they found themselves increasingly at odds after Pushkin was killed in January of that year. In response to his death, there was such an outpouring of public grief and anger that Nicholas I all but banned the publication of anything to do with the tragedy. (In fact, it was for his poem on Pushkin's death, "Smert' poeta" ["Death of a Poet," 1837], that Lermontov first got into serious trouble with the authorities.) As the minister of education, Uvarov was largely responsible for keeping a lid on expressions of grief in the press and he insisted on personally approving any publications on Pushkin before releasing them to the censor's office.[101] In 1834–36 Uvarov was often in conflict with Pushkin, who managed to circumvent Uvarov's censorship regime, in large part, by dint of his personal relationship with the tsar. In 1836 Pushkin also wrote a vicious satirical ode, "Na vyzdorovlenie Lukulla" ("On the Recovery of Lucullus"), targeting Uvarov, and he circulated epigrams accusing Uvarov of giving important posts to men he fancied, thus publicly "outing" him.[102] For this and other reasons, Uvarov enforced the ban with especial vigor. Zhukovskii managed to get an article through directly to Nicholas I, and when the tsar approved the article (after censoring it), Zhukovskii sent it to Uvarov with the following letter. At such a tense moment, in the midst of toothsome political maneuvering, and twenty years after Arzamas disbanded, Zhukovskii wrote an exceedingly domestic letter to Uvarov, one so rooted in Arzamasian discourse that it had to be accompanied by an "official" letter in which Zhukovskii made his request in the language of state.

> I'm sending you, *Starushka* [Uvarov's Arzamas nickname], an official letter and with it this small Arzamasian howl; and with this Arzamasian howl an article about Pushkin's death in two, so to speak, copies, with this little explanatory story: I presented the copy marked "No. 1" personally to His Majesty the Emperor with a request for permission to publish it in *Sovremennik* [*The Contemporary*]. His Majesty read the manuscript, made some comments, and instructed me to cut some things. On His Majesty's instructions I cut everything relating to him and I cut everything where I mention foreigners by name, which you can see for yourself if you compare No. 1 with the unnumbered copy. The latter is being submitted to the censor's office. Be so kind, *Starushka*, old fellow, to cast upon these pages scribbled-over with goose quill those parts of your being in which from the time of Adam is contained the visual faculty of the sons of man. Read with your characteristic reasonableness, so befitting a minister of education selected for this high position by dint of the monarch's trust, the pages which have flowed from beneath my pen, and be so kind as to thrust this creation into the gaping maw of the censor's office, that famished cow which grazes on the plump pastures of literature and chews its cud with some kind of philosophical selflessness; be so kind as to prescribe to this cow that it quickly chew up my article and quickly spit it out so that I might immediately submit the cud for printing in *Sovremennik*. In any event, I wish you all providence, and for prompt execution of my request, I shall send you from Arzamas, where I hope to be, a fat goosey goose, with which I take your leave. *Svetlana*[103]

Such levity in such circumstances is, to say the least, difficult to understand at first. Zhukovskii of course knew about Pushkin and Uvarov's struggles over the censorship of the journal *Sovremennik*, which Pushkin launched the previous year, and he knew very well how poorly Uvarov had conducted himself.[104] It seems unlikely that Zhukovskii had any genuinely friendly feelings toward Uvarov, and they were certainly not close. Meanwhile, such familiarity with the minister of popular education – Arzamasian or not – was highly risky, even for someone with Zhukovskii's standing at court (he was, at the time, the Grand Duke Alexander's tutor). As it was, Uvarov was making life difficult for Zhukovskii, and they had never been friends. The only other letter from Zhukovskii to Uvarov that I have been able to find is written in an entirely un-Arzamasian tone.[105] Of his Arzamasian correspondents, Zhukovskii was *na Vy* only with Uvarov. In a word, the social distance and the power asymmetry were very great, and this was a very weighty FTA. Yet, his letter is in no way obsequious. Apparently, though, Zhukovskii chose the right approach to Uvarov because the article was published in the May issue of *Sovremennik*.

"The 'Arzamasian' tone of the letter was meant to remind Uvarov of his youth and of his duty to the memory of the 'Arzamasian brotherhood,'" notes Oleg Proskurin in his commentary on the letter.[106] In fact, as I remarked earlier, this Arzamasian tone was so pronounced that Zhukovskii had to enclose the previously quoted letter inside another letter written in non-Arzamasian prose. From this, we can conclude that Zhukovskii thought using "Arzamasian play" (*arzamasskii smekh*), an entirely unofficial discourse, was a good strategy for getting what he wanted.

Let us consider two questions. First, what does this "Arzamasian tone" in Zhukovskii's letter consist of? Most obviously, there are the symbols of Arzamas: the nicknames (Svetlana and *Starushka*), the idea of the "return to Arzamas," the goose, and so on. The drawn-out metaphor of the censorship cow with its physiological detail is also reminiscent of Arzamasian galimatias, as is the absurdly extended periphrasis of "eyes" ("that part of your being ... ").[107] The second question, then, is what does this tone accomplish here? As Proskurin says, it was meant to remind Uvarov of the social connections of his youth. But to what end?

Clearly, Zhukovskii thought that this appeal to their domestic relations of twenty years ago, however contrived they might have been, was the most effective strategy available to him for redressing the face threat. Zhukovskii threatens Uvarov's positive face by going directly to the tsar, thus disregarding Uvarov's claim to power in the matter. The domestic language of the letter also threatens Uvarov's positive face by challenging the authenticity of Uvarov's rank and status in society and state. What is more, he threatens Uvarov's negative face by making a request of him, encroaching on Uvarov's freedom from imposition. Given that the FTAs are quite weighty, Zhukovskii takes "redressive action" in order to ameliorate these threats and in order to improve the chances that his request will be granted.

The form of redressive action that he chose is "positive politeness." The ingroup language (the "Arzamasian tone") of the letter serves to indicate that, in some respects, Zhukovskii wants the same things Uvarov wants, "by treating him as a member of an in-group, a friend, a person whose wants and personality traits are known and liked."[108] Instead of giving deference, apologizing for the FTA, hedging, going on record as incurring a debt, or doing the other things one often does to attend to negative face when making requests, Zhukovskii seeks to cast Uvarov as an equal member of the same group (who just happens to be minister of popular education and a hated enemy of Zhukovskii's recently deceased friend, Pushkin) and to pay him compliments. By treating Uvarov as an ally, Zhukovskii underscores their old, Arzamasian connection, which presupposes a commonality of interests. This commonality implies that the request is made in the interests of both parties, that granting the request will be beneficial to both, and that Zhukovskii's request does not signal any disrespect.

Meanwhile, returning to the politeness equation (social distance + relative power asymmetry + imposition = weightiness), this positive politeness encodes a low weightiness. In other words, the form of politeness Zhukovskii chose is designed to make it seem as though there was not much chance that Uvarov might lose face. Moreover, it signals that Uvarov is a social equal, which, given the realities, was quite risky and not a little impudent. It stands to reason that positive politeness is less drastic a redressive action than negative politeness.[109] This is the difference between "Give me a cigarette, my man" and "I beg your pardon, but I don't suppose I could trouble you for a cigarette? I've just run out and I can pay you back." The former relies on a sense of belonging and mutual dependence ("We're in the same boat"), whereas the latter "is oriented mainly toward satisfying (redressing) [the addressee's] negative face, his want to maintain claims of territory and self-determination."[110] The former employs only "my man," while the latter employs an apology, an acknowledgment of the imposition, and a promise of reciprocity. Again, the weightiness of the FTA predicts the kind of politeness one chooses for performing that FTA. Using positive politeness, therefore, indicates that one does not think that the FTA is very weighty. This means that Zhukovskii is projecting or encoding low values for two variables of weightiness – low social distance and low power asymmetry – in the form of his request while in no way downplaying the imposition.[111] In a word, "Arzamasian play" serves here to project a social unity that does not exist. And that is how Zhukovskii managed to get the censor's stamp on the article so quickly. That "Arzamasianness" could be used as a politeness strategy nearly twenty years after Arzamas disbanded shows just how forceful it was. Moreover, the impulse to use it in this way so long after the fact suggests that one of its primary original functions was to serve as the glue binding the Arzamasians together, making it easier and more rewarding to do things for one another, to build and reify social corporation.

Recall that the Arzamasians rejected the conflation of, in Vigel''s words, the Table of Ranks with the Table of Talents. Now, rank was a means for regimenting social interaction. In terms of politeness, one took into consideration whether a person was his "superior" (*vysshii*), "equal" (*ravnyi*), or "inferior" (*nizshii*). In other words, the state sought with its ranks to regulate the factor of "power asymmetry" described earlier; one was supposed to know how risky a FTA was by referring to his position in the Table of Ranks, as well as the position of the addressee. These terms were inscribed even in the translations of Latin etiquette manuals. In one, for example, we read that on a stroll in the park one should walk three feet behind and to the right of superiors, abreast of equals, and four [sic] feet ahead and to the left of inferiors.[112] Society, of course, had its own means for regulating relative social power: money, style, looks, connections, "character," and so forth.

The Arzamasians rejected this regimentation, and their refusal to operate on these prescribed terms (at least within Arzamas) angered some their contemporaries. For example, in a denunciation to the gendarmerie, Faddei Bulgarin condemned the Arzamasians' behavior on all three fronts. "With equals they were intolerable, arrogant, inferiors they treated like field slaves, and they criticized all superiors *behind their backs* and sent them up in epigram form."[113] Not only was the politeness (actually, "rudeness" that projects intimacy) the Arzamasians adopted a rejection of regimentation, it was also part of how they defined themselves.

One way to test whether "Arzamasianness" and rudeness are concomitant is to compare conduct with non-Arzamasians to conduct within the group. There are many examples of this. Zhukovskii, for example, opens a letter to Ivan Dmitriev in 1816 (the apex of Arzamas) thus: "Dear Sir, Ivan Ivanovich. I had the pleasure of receiving your pleasant letter and your book. From all my heart I thank Your Excellency for this priceless gift."[114] Two months later, the opening of his letter to Derzhavin is similarly formal: "Dear Sir, Gavrila Romanovich. I hasten to fulfill the promise I made to Your August Excellency; I am sending the German transla- tion of your ode, 'Vel'mozha.'"[115] Compare these formal openings to the opening of a letter to Viazemskii from the same month: "What's happened to you? You don't write me and you're not answering my letter."[116]

True, Zhukovskii is similarly abrupt with many of his friends, not just Arza- masians. That same year, for example, he opens a letter to Nikolai Gnedich: "I'm returning the signed ticket, and I thank dear Hexameter for the tobacco."[117] Obvi- ously, the relative "rudeness" here is to some degree merely the language of friend- ship, of genuine intimacy. And distinguishing specifically Arzamasian rudeness from the normal rudeness associated with intimacy requires longitudinal analysis of the interaction between two people who both joined Arzamas to see whether the nature of this interaction changed with the addition of Arzamasianness. Luckily, we have a well-documented correspondence between two Arzamasians, Viazemskii and Aleksandr Turgenev, from 1812 until Turgenev's death in 1846.[118] This gives us the opportunity to trace their interaction from well before Arzamas through the period of its activity and beyond.

I have attempted a crude "statistical" analysis of politeness (specifically, social distance and power asymmetry) in these letters. As an index, I have chosen the fre- quency of requests.[119] According to Brown and Levinson, the surest way to avoid threatening anyone's face is to avoid FTAs altogether. This, again, is common- sensical: we are very reluctant to make requests or ask even very small favors of people who are quite socially distant from us and/or have greater social power. Because the capacity of politeness to redress face threat is not unlimited, and not all FTAs *can* be redressed, the very fact of making a request indicates that one or more of the following three conditions is in force: (1) the social distance is not too great; (2) power asymmetry is not too high; (3) the request is sufficiently insignificant as to downgrade any risk of threatening face. Further, a request threatens not only the negative face of the addressee, but also the positive face of the person making the request, who may, for example, incur a debt to the addressee in making the request. In any case, I think it is plain enough that people who are closer to one another make more requests of each other, and that people seeking to foster or simulate social proximity more readily take on the risk of making a request, especially if the desire to increase social proximity is perceived to be mutual.

I compared the frequency of requests in two periods: 1812–13 (pre-Arzamas) and 1816 (Arzamas). The years 1812–13 are sufficiently distant from the organiza- tional meeting of Arzamas (October 14, 1815) to avoid any "contamination." I used two years in the first sample because the correspondence itself (or at least the letters that have been preserved) was much less frequent prior to the founding of Arza- mas. In 1816, on the other hand, the correspondence was at its most "Arzamasian": twenty-eight of the thirty-three letters from 1816 (85 percent) mention Arzamas or Arzamasians by name. Analyzing the frequency of requests in the correspondence of Viazemskii and Turgenev is particularly interesting because they had very little face-to-face interaction in those years. The relationship is almost entirely episto- lary in nature.

In 1812 and 1813 there are .842 requests per page: sixteen requests over nineteen pages.[120] In 1816, there are 2.4 requests per page: seventy-two requests over thirty pages.[121] From one period to the next, the frequency of requests nearly *triples*. Naturally, there are any number of other factors that might contribute to this rise in frequency: the war with its privations, the mobility of the correspondents, and so on. Moreover, we can have no idea how representative a sample the extant letters are. Nonetheless, the rise of frequency does correspond to the founding of Arzamas, and given the pivotal role Arzamas plays in the correspondence, it is not unreasonable to posit a correlation. This is especially true because the change is so dramatic. Further, the politeness strategies employed in these requests are the same found in other Arzamasian requests, which most often fall under Brown and Levinson's category of "bald, no redressive action" or relatively weak politeness strategies. Some representative examples, with reference to Brown and Levinson's typology of politeness strategies:

- On April 20, 1816, Viazemskii writes Turgenev: "Вели ко мне скорее выслать для подписчиков второй том Жуковского и потребуй от Кашкина записку о числе экземпляров первого тома, высланных ко мне в разные времена [Give the order to send me quickly the second volume of Zhukovskii for the subscribers and demand of Kashkin a note with the number of copies of the first volume sent to me at various times]."[122] *Strategy*: No redressive action, bald.

- In October, 1815, Zhukovskii writes to Viazemskii, informing him of the founding of Arzamas. He closes the letter: "Приезжай, чтобы заслужить свое место в нашем клубе [Come [to Petersburg] to earn your place in our club]."[123] *Strategy*: Positive politeness. 5.3.2. "Assert reciprocity."

- On November 26, 1815, Dashkov writes to Viazemskii: "Приезжайте скорее к нам, хотя недели на две [Come visit us soon, at least for a couple weeks]."[124] *Strategy*: No redressive action, bald.

- In December 1815, Zhukovskii writes Viazemskii: "Присылай письмо липецкого жителя и критики [Send me the Lipetsk resident's letter and the critical articles]."[125] *Strategy*: No redressive action, bald.

- On April 26, 1816, Zhukovskii writes Viazemskii: "Кстати об Арзамасе: переписаны ли речи и протоколы? Прошу мне прислать оригиналы [Apropos Arzamas: have the speeches and protocols been copied? I request that the originals be sent to me]."[126] *Strategy*: Negative politeness. 5.4.4. "Impersonalize Speaker and Hearer."

Membership in Arzamas entailed a significant reduction in the risk of face threat. This cannot be said of any of the period's other well-known literary societies, to which, as detailed earlier, the Arzamas domesticity was conceived as a counterpoint. Beseda, in particular, with its regimentation of social power and social distance and its codification of face, was not meant to foster genuine intimacy between members. We would search in vain for any semblance of domesticity in Beseda. The contained egalitarianism ("contained" in that it did not extend beyond the confines of the group) of the Arzamasian letters is also motivated in part by literary convention. As Todd notes, "The Arzamasians wrote their letters for equals; the genre required this relationship between author and recipient."[127] This is a key point. Todd also observes that the familiar letter was an ideal form for cultivating the intimate discourse of Karamzin's sentimentalism as a counterpoint to the bombast of Shishkov's Romantic, nationalistic, biblical language. Thus, the Arzamasians did not so much choose the genre as it chose them: it was simply the best available form for doing what they instinctively felt needed doing. One of the things they wanted to do was institute a hierarchy of literary reputation based on the anarchy of talent and personality rather than the ironclad order of the Table of Ranks. The letters and the interaction recorded in them were an extremely suitable vehicle for precisely this purpose.

To sum up, impoliteness in the form of direct, bald FTAs and relatively weak politeness strategies served two purposes in Arzamas. First, it encoded a certain kind of equality, an absence of power asymmetry. Second, it encoded social proximity. The Arzamasians wanted to project equality because they found the conventional means for regulating power asymmetry (such as the regimentation of relationships in Beseda) both ethically repugnant and an obstacle to their modernization aims. The raw intimacy of their letters is partly a side effect of their efforts to construct a mostly artificial domesticity. It is also, in large measure, genuine. As they met more and more frequently and provided more and more favors for one another, some of the Arzamasians did genuinely grow close. The group, much as they intended, produced some very lasting and very literary friendships, most of which were either initiated or strengthened by participation in Arzamas. And, genuine or not, the closeness projected in Arzamasian *shalosti* was so strong that it could still be used effectively many years later to get things done in literary institutions – effectively enough that Zhukovskii chose it as a rhetorical strategy when he approached Uvarov about getting his obituary of their beloved Cricket published twenty years later.

3

The Green Lamp

Sexual Banter

The Semenovskii Regiment mutiny in October 1820 spurred a general crackdown on unsanctioned assembly of all sorts, and the familiar literary societies that had begun to multiply rapidly in the late 1810s were among the targets. One tale of this crackdown comes to us from Filipp Lialikov's memoir of his student days. Lialikov, later a prominent education official, recalls a literary society that he and fellow students started in the fall of 1820, and which was shut down almost immediately. "We decided to form a literary society, that is, to read works we wrote especially for the group and to analyze them critically. About a dozen of us signed up. I. V. Titov provided his spacious apartment in Golutvino, near the Nikola church on the other side of the Moscow River, for our meetings. We got together about three times; then we hear that the neighborhood police has us under surveillance, and then the landlord informs Titov that unless the gatherings are brought to a halt, he cannot allow him to remain in his house. Nothing to be done. We had to quit. And that is how the most innocent and pure thing imaginable came to an end."[1]

As Lialikov's account suggests, the authorities were very much on the lookout for any kind of informal gathering, any manifestation of orchestrated domesticity. This was a different time than the heyday of Arzamas, just five years prior. Historiographic convention has it that 1818 was a watershed year for Russian culture, especially political culture. The years immediately following the Russian victory over Napoleon were a period of great expectations and relative freedom for reform-minded elites. But Russians hoping for democratization and modernization had become disillusioned by 1818: their hopes for a constitution were dashed in late 1817; under Alexander's leadership, the Holy Alliance quashed dissent all over Europe; Arakcheev came into his own in 1817; and later the wave of European revolutions in 1820–21 cemented a strain of violent, reactionary paranoia in the regime. The late Alexandrine period (1818–25) was a period of increasingly heightened state scrutiny of private life. As we have seen, Alexander I was kept informed of even the most trivial misbehavior, and often meted out punishment himself. By 1820, the social and aesthetic experiment of Arzamas would not have been possible. Collectives formed outside the contexts of state and society now inspired fear in the state administration. The Arzamasian retreat to domesticity very swiftly became an untenable option.

The disbanding of the students' literary society described by Lialikov was not an isolated incident. According to the Decembrist Ivan Burtsev, "during the investigation of the Semenovskii Regiment incident, the police uncovered many secret societies in St. Petersburg."[2] One of them was the Green Lamp. The Lampist Iakov Tolstoi later testified, "Once, a [Green Lamp] member, retired Colonel Zhadovksii, announced to the society that the government had information about it and that we were in danger, not having permission to create the society."[3] We can date Zhadovskii's announcement to late 1820, and we know his information was correct because the following spring the gendarmerie submitted a report to the tsar on their investigation, which names the Green Lamp as one of the secret societies uncovered.[4]

Not surprisingly, then, given the political climate, we have scant knowledge of familiar literary societies in the late 1810s and early 1820s. The Green Lamp is in some respects an exception to this rule. We know a bit about it, and this is due to one simple fact: Pushkin was a member of the Green Lamp.[5] As with anything related to Pushkin, the Green Lamp has been picked over thoroughly.[6] It has also been extremely politicized over the years, and the accepted version of the group's history and creative output, now ubiquitous, stems from Stalin-era manipulation, concealment, and distortion of the available documentary evidence. The pressure to establish Pushkin's credentials as a revolutionary and earnest proto-Bolshevik led scholars to greatly overemphasize the role of the Welfare Union (*Soiuz bla-godenstviia*) in the Green Lamp. As a result, generations of Russian schoolchildren and university students have been taught that the Green Lamp was nothing more and nothing less than a propaganda arm of the Welfare Union, the first political formation of the radical movement that later came to be known as "Decembrism." According to this version, Pushkin was, through the Green Lamp, "connected without his knowledge" to the Welfare Union.[7] In fact, as Igor Nemirovsky has recently demonstrated, Pushkin was not connected to the Decembrist societies for the simple reason that they wanted nothing to do with him. According to the Decembrist Ivan Gorbachevskii, the Decembrist leadership (namely, the Supreme Duma) actually forbade Southern Society members from even becoming acquainted with Pushkin "because of his character and cowardliness, because of his dissipated lifestyle, he would immediately make a denunciation to the authorities about the existence of the Secret Society."[8] As Nemirovsky shows, Gorbachevskii's disparagement of Pushkin was actively and consciously concealed by scholars during the Soviet period, and they evidently hoped that it would eventually be expunged from the historical record.

Despite this long history of ideologized scholarship, careful distillation of Soviet research on the Green Lamp and examination of the primary materials, scant as they are, makes possible the reconstruction of certain indisputable facts. There were at least sixteen members of the Green Lamp. These included well-known writers like Aleksandr Pushkin, Anton Del'vig, Iakov Tolstoi, Fedor Glinka, Nikolai Gnedich, and Arkadii Rodzianko. Most meetings were held at the home of the brothers Nikita and Aleksandr Vsevolozhskii, where Children's Clinic #27 at 35 Prospekt Rimskogo-Korsakova now stands, across the street from the Nikola church square. Other members included the prominent proto-Decembrists Sergei Trubetskoi and Aleksandr Tokarev. Most Lampists were military men; almost half were veterans of 1812, like the guardsmen Iakov Tolstoi, Fedor Glinka, Fedor Iur'ev, Dmitrii Barkov, Pavel Mansurov, and Ivan Zhadovskii, a retired colonel. Many Lampists later had distinguished careers, like Dmitrii Dolgorukov, who became a senator; Aleksandr Ulybyshev, who was the editor in chief of *Journal de St.-Pétersbourg* for eighteen years; and Iakov Tolstoi, who rose to the rank of general as Russia's most important spy in France.[9] Besides these sixteen, there likely were more members (Tolstoi says "upwards of twenty" in his 1826 letter to the tsar), but they left no trace in the Green Lamp archive, and their membership is not attested in any other documents.[10] The Green Lamp held at least twenty-two meetings between March of 1819 and late fall of 1820. Members were admitted to the society only on the basis of a unanimous vote. They were sworn to secrecy. They were required to present any new works to the Green Lamp before publishing them. The presidency of the society was an elected and rotating office. Members were obliged to have a ring with the Green Lamp insignia (an oil lamp and an anchor) on it. There was also a "statute" that required the members to write and speak freely. Members presented works of four types at Green Lamp meetings: poems, historical works (essays and anecdotes, historical-educational projects and outlines), journalism, and theater criticism. Reading and discussing poetry was the Green Lamp's main raison d'être, and poetry, much of it unpublished, makes up the bulk of the group's archive. The textology of the archive reveals a literary collective that worked over member contributions with great thoroughness. It is not for nothing that many Pushkinists have characterized Pushkin's involvement in the group as one of the most important episodes in his literary biography, for it was a true poet's workshop, and the only one of which Pushkin was a member.

Literary historians of the Golden Age commonly speak of Arzamas and the Green Lamp in the same breath, and the latter is often cast as a continuation of the former. On the whole, there is good reason for this. The Green Lamp in some respects modeled itself after Arzamas: it, too, had a mocking system of parliamentary procedure and a host of other humorous rituals. Thirty years after the fact, Iakov Tolstoi, for example, recalled that the host of the Green Lamp meetings, Nikita Vsevolozhskii, kept a young Kalmyk servant boy, who was required to attend all Green Lamp proceedings. Whenever a member let fall a vulgar phrase (*poshloe slovtso*), the boy was required to regale the offender with the military salutation "*Zdraviia zhelaiu!*" (I wish you health!).[11] Like Arzamas, the Green Lamp demanded participation from all its members: even the dilettantes among them contributed essays, theater reviews, and verse. As in Arzamas, there were plenty of political discussions in the Green Lamp, though it would be folly to speculate on their content given the paucity of evidence currently at our disposal. Like the Arzamasians, the Lampists took up domestic genres, especially the familiar verse epistle. And they also created a very specific, in-group language. Finally, the Green Lamp shared one important member with Arzamas – Pushkin.

One of the key differences between Arzamas and the Green Lamp is the role of libertinism. The Arzamasians never rejected moral convention in the extreme way that became the hallmark of the Green Lamp. As Lotman points out, the focus on salon behavior (*salonnost'*) characteristic of Arzamas was completely absent in the Green Lamp. Arzamas and the Green Lamp, he says, were very similar in many respects: the same rejection of *arakcheevshchina*, the same focus on "familiar directness" (i.e., the rudeness of intimacy) and anti-officialdom (*neoffitsial'nost'*).[12] Yet, the "dual influence" of radical politics and libertinism on the Lampists had the result that "the [Arzamasian] orientation toward salon culture was foreign to the Green Lamp."[13] Whereas Arzamas was simultaneously a phenomenon of society and domesticity, the Green Lamp was conceived in opposition to society norms and values. The Arzamasian self-image excludes extreme drunkenness and profligate sex. Indeed, drunkenness was to be despised: it was the centerpiece of some of the Arzamasians' cruelest epigrams. Their *shalosti* were thoroughly frivolous, but there is a kind of properness even to their frivolity. The Lampists, on the other hand, constructed a self-image that was all about flouting moral convention, about reveling in frivolity, drink, and wild sexual abandon. By comparison, the Arzamasians' fabled jellied-goose dinners seem extraordinarily chaste.

To some extent, this divergence is a reflection of the differences between the groups' respective aesthetic ideologies. The Green Lamp is self-consciously rooted in discourses of eighteenth-century French libertinism, whereas Arzamasian aesthetics, following Zhukovskii, bore little relation to that tradition. And unlike Arzamas, the Green Lamp shunned literary polemic in general, and in published form in particular. Only three of the twenty-five poems in the Green Lamp archive are pronouncedly polemical: Tolstoi's "Tarakan-ritor" ("The Rhetorician Cockroach," composed 1819), Barkov's "Prigovor bukve Ъ" ("A Death Sentence for the Letter Ъ," composed 1818?), and Tolstoi's "K Emel'ianovke" ("To Emel'ianovka," composed 1819, published 1821). Only the latter was published in the 1820s, and only with major revisions, including the removal of a lengthy ad hominem polemical attack (on whom exactly, I am not yet sure).[14]

Perhaps most importantly, though, the role of libertinism in the Green Lamp was significantly greater due to the changes in the sociopolitical climate that took place in Russia between 1815, when Arzamas formed, and the first meetings of the Green Lamp in 1819. In a word, the political significance of forming an underground literary society was strikingly different. As the organs of state encroached further and further into the domestic realm in the mid to late 1810s, unofficial social formations flourished, ranging from the somber cells of the Welfare Union to the hilarity of the Green Lamp and the infantilism of schoolboy societies like Boratynskii's "Society of the Avengers" or M. A. Dmitriev's "Society of Loud Laughter." The observance of absurd rituals and charters (often parodies of Masonic rites) in these societies is a comic "refusal to take the whole world of state values seriously."[15]

After 1818, the regime, from non-commissioned policemen to the tsar himself, began to view any unofficial gathering as potentially dangerous. And they were probably right to do so. Familiar societies were by nature a refuge from the symbols and structures of power – uniform, rank, title – that increasingly regulated the behavior of the nobility under *arakcheevshchina*. This is true not only of societies like Arzamas and the Green Lamp, which adopted republican charters and parliamentary procedure (albeit jokingly). According to one memoirist, even in the Masonic lodges of the late 1810s, "any kind of man could breathe and speak freely; inside the Lodge, hierarchical differences in rank and station, which were so sharply prominent and so strictly observed outside, were smoothed over."[16] Various measures were taken to prevent such groups from forming. And the authorities were wont to shut down any such organizations that popped up. By late 1820, Alexander I had received several reports of various secret societies bent on overthrowing the monarchy. The result was the disbanding of the Welfare Union, and more intrusive measures for controlling the conduct, speech, and even thought of the urban gentry. By August 1822, Alexander was so alarmed by the continued existence of secret societies in Russia that he banned all Masonic lodges and all "secret societies" of any kind – that is, all social formations and assemblies that existed outside the contexts of society and state without formal permission. He was so concerned, in fact, that he ordered Viktor Kochubei, the minister of the interior, to institute a new set of policies: all secret societies were to be shut down; all members of any secret societies were to sign a pledge that they would not participate in any such groups in the future, and anyone who refused was to be discharged; all governors and commanders (*Glavnoupravliaiushchie*) were to be held responsible for preventing the formation of any new societies in the future; further, ALL military and civil personnel under their command were to pledge that they are not, and will not be in future, a member of any secret society.[17]

It was in this political climate that the Green Lamp came into being. Unlike Arzamas, it was a secret society that the membership assiduously concealed even from their closest friends.[18] As I've already mentioned, members were required to take an oath of secrecy upon joining the group; a "statute" required Lampists to speak freely at meetings; members wore rings with the Green Lamp seal; and the group developed a whole code language with its own, peculiar, conspiratorial semantics.[19] At the most fundamental level, the Lampists were asserting a right to assembly that the tsar at that time did not grant his subjects. And herein lies the main difference between Arzamas and the Green Lamp: the Green Lamp was an illegal and secretive association of (mostly) young clerks and officers, whereas Arzamas was a gathering of some of the country's most powerful technocrats, courtiers, and military men, which convened with the blessing, and even encouragement, of the court.

Another important difference between the Green Lamp and Arzamas has to do with geography and genre. Whereas the Arzamasians were often spread all over the empire and abroad, the Lampists were usually all living in Saint Petersburg and saw each other weekly and, in some cases, even daily. Perhaps as a result, they did not take up the familiar letter with anything approaching the Arzamasians' verve. We have only a handful of Lampist letters, most written after the group had disbanded and several members, including Pushkin, had gone into exile or been transferred. The very different tone and the very different character of their letters' "literariness" underscore the aesthetic, political, and behavioral divide that separated the two groups. The most famous of these letters is Pushkin's postscript to the Lampist Pavel Mansurov, which he wrote in October 1819, just a few months after the Green Lamp first convened. Mansurov had recently been transferred to Novgorod to serve in the Arakcheev colony there, and Pushkin sends him news of the Lampists:

> With difficulty, I have convinced Vsevolozhskii to allow me to write you a few lines, dear Mansurov, you amazing-Circassian [*chudo-Cherkes*]! Are you well, my joy; are you jolly, my delight – do you remember us, your friends (of the male sex) ... We have not forgotten you, and every day at half past seven we memorialize you at the theater with applause and sighs – and we say: Pavel, our light! what's he doing now in great Novgorod? he envies us – and weeps for Kr ...... (from his lower duct, naturally). Every morning the winged maiden flies to rehearsal past the windows of our Nikita, as in the past telescopes and cocks are raised toward her – but alas ... you don't see her, she doesn't see you. Let's leave off the elegies, my friend. I will give you a historical account of our friends. Everything is as it was; the champagne, thank God, is healthy – and so are the actresses – the one is getting drunk up, and the others are getting fucked – amen, amen. That's as it should be. Iuriev's chancre [*khuerik*], thank God, is healthy – I've got a little one opening up; and that's fine. Vsevolozhskii N. is gambling; a column of chalk dust! the money showers down! Sosnitskaia and Prince Shakhovskoi are growing fatter and stupider – but I'm not in love with them – though I did call him out for

his lousy comedy, and her for her mediocre acting. Tolstoi is sick – I won't say with what – I've got a lot of cocks in my letter as it is. The Green Lamp is smoking – it seems it will burn out – and it's a pity – there's still oil (i.e., the champagne of our friend). Are you writing, my compeer – will you write me, my cutesthy [a lisping *kholosen'koi* for *khoroshen'kii*]. Tell me about yourself – about the military settlements. I need all of this – because I love you – and I hate despotism. Farewell, deary.

    Cricket A. Pushkin.[20]

Pushkin signs off with his Arzamas nickname, "Cricket," and in some respects, this letter is indeed a hypertrophic interpretation of Arzamasian epistolary convention – isolated verbal tricks borrowed from Arzamasian letters are swollen to the bursting point, especially non-standard, "oralistic" punctuation. Pushkin, of course, employs here the same strategies of positive politeness characteristic of the Arzamasian letters: in-group identity markers and a finely calibrated rudeness that projects intimacy. We also see here cross-fertilization with the epistolary style of Viazemskii, who appears to have been Pushkin's most important model in this genre at the outset of his career. The repetition of an obscenity and the subsequent expression of concern that the letter is already too full of them is a compositional scheme Viazemskii also employs. For example, a few months later, in his letter to Pushkin of April 30, 1820, he repeats the words "shit" (*govno*) and "to shit" (*srat'*) and derivations from them no less than seven times in the first paragraph, which he closes, "Well, that's a shitty beginning to my letter."[21]

There are a few things in this letter, however, that mark it as distinctly *un-*Arzamasian. First, there is the open political speech ("I hate despotism" – in reference to *arakcheevshchina*), which, though comically deflated by the context, could not have appeared in an Arzamasian letter. This is a function of projected audience. Though it certainly cannot be said that Pushkin was especially careful about watching his political tongue during his Petersburg period, such extreme looseness does not figure in letters that he expected would be circulated widely. The Arzamasians, for their part, did not ever engage in such speech in their letters precisely because they were meant to be shared, semi-public documents. (Recall, for example, Zhukovskii's complaint about Turgenev's lack of discretion in this regard.) It is also likely that they simply *expected* that these letters would be intercepted and read by the police. In any case, most of the Arzamasians were very politically powerful, highly placed statesmen and bureaucrats who did not lack venues for political expression. Indeed, for the prime instigator of Arzamas, Sergei Uvarov, the very existence of the group was a form of political expression – a "calling out to Europe," as Mariia Maiofis characterizes it. The Lampists, on the other hand, were drawn from the ranks of card-sharps, adjutants, theater mavens, lowly clerks, and under-officers who lacked any public venue even for theater criticism, much less political expression.[22]

Another un-Arzamasian feature of this letter is the obscenity. With very rare exceptions (Viazemskii being the chief culprit), the Arzamasians do not use obscenity in their letters. Again, this is a function of projected audience: the Arzamasian letters were not only domestic texts, but also society texts (often with a thick veneer of faux domesticity), which were sometimes read in mixed salon company. As Lotman notes, the Green Lamp positioned itself very much in opposition to both society and state, and therefore rejected salon culture. And Pushkin wrote this particular letter secure in the knowledge that there was little danger the addressee would be showing around Pushkin's description of his own weeping privates in society – even if he could, which he could not because he was stationed at a remote Arakcheev colony.

A connected, but distinct un-Arzamasian feature is the sexual frankness of the letter. Irina Paperno writes, "There arose a peculiar cult of circle speech, of 'friendly banter' [*druzheskie vraki*], of domestic language, with a special semantics that was understandable only to 'insiders' [*svoi*]. The intimacy of this insider language in the Green Lamp and Arzamas, and later in Pushkin's circle of the mid-1820s and 1830s, was underscored by the risqué topics, swearing, and indecencies that became a defining characteristic of this language."[23] A distinction must be made, however, between the use of vulgarity in the Green Lamp and in Arzamas: Pushkin's letter to Mansurov far exceeds any Arzamasian letter in its vulgarity. Beyond the preoccupation with genitalia and venereal disease, which appear without any of the periphrasis and intertextual puns of Arzamasian sexual discourse, an object of sexual desire is even called by name (according to the commentaries published by the Russian and, later, Soviet Academies of Sciences, "Kr ......" refers to the fifteen-year-old dancer Mariia Krylova), something unthinkable in the comparatively chaste Arzamasian interpretation of the genre. As we shall see, such frank sexual banter is in fact a defining characteristic of the Green Lamp, and it was by no means an apolitical discourse. Libertine discourse here, as in other places and in other times – eighteenth-century France or Italy, for example – is fueled by "resistance to the growing predominance of the public over the private."[24] There is ultimately no discourse more domestic than the discourse of sex. Hence the connection between *shalosti* and sex: recall Vul'f and Boratynskii's use of the word *shalost'* to describe uncondoned sex acts.

The Green Lamp employed some of the same techniques to construct and insulate domesticity – rudeness, code language, and so on – that Arzamas did. Given the increased risks of constructing domesticity, though, they employed other practices as well: oaths of secrecy and nonstop sexual banter. The latter has been neglected almost completely in the scholarly literature; in fact, it has often been assiduously concealed. It is, meanwhile, perhaps the most important hallmark of the domesticity constructed in the Green Lamp. In the following analyses of Lampist poems, one by Anton Del'vig and one by Arkadii Rodzianko, I explore the forms and functions of sexual banter in the Green Lamp on the, so to speak, "micro-philological" level. I take as my conceptual starting point Geoffrey Leech's "banter principle" discussed in the preceding chapter.[25] This is the idea that "surface rudeness" (i.e., rudeness patently not intended to offend) can be used to cement the boundaries of social contexts and strengthen bonds between interactants. According to Brown and Levinson, bringing up taboo topics such as sex in conversation is one of the "intrinsic" face-threatening acts, which indicate that the speaker "doesn't care about (or is indifferent to)" the hearer's positive face.[26] Naturally, this is entirely context-dependent. In some contexts, taboo topics are completely appropriate, but the onus for assaying this "appropriateness" is on the speaker. When she or he miscalculates appropriateness, face threat occurs. As with any FTA, a large part of how we evaluate the "appropriateness" of taboo speech in a given context, according to Brown and Levinson, is by correctly evaluating its weightiness – that is, by correctly assessing social proximity and relative power. This is, of course, very commonsensical: people engage in sexual banter only when interactants are very close socially or when they want to project such closeness. It can also be used to assert imbalances in social power – hence the use of sexual banter to degrade. Looking at sexual banter in the poetic *shalosti* of the Green Lamp gives us an opening on the ways in which they used poetry to consolidate a group identity.

Arkadii Rodzianko's "Ligurinus"

Arkadii Rodzianko is one of the most forgotten of the Golden Age's forgotten poets.[27] He has received some limited scholarly attention, mostly due to his association with Pushkin during the latter's Petersburg period, but we still know relatively little about him, despite the fact that he was an important and well-known figure of the day's literary scene. The oldest of seven children, Rodzianko was born to a prominent Poltava family in 1793. He was educated at the Moscow Pansion and moved to Petersburg in 1814, where he joined the Life Guards. There he met Derzhavin, who liked his poetry, and started publishing soon thereafter. Another admirer, Sergei Aksakov, was to read the young Rodzianko's poem "Razvaliny Gretsii" ("Ruins of Greece") at a Beseda meeting, but Derzhavin died and Beseda disbanded before he got the chance. Rodzianko retired from the Life Guards to his Poltava estate in 1821, soon after the gendarmes uncovered the Welfare Union, with which he was associated. He continued publishing after retirement, though more rarely, and died in the late 1840s. There are about twenty-eight known publications of his works.[28] Of his unpublished work, we have some album inscriptions attributed to him, a number of letters, and a 448-page manuscript collection of 151 of his poems, which he compiled in 1838–40 (hereafter, "the RGB collection").[29]

Among the Lampists, Rodzianko is particularly interesting. His reception has shifted over the years in much the same way as the perception of the Green Lamp. His contemporaries regarded him principally as a light, Epicurean poet. For example, in 1823 Aleksandr Bestuzhev-Marlinskii called him "a carefree bard of mirth and love."[30] (Interestingly, this is exactly what Fedor Glinka had called Pushkin in an 1820 epistle composed just weeks before Glinka's boss, the governor-general, informed him that Pushkin was under surveillance.[31]) For his part, Pushkin called Rodzianko by various names: "the Ukrainian Piron" and "the Local Deputy [*namestnik*] of Phoebus or Priapus."[32] Pushkin also called him "the Bard of Socratic Love" – which is to say the Bard of Homosexual Love.[33] Modzalevskii writes, "Pushkin's name for Rodzianko, 'the Bard of Socratic Love,' is ironic; Rodzianko wrote poems which, due to their indecent content, were, for the most part, inappropriate for publication."[34] Pushkin takes the term "Socratic love" from Voltaire's entry on male homosexuality ("Amour nommé Socratique") in his *Dictionnaire philosophique*.[35]

Modzalevskii held a view of Rodzianko that is in line with the opinion generally held by prerevolutionary scholars.[36] Though he probably never saw the RGB manuscript collection, Modzalevskii is quite correct that Rodzianko was the author of many poems that were "inappropriate for publication." Of his 151 known poems, perhaps half would not have passed the censors. In any case, for Pushkin, the most salient aspect of Rodzianko's reputation as a poet was his taste for erotica, and homosexual erotica in particular. And Rodzianko's reputation as "the carefree bard of mirth and love" survived well into the twentieth century, until it was challenged by the esteemed Soviet literary historian Vadim Vatsuro, who proclaimed

Rodzianko a civic poet.[37] His 1969 article on Rodzianko remains the most substantive treatment of Rodzianko's poetry and is a central text of the so-called Golden Collection (*Zolotoi fond*) of Russian literary history. In her recent book, for example, Mariia Maiofis cites it as an exemplary analysis of the interrelationships between political and literary life of the 1810s.[38] The problem with Vatsuro's account, however, is that he disregards (and, in fact, even conceals) the larger part of Rodzianko's oeuvre – namely, the domestic poems for which he was famed among his contemporaries – in order to make the case that Rodzianko's literary reputation as a "semi-pornographic poet" is merely an "aberration" and "legend" and that Rodzianko was actually a civic poet. Thus, the analysis Maiofis praises and builds on is in fact deeply flawed and incomplete, and still in need of correction.

The source of Vatsuro's confusion was an inability (shared by many Soviet literary historians) to acknowledge the concomitance of "serious" political thought and speech on the one hand, and domesticity on the other. To them, this seemed a paradox. In fact, though, it was not a paradox at all, and Rodzianko often equated domestic hedonism with political opposition. For example, in his satire "Dva veka" ("Two Ages," composed 1822), liberal bombast is a wine-soaked affair. He describes the "unschooled swarm" of liberal guardsmen that gathered around people like Pushkin and Aleksandr Turgenev:

И как пощаду дать их сборным вечерам,

....

Где мыслей в дерзости ум высший признают
И с веком наравне средь пьянственного пира
Где весит прапорщик царей и царства мира,
Полн буйства и вина, взывает: «Други, дам
Я конституцию двумстам моим душам!».[39]

[And how can one forgive their assembly soirees ... Where impudence is regarded the highest wit, and like the rest of the age, amid the drunken feast, where a corporal sits in judgment of tsars and of the kingdoms of Earth and, full of unruliness and wine, calls out: "Friends, I shall grant a constitution to my two hundred slaves!"]

In his epistles to Pushkin, Rodzianko further develops this nexus of domestic profligacy and political opposition. He praises Pushkin as a leader of the youth, a revolutionary figure, but he also describes him as a "rake and a spendthrift of the sacred gift of poetry."[40] In fact, it is precisely because Pushkin is so "unserious" that Rodzianko praises him. Long before he came to the Green Lamp, Rodzianko was writing verse in this vein. His unpublished poem, "Vostorg" ("Rapture," 1815), is a good example:

Пусть Ахиллъ блистаетъ боемъ,
Артаксерексъ – златымъ вѣнцомъ,
Не хочу я быть героемъ,
Не хочу я быть царемъ –

Я герой, коль восхищаю
Нѣжной лирой дѣвъ младыхъ,

Въ играхъ, въ пляскѣ побѣждаю
Всѣхъ соперниковъ моихъ.

Царь я, коль въ прохладныхъ тѣняхъ
Кипрскимъ упоенъ виномъ
У любезной на колѣняхъ,
Засыпаю сладкимъ сномъ![41]

[Let Achilles be famed for his prowess in battle, and let Artaxerxes – for his golden laurels, I do not want to be a hero, I do not want to be a king. I am a hero when I charm young maidens with a tender lyre, when I outdo all my competitors in games and dance. I am a king when, intoxicated on Cyprus wine, I fall into a sweet sleep on my beloved's lap in the cool shade.]

For Rodzianko, this Horatian devotion to peaceful, sensual reverie is an antipode to civic values – be they the values of the regime or of those who plotted against it.[42] It should not be forgotten that Rodzianko was by no means apolitical, and that this is therefore to some extent a poetic pose. Yet, as Vatsuro convincingly argues in his article on Rodzianko the civic poet, there was a distinct ambivalence to Rodzianko's politics. First and foremost, he strove to maintain ideological independence. While associating with circles of various political stripes, he identified himself fully with none.

Very little is known about Rodzianko's involvement in the Green Lamp. Among his surviving texts, we do not find the kind of self-referential verse about the Green Lamp that Iakov Tolstoi and Aleksandr Pushkin produced in great quantities. His single recorded comment on the group comes to us second-hand, from Lieutenant General Mikhailovskii-Danilevskii, a highly placed military and political figure. Mikhailovskii-Danilevskii writes in his memoirs of a conversation with Rodzianko, who, purportedly, told him that "when he was living in Petersburg about six years previous, he was in a society of young men who gathered for literary readings at Vsevolozhskii's house, where they recited anti-tsarist and anti-government poetry every time [they met].… This society was called *The Lampists*."[43] The Green Lamp stopped meeting in 1820, so the conversation Mikhailovskii-Danilevskii reports must have taken place in 1826–1827. Rodzianko presented an ode to Mikhailovskii-Danilevskii in 1824 in which he compares him to Maecenas, but one assumes that he would have nonetheless been rather circumspect with someone like Mikhailovskii-Danilevskii in 1826.[44] Rodzianko was involved with the secret societies in 1819–20 and therefore under investigation for involvement in the previous year's Decembrist Uprising. For his membership in the Green Lamp he even earned an entry in the Investigatory Commission's *Alfavit Dekabristov* (1827), an alphabetically organized compilation of the conspirators' resumes. (His case was dismissed because the Investigatory Commission concluded that the Green Lamp "had no political goal.") As such, whatever Rodzianko may have told Mikhailovskii-Danilevskii about the Green Lamp must be taken with a grain of salt.

Vatsuro is puzzled by the fact that Rodzianko, with his "dubious reputation of a semi-pornographic poet," would join the Green Lamp in 1819.[45] He asks, "How are we to explain his appearance in a literary society with a political bent?"[46] In fact, it would have been more surprising if Rodzianko had *not* joined. He had, after all, been in the thick of Saint Petersburg literary life since 1815, and we have documentary evidence that he was acquainted with several key Lampists nearly two years before the group's inaugural meeting in March of 1819.

In November 1817 Rodzianko was inducted into the Free Society of Amateurs of the Letters, Sciences, and Arts (VOLSNKh), which already counted Fedor Glinka among the membership.[47] More Lampists were inducted in the months that followed. The minutes for the August 8, 1818, meeting of VOLSNKh list the Lampists Fedor Glinka, Anton Del'vig, and Aleksandr Pushkin as present for a recitation and discussion of Rodzianko's poem titled "K Ligurinu (podrazhanie drevnim)" ("To Ligurine [An Imitation of the Ancients]," composed 1816). In a word, Rodzianko's literary connection with his fellow Lampists was already more than a year old by the time the Green Lamp convened. There is, furthermore, reason to suspect that Rodzianko may have known Pushkin even longer. In an 1817 epistle he invites a certain "P ......" to join him for a night of revelry. Though this initial cannot yet be decoded with complete certainty, several things suggest that it stands for "Pushkin."[48] Their literary relationship, therefore, quite possibly predates the Green Lamp by over two years.

One of the very few known rules of the Green Lamp is that members were admitted by unanimous consent. Therefore, something about Rodzianko's literary and social reputation must have been attractive to the Green Lamp. In a word, it is not so much that Rodzianko chose the Green Lamp, but that the Green Lamp found what Vatsuro calls his "dubious reputation of a semi-pornographic poet" in keeping with some of their principal aesthetic and social values. What is more, the poetry preserved in the Green Lamp archive evinces a taste for the "light" and the "frivolous" – in a word, for the domestic.[49] Thus, bringing on board "the carefree bard of mirth and love" was fully in line with the group's remarkably cohesive literary tendencies.

Another of the few known rules of the Green Lamp stipulated that authors present any work they wished to publish to the membership for critique before publishing it. Only one of Rodzianko's texts is preserved in the Green Lamp archive: the same poem, "To Ligurinus," that he presented to VOLSNKh in August 1818, but never published. However, he did publish at least two poems in 1819: "Derzhavin," an ode written on the occasion of the poet's death, and "Poslanie k A. S. Norovu" ("Epistle to A. S. Norov").[50] If he followed the Lampists' rules, he must have presented these poems to his fellow Lampists as well, but they were not preserved in the archive. In Rodzianko's RGB manuscript collection, we find forty-seven poems dated prior to 1819, most of them on Horatian themes sympathetic to the Lampists. In all likelihood, he presented many of these as well. In general, Rodzianko was eager for feedback on his work in the late 1810s and sought multiple venues for non-print dissemination of his work. Besides his involvement in the Green Lamp and VOLSNKh, he was a permanent fixture at the salon of Princess Khilkova, the daughter of Rodzianko's Ukrainian compatriot, D. P. Troshchinskii. According to one contemporary, "Arkadii Rodzianko would not print anything without first giving a trial reading in Troshchinskii's parlor."[51]

Let us turn now to Rodzianko's only text in the Green Lamp archive, the poem titled alternately with the Latinate "K Ligurinusu" and the Gallicized "K Ligurinu," which he dates 1816. Before bringing it to the Green Lamp two years later, he revised the poem in ways that tell us a great deal about the proclivities and tastes of the group. There are two known texts of "K Ligurinusu," one from the RGB manuscript collection (hereafter, "the RGB text"), and the other from the Green Lamp archive (hereafter, "the Green Lamp text").[52] The RGB text has corrections made in pencil. Unfortunately, though the Green Lamp text has been authenticated as an autograph by Tatiana Krasnoborod'ko at Pushkin House, and we know what Rodzianko's handwriting looked like, we cannot say for certain whether the pencilled corrections to the RGB text are in his hand. At any event, there are thus three redactions here: the Green Lamp text, the RGB text, and the corrected RGB text. As the pattern of variation shows, the uncorrected RGB text is the earliest redaction, and it is probably this text that Rodzianko presented to VOLSNKh in 1818.

Boris Modzalevskii, who first published the Green Lamp text in the 1920s, and Vatsuro, who discovered the RGB text in the 1960s, both comment in passing on the poem. Modzalevskii was unable to attribute the poem, and its author remained unknown for forty years until Vatsuro discovered the RGB text. Modzalevskii notes an important subtext for the poem, Ovid's story of Hyacinthus and Apollo.[53] For his part, Vatsuro calls it a translation from Book 5 [*sic*] of Horace's ode, but, as I discuss later, it is not anything like a translation of Horace's Ligurinus odes (*Odes* 4.1 and 4.10).[54]

Of primary interest here are the textological variants, because they allow us to trace the ways in which Rodzianko changed the poem in order to make it better fit the literary ethos and tastes of the Green Lamp. Presented here is the Green Lamp text together with the variants from RGB. The plain text in brackets represents the variants in the RGB manuscript. The italicized text in brackets represents the corrections to that text. The translation is of the Green Lamp version.

[Къ Лигуринусу]
[1816го Года]

[Латонидъ часто] оставляетъ
Свой двухолмистый Геликонъ
Поля и рощи пробѣгаетъ
За нимфою [Дафною, *нимфою*] пугливой онъ
Но чаще отъ высотъ Тайгета
Къ долинамъ гдѣ Пеней [Эврот, *Пеней*] шумитъ
Приманиваетъ Бога свѣта
Золотокудрый Гіацинтъ.

Тамъ житель неба голубова,
Свою Божественность забывъ
Цѣлуетъ ловчаго младова
Подъ сенію пріютныхъ ивъ,
Панъ зритъ ихъ ласки молчаливо [молчаливы;]
И Цинтія царица сновъ
Полускрываетъ ликъ стыдливой
За дымъ сребристыхъ облаковъ.

Во взорахъ отроковъ прекрасныхъ [Во взорахъ женщины прекрасной]
Иль полногрудыхъ дѣвъ младыхъ
Грозитъ равно Богъ чувствій страстныхъ [Грозитъ равно Богъ нѣги страстной]
Жестокимъ жаломъ стрѣлъ своихъ;
И Нимфѣ близь тебя дрожащей,
Урокъ любови первый дать

Равно прелестно, какъ горящій [Прелестнѣй, чѣмъ рукой горящей]
Цвѣтъ друга юнаго сорвать! – [Мальчишку друга обнимать.]

Что думать, Лигуринусъ милой!
Летящій мигъ ловить спѣши
Пока восторги лёгкокрылы
Доступны жаждущей души!
Скорѣй въ свой уголокъ уютной.
Эроту часикъ подари
Невѣждамъ дверью неприступной
Храмъ наслажденья затвори!

Тамъ – въ нишѣ тайномъ другъ мой, чаще
Лобзать тебя уста горятъ
Которыхъ поцѣлуи слаще
Чемъ первой розы ароматъ,
Чемъ многорощныя Гиметы
Благоуханный, чистый медъ
Или струя подземной Леты,
Ліющая забвенье бѣдъ. –

[Latonides often leaves his two-peaked Helicon and runs through the fields
and copses after a timorous Nymph: but more often, golden-curled Hyacinthus draws the god of light down from the heights of Taygetos to the valleys
where [the] Peneus roars [*shumit*]. This resident of the blue sky, forgetting
there his godliness, kisses the young huntsman under the protection of the
sheltering willows; Pan looks upon their caresses silently, and Cynthia, the
queen of dreams, half covers her bashful face behind the smoke of silvery
clouds. The god of passionate feeling threatens with the cruel point of his arrows equally in the gazes of beautiful boys or full-breasted young maidens;
It is equally marvelous to give a first lesson in love to the Nymph trembling
near as it is to pluck the burning flower of a young friend. What to think,
dear Ligurinus! Hasten to catch the fleeting moment while the light-winged
delights are still available to [your] thirsting soul. Hurry to your cozy little
corner! Grant a little time to Eros and lock the ignorant out of the temple of
pleasure with an impenetrable door! There – in a secret niche, my friend, lips
more often burn to kiss you, lips whose kisses are sweeter than the aroma of
the first rose, than the fragrant, pure honey of many-copsed Hymetus or the
stream of the subterranean Lethe, which pours the oblivion of woes.]

My as yet hypothetical reconstruction of the chronology of these texts' provenance is as follows. The RGB text, though put to paper in 1838–40, is a fair copy
of the first, original 1816 text. Rodzianko revised this text at some point in 1818–20
for presentation at the Green Lamp, which resulted in the Green Lamp text of the
poem. Soon after the RGB manuscript collection was completed, Rodzianko or
someone else familiar with the Green Lamp text made corrections to the 1816 RGB
text. Except in the third stanza (more on this later), these corrections reinstate lexical variants from the Green Lamp text. It is, of course, also possible that the RGB
and the Green Lamp texts were both extant and perhaps even in complementary

distribution in 1818–20. It is even possible that the Green Lamp text was actually put to paper during a meeting of the group, and the revisions were introduced on the spot. In any event, given the pattern of variation, it seems clear that the Green Lamp text is a second redaction. In lines four and six of the first stanza, we have the same pattern of lexical variation: Green Lamp variant → RGB variant → Green Lamp variant reinstated in penciled corrections. Thus: "Нимфою [Дафною, *нимфою*]" and "Пеней [Эврот, *Пеней*]." Obviously, if, twenty years after the fact, Rodzianko had introduced the variants "Дафна" and "Эврот" when compiling the RGB manuscript collection in 1838, there would be no reason to reinstate the Green Lamp variants. Therefore, we can conclude that the RGB text must be the earlier redaction and the Green Lamp text a later one. The implications of this conclusion for our picture of the Green Lamp are clear. Rodzianko, remember, was already well acquainted with some Lampists before the group convened and he knew their tastes. There can be no doubt that revisions he made to the RGB text in order to present it to the Green Lamp reflect his perception of this very particular audience. Most telling are the changes he made to the third stanza.

Before turning to the third stanza, however, let us pause on the lexical variants from the first stanza to get a sense for Rodzianko's poetic practice. In the first redaction, the RGB text, the fourth line of the first stanza reads "За *Дафною* пугливой онъ," which Rodzianko revised to read "За *Нимфою* пугливой онъ" in the Green Lamp text. One might speculate that Rodzianko wanted the "Nymph" of the first stanza to parallel the "Nymph" in the third stanza ("И *Нимфе*, близъ тебя дрожащей"). It is also quite possible that he is tapping into an inside joke: as I discuss at length later, "nymph" was a loaded word in the lexicon of the Lampists' literary-social milieu, which often meant, simply, "prostitute."

The lexical variation in the sixth line of the first stanza ("К долинамъ гдѣ *Эвротъ* / *Пеней* шумитъ") is a bit more difficult to explicate. It appears that Rodzianko here conflates the toponym "Peneus" (two rivers, one in Peloponnesia and one Thessaly) with the theonym "Peneus" (the god of rivers and the father of the nymph Daphne). In this, he follows Ovid, who speaks of "the banks of her [Daphne's] father" (*Metamorphoses* 1.815). As the subject for the aural verb *shumet'* ["to be noisy"], "Peneus" is therefore ambiguous: the verb can take as a subject both the theonym and the toponym. Here, in "K Ligurinusu," it makes more sense to read it as a theonym because the location is the plural *doliny* ("valleys"). A river like the Peneus or the Eurotas can "be noisy" only in one valley, whereas the god of rivers can "be noisy" in any number of valleys. This reading, however, is complicated by the fact that this ambiguous "Peneus" was for Rodzianko's generation a conventional location for the representation of Apollo's amorous pursuit of nymphs. The ambiguity is both geographical – because we cannot know whether the referent is the Peloponnesian Peneus River or the Thessalian Peneus River – and semantic-categorical because we cannot know whether the referent is the god Peneus or a river. We see the same ambiguity, for example, in Pushkin's Latinate "Rifma" ("Rhyme," 1832), where Apollo falls in love with Echo on the banks of (the?) Peneus: "Эхо, бессонная нимфа, скиталась по брегу Пенея. / Феб, увидев ее, страстию к ней воспылал"[55] (Echo, the sleepless nymph, was scrambling along the bank of (the) Peneus. / Phoebus, seeing her, was inflamed with passion for her). All the same, it is perhaps a bit surprising that Rodzianko would twice reject the variant "Eurotas" in favor of the ambiguous "Peneus." The Eurotas, after all, is the river which flows through Hyacinthus's native Sparta, and it is here Ovid places his story of Apollo's love for the boy and his accidental killing (10.164–220). This toponym certainly hews closer to Rodzianko's Ovidian subtext. If my reading of "Peneus" as a theonym rather than a toponym is correct, however, it would seem that Rodzianko sought to make his geographical setting less specific, which in turn makes his reliance on multiple subtexts possible. That is, were all the toponyms strictly Ovidian, the Horatian subtexts would be less effective. Perhaps this evident urge toward the general over the specific also explains his preference for the common noun "Nymph" over the proper noun "Daphne."

The variants in the third stanza, as yet unremarked in the scholarly literature, are by far the most significant. Before taking this overtly homoerotic text to the Green Lamp for discussion, he made it even more strongly homoerotic. This is important because – and this cannot be stressed enough – there was a very powerful taboo on homosexuality in Rodzianko's Russia.[56] On the very few occasions when references to homosexuality did gain some circulation (though never in print), they were usually ad hominem attacks, such as Pushkin's epigram accusing Sergei Uvarov of granting the post of vice president of the Academy of Sciences to Prince Dundukov-Korsakov because he fancied him ("Because he has an ass.").[57] "K Ligurinusu" is not the only Rodzianko poem that treats "Socratic love," and I will discuss others later. None of these poems was ever published, and none of them were written with the intention of publishing them. In a word, Rodzianko thought of these poems as thoroughly domestic texts. That he would revise the third stanza of "K Ligurinusu" as he did before presenting it to the Green Lamp shows that he perceived the Green Lamp as a very permissive, domestic context.

RGB

Во взорахъ женщины прекрасной
Иль полногрудыхъ дѣвъ младыхъ
Грозитъ равно Богъ нѣги страстной
Жестокимъ жаломъ стрѣль своихъ;
И Нимфѣ, близъ тебя дрожащей,
Урокъ любови первый дать
Прелестнѣй, чѣмъ рукой горящей
Мальчишку друга обнимать.

[In the gazes of a beautiful woman
And of busty young maidens
The god of passionate languor
    threatens equally

With the cruel sting of his arrows;
And to give a first lesson in love
To the Nymph trembling near you
Is more marvelous than with a
    burning arm
To embrace a young boy friend.]

GL

Во взорахъ отроковъ прекрасныхъ
Иль полногрудыхъ дѣвъ младыхъ
Грозитъ равно Богъ чувствій страстныхъ
Жестокимъ жаломъ стрѣль своихъ;
И Нимфѣ близъ тебя дрожащей,
Урокъ любови первый дать
Равно прелестно, какъ горящій
Цвѣтъ друга юнаго сорвать! –

[In the gazes of beautiful boys
And of full-breasted young maidens
The god of passionate sensations
    threatens equally

With the cruel sting of his arrows;
And to give a first lesson in love
To the Nymph trembling near you
Is equally marvelous
As it is to pluck the burning flower
    of a young [male] friend.]

Rodzianko equivocates here between homonormativity and heteronormativity. In the earlier RGB text, the balance is tipped in favor of the Nymph: "And to give a first lesson in love / To the Nymph trembling next to you / Is *more marvelous* than with a burning arm / To embrace a young boy friend." But in the Green Lamp text, there is a complete affirmation of bisexuality: beautiful boys are equally sexually attractive as "full-breasted young maidens," and deflowering either is "*equally marvelous*" (italics mine in both examples).

This textological exercise gives us an analytical window on the reception contexts in which Rodzianko operated. The variants thus become part of a *social* artifact, a record of linguistic behavior. There are four contexts to consider here: publication, VOLSNKh, the Green Lamp, and the salons Rodzianko frequented. Each corresponds in different ways to our larger, hermeneutic contexts – state, society, domesticity. Let us consider the social/behavioral meaning of presenting "K Ligurinusu" in each of these contexts.

First, we have publication. Because everything published had to pass the censors, publication was state-controlled, and therefore in the state context. And because the primary intended audience of published poetry was the educated, Westernized nobility, the reception context of publication was also a society context. Rodzianko could not have published "K Ligurinusu." We can surmise that he thought it one of his best works because he selected it for presentation at two different literary societies. He therefore would have published it if he could have. This means that, even in its "milder" redaction, the poem ran against the norms governing what was permitted in print; there was no use even trying to get such a poem past the censors. Thus, it was conceived and composed both outside of this system of norms and, in some sense, counter to it.

Second, we have VOLSNKh, where Rodzianko presented the poem on August 8, 1818. VOLSNKh was also a state context. As described earlier, in its heyday, the Free Society was licensed by Alexander's administration and supported by it. The membership included many of the day's most influential political figures, and competing parties within the administration staged important political struggles in VOLSNKh. Declaiming an unpublishable, domestic poem in this context is, of course, a *shalost'* of the first order – a transgression of contextual boundaries. Perhaps it was this daring that gained Rodzianko the respect of the soon-to-be-Lampists who were in the audience that day: Glinka, Pushkin, and Del'vig. It was all the more daring since, as a pupil of Aleksei Merzliakov who once enjoyed the favor of Beseda, Rodzianko doubtless came to VOLSNKh in 1817 as a latter-day anti-Karamzinian (which he most definitely was), a new addition to the ranks of Shishkov's supporters in VOLSNKh who had purged the Arzamasians from the society five years before. "K Ligurinusu" was the first of nine Rodzianko poems presented at VOLSNKh in 1818–1819 (he stopped attending meetings in early 1819, just as the Green Lamp was starting up). It is interesting to note the title of Rodzianko's poem as recorded in the VOLSNKh minutes: "K Ligurinu (podrazhanie drevnim)." Instead of the Latinate spelling "Ligurinus," which Rodzianko uses in the RGB title, we have a Gallicized spelling (Ligurine) and what would seem to be a completely superfluous subtitle describing the poem as a stylization of classical poetry (who would think otherwise of a poem that opens with the rather obscure matronymic "Latonides"?). By contrast, the Green Lamp text is not even titled, and part of the first line was lost to a torn corner – even the poor-quality paper and the careless handwriting marks it as an unofficial, domestic document.

Third, we have the Green Lamp, which of course strove to be a domestic context and to seal itself off from any intrusions from society and state. This is really the "home context" for "K Ligurinusu," and the poem was part of the Lampists' cohesive corpus of "Horatian" texts (shortly I will further explain the meaning of "Horatian" for the Lampists). This is also the only context where we know for certain which redaction of the poem Rodzianko presented. Of the two existing redactions, he chose the one that more forcefully ran against the norms of poetic speech. Clearly, there was something in this flouting of convention and mores that Rodzianko thought would appeal to the sensibilities and tastes of the Green Lamp.

Fourth, we have a hypothetical context: the salon. There is no direct evidence that Rodzianko presented "K Ligurinusu" anywhere but VOLSNKh and the Green Lamp, but imagining this very probable scenario is nonetheless instructive. Rodzianko was a habitué of the salon of Nadezhda Khilkova, his childhood friend from Ukraine. She came in 1815 with her father, Dmitrii Troshchinskii, to Saint Petersburg, where she died two years later.[58] Rodzianko greatly admired Khilkova and her family and composed a madrigal to her in 1815, soon after her arrival to the capital, as well as an ode to her father.[59] A recent transplant to Petersburg, Khilkova's salon was probably not typical of Petersburg society. The Troshchinskii family was famed for their entertaining. As a frequent summer guest at their estate in his childhood and adolescence, the young Rodzianko was treated to many a merry evening laughing at Troshchinskii's troupe of jesters and taking part in home theater productions. Khilkova's Petersburg salon was no doubt an equally jolly setting. Though certainly a society institution, it was probably more permissive than most Petersburg salons. And as Khilkova's family friend and Ukrainian compatriot, moreover, Rodzianko probably conducted himself there as an intimate. In terms of politeness theory, his interaction with Khilkova at the salon reflected high social proximity and no imbalance in relative power. As such, he had to worry about attending to her positive and negative face much less than other attendees, and his measure of "appropriateness" was therefore much different than theirs. Reciting "K Ligurinusu" in this setting, in either redaction, would have been an assertion of domestic relations with the hostess, an attainment many salon attendees sought fervently.

Turning from these pragmatic and behavioral considerations back to the literary form of "K Ligurinusu," the first issue I should address is its subtexts. The existing scholarship on "K Ligurinusu" amounts to a grand total of seven sentences: Modzalevskii links it to Ovid, and Vatsuro mistakenly calls it a translation of Horace's *Odes* 5.10. It requires further intertextual and contextual analysis. As a student at the Moscow University Noblemen's Pansion, Rodzianko no doubt studied Ovid and Horace thoroughly. Yet, "K Ligurinusu" is by no stretch of the imagination a translation of Horace, *Odes* 4.10, the ode Vatsuro has in mind. That ode makes no mention of Hyacinth or Apollo. It reads:

O lad still cruel and powerful thanks to Venus,
when suddenly scraggly down intrudes on your vanity,
the locks that flick your shoulders are shorn, and whiskers
shadow and roughen your face, whose color surpasses
the scarlet rose's now, Ligurinus, seeing

another self in the mirror, you will mutter, "*Heu*!
Why is my attitude different today than in boyhood?
And why do these feeling not restore my looks?"[60]

This is the continuation of *Odes* 4.1, in which Horace entreats Venus to train
Cupid's "cruel arrows" on another heart, that of a younger, richer man more able to
bring happiness to his beloved. It concludes with the following stanzas:

But why [*eheu!*], Ligurinus,
does a tear occasionally line my cheek?
Why does an awkward silence
trip my tongue in conversation?

At night I dream we embrace,
or I breathlessly chase you across the grassy
Field of Mars, you callous
boy, or through the churning water.[61]

Thus, Odes 4.10 is the spiteful response of a petulant suitor to a boy who has
rejected him: "Someday you, too, will be old."

Nor is "K Ligurinusu" a retelling of the myth of Apollo and Hyacinthus from
Ovid (*Metamorphoses*, 10.164–220). That myth relates the origins of the hyacinth:
when Apollo accidentally killed his beloved Hyacinthus with a stray discus, he
caused the boy's spilt blood to turn into the purplish-red flowers that thereafter
covered the hills of Sparta in springtime. In "K Ligurinusu," Rodzianko brings in
the myth of Hyacinthus as an image of the fleetingness of youth and life, as well as
homosexual love for a boy. But he performs a significant twist on Ovid: his lyrical subjects' kisses are *sweeter* than the afterlife and the honey of Hymetus or the
scent of the roses (hyacinths) that will commemorate the object of his desire after
death – after it is too late to pursue earthly delights. In a sense, Rodzianko inverts
the position of Ovid's Apollo, who, as an immortal, is doomed to permanent material existence – for him, there is no hope of an elegiac reunion in the afterlife, which
sharpens his grief. Rodzianko, to the contrary, is inclined to revel in his material
existence.

Rodzianko's skepticism of the afterlife in "K Ligurinusu" grows out of an
influential thematic line of the late 1810s that celebrates the mortal and corporeal
over the spiritual, and earthly existence over the afterlife. This line is most evident
in the poetry of the Arzamasian Denis Davydov. As Irina Semenko explains, it
arose in part as a reaction to the ubiquitous preciousness of posthumous, elegiac
reunions in Russian poetry of the early 1810s.[62] In a poem called "Katai-valiai"
("Giddyap," 1820), which he dedicated to Davydov, Viazemskii sums up the world
view of Davydov's lyrical subject most succinctly:

Какой-то умник наше тело
С повозкой сравнивать любил
И говорил всегда: «В том дело,
Чтобы вожатый добрый был».
Вожатым шалость мне досталась,

Пускай несет из края в край,
Пока повозка не сломалась,
    Катай-валяй![63]

[Some smart fellow liked to compare our body to a wagon, and used to always say: "The thing is to have a good driver." I wound up with a *shalost'* for a driver, so let the wagon carry me from place to place until it breaks, Giddyap!]

Among the Lampists, all young men and adolescents, this thematic line appears to have gained currency in a slightly altered, more Horatian key. They transformed it into a call to hedonism as a way to glory in an ephemeral youth and to prepare for old age and death. For example, in Del'vig's poem "K mal'chiku" ("To a Boy," composed 1814?, published 1819), the lyrical subject instructs his addressee to bring up plenty of wine from the cellar to meet the sunrise and reminds him that, in old age, it is nice to drink from the cup of one's youth and to "Deceive the imagination / And to peer into the past."[64] As in Del'vig's other Green Lamp poems, the textology of "K mal'chiku" carries the imprint of his fellow Lampists' critique. He published it twice, once in February 1819, right before the Green Lamp convened, and once ten years later, in his 1829 collection. These two published texts differ significantly, but all the variants of the 1829 text are in evidence in the text preserved in the Green Lamp archive. Thus, the "workshopping" of this poem at the Green Lamp resulted in its definitive text. From this we can only conclude that, in its final redaction, "K mal'chiku" was acceptable to Del'vig's fellow Lampists. There certainly can be no doubt that Del'vig's theme was sympathetic to Pushkin, who takes it up in an 1819 epistle to Mikhail Shcherbinin (who may or may not have been a Lampist), which some scholars consider part of his so-called Green Lamp cycle. Pushkin knew "K mal'chiku" well. In fact, the manuscript of "K mal'chiku" in the Green Lamp archive has a revision made in Pushkin's hand. The second stanza of Pushkin's epistle to Shcherbinin bears unmistakable traces of Del'vig and even appropriates one of his characteronyms, "Fanni," which I discuss at length later:

И мы не так ли дни ведем,
Щербинин, резвый друг забавы,
С Амуром, шалостью, вином,
Покамест молоды и здравы?
Но дни младые пролетят,
Веселье, нега нас покинут,
Желаньям чувства изменят,
Сердца иссохнут и остынут,
Тогда – без песен, без подруг,
Без наслаждений, без желаний,
Найдем отраду, милый друг,
В *туманном сне воспоминаний!*
Тогда, качая головой,
Скажу тебе у двери гроба:
"Ты помнишь Фанни, милый мой?" –
И тихо улыбнемся оба.[65]

[And is this not how we lead our days while we are still young and healthy, Shcherbinin, you frisky friend of fun: with Amour, *shalost'*, and wine? But our young days will fly past, merriment and languor will abandon us, our feeling will betray our desires, our hearts will dry out and grow cold, and then – with no songs, no girlfriends, no pleasures, no desires – we shall find joy, dear friend, *in the foggy dream of remembrance!* And then, shaking my head, I shall say to you at the door to the grave: "Do you remember Fanni, my dear friend?" – And we will both quietly grin.]

At the same time, in the poetry of the Lampists, hedonism could provide freedom not only from the fear of death and old age, but from suffocating social discourses as well. Hedonism and freedom was a natural collocation for the Lampists. By the time he joined the Green Lamp in 1819, Rodzianko had been employing this thematic nexus (hedonism – mortality – freedom) for several years in his poetry. His unpublished poem "Udovol'stviia zhizni" ("Pleasures of Life," composed 1815) is a representative example:

Пусть кто хочетъ ищетъ славы
Сладко, сильно говорить.
Я люблю одни забавы
И учусь искуству [*sic*] пить.

Прочь со скукой наставленій
Умъ словами обольщать:
Всѣ оттѣнки наслажденій, –
Вотъ что я желаю знать;

Обойми меня Лилета!
Старъ я, не румянъ и сѣдъ;
Но горитъ душа поэта
И ущерба въ сердцѣ нѣтъ.

Дайте винъ! – Средь пированій
Пусть разсудокъ дремлетъ нашъ!
Мы умремъ! – тамъ нѣтъ желаній,
Нѣтъ нектара полныхъ чашъ.[66]

[Whoever wants to, let him seek glory, speak sweetly and strongly. I like only fun and I study the art of drinking. The tedium of lessons be gone, [be gone] the tricking of the mind with words: all the hues of pleasure – that is what I wish to know. Embrace me, Lileta! I am old, pale, and gray; but my poet's soul burns yet, and there's no damage to my heart. Pass the wine! – Amid the feasting let our reason drowse! We shall die! – there are no desires, no cups full of nectar there.]

As we see in "K Ligurinusu," the thematic association of mortality-avoidance and sensual pleasure was particularly important in Rodzianko's homonormative poems. In the RGB collection, Rodzianko places "K Ligurinusu" together with an earlier poem, "K drugu. Podrazhanie Goratsiiu" ("To a [male] friend. An imitation of Horace," 1814).[67] The lyrical subject of "K drugu" is a young man who invites a boy to visit him in the night. As in "K Ligurinusu," he attempts to seduce his addressee by citing the fleetingness of youth and telling him not to worry about the future (old age and death), but to make the most of the present before he is ruined by experience, marriage, and so on. The third and fourth stanzas read:

Другъ, жить спѣши, пока ланиты
Зарею младости горятъ;
Пока и Музы и Хариты
Съ улыбкою на тебя глядятъ;
Скорѣй бокалъ съ виномъ кипящимъ,
Любви безпечно руку дай;
И наслаждаясь настоящимъ
О будущемъ не помышляй.

Жизнь, счастье смертныхъ – сонъ прелестный:
Невидишь и неслышишь ты,
Какъ невозвратно въ край безвѣстный
Несутся юности мечты;
Очарованье исчезаетъ,
И опытъ свѣточью своей
Послѣдни грезы прогоняетъ,
И съ ними щастье нашихъ дней. –

[Friend, hasten to live, while your cheeks still burn with the dawn of youth; while both the Muses and the daughters of Venus look upon you with a smile; hurry with a glass of bubbling wine, give your hand to love without a care; taking pleasure in the present, do not think of the future. Life, the joy of mortals – is a marvelous dream: You can neither see nor hear the dreams of youth fly irrevocably to an unknown place; the charm disappears, and experience will chase off the last reveries with its torch, and with them – the happiness of our days.]

And, just as in "K Ligurinusu," the last stanza puts the preceding Horatian meditations on mortality and the fleetingness of youth to the practical purpose of seducing the addressee:

Оставьже старости унылой
Воспоминаніями жить;
Ты любишь, ты любезен милой,
Умѣй щастливый мигъ ловить;
Спѣши украдкой, молчаливо,
Подъ скрытое межъ липъ окно:
Любовью робкой, торопливо
Тебѣ отворено оно.

[Leave it to gloomy old age to live by recollections; you love, you are lovely, my dear, catch this happy moment; Hurry furtively, silently, to a window covered by lime trees: it has been hurriedly cast open by a timid love.]

By way of conclusion, let us consider another poem from the RGB manuscript collection, Rodzianko's "Poslanie o druzhbe i liubvi Avramu Sergeevichu Norovu" ("Epistle on Friendship and Love to Avram Sergeevich Norov"). According to the date in RGB, Rodzianko composed the poem in 1818, and he published a heavily redacted version of it in late 1819, a few months after the Green Lamp convened.[68] As such, this poem was certainly known to the Lampists, and they likely discussed it at one of their meetings. Perhaps more interesting than the epistle itself is a postscript attached to it, which is dated 1838.

"Poslanie o druzhbe i liubvi" compares "love" and "friendship." "Love" is the irrational and volatile connection between men and women; "friendship" is the lofty, spiritual connection between men. The rejection of heteronormativity is, of course, quite plain, and Rodzianko discounts the offense his associated misogynistic rhetoric might cause:

> Пускай прекрасной полъ мной будетъ недоволенъ,
> Узнавъ тебя, мой другъ, я въ выборѣ неволенъ,
> И долженъ дружество по гробъ боготворить![69]

[I care not if the fair sex be angry with me, having met you, my friend, I am not free to choose and must worship friendship to my grave.]

Acknowledging that his position flies in the face of social norms, Rodzianko makes an extended tour through history in order to argue that "love" is the root cause of slavery and hardship, while "friendship" will lead to freedom, prosperity, and virtue:

> И дружество посмѣть любви предпочитать? –
> Чтобъ мнѣніе мое предъ свѣтомъ оправдать,
> Во глубину началъ и ихъ послѣдствій вникнемъ.[70]

[And dare to prefer friendship to love? – to defend my opinion before society, let us penetrate the depths of the causes and their effects.]

Rodzianko composed a postscript to this epistle when compiling the RGB manuscript collection in 1838, and reading it, we get a sense of what the epistle meant to him by observing Rodzianko reading himself. In the postscript, it turns out that he was right, that youth has passed, and, as he put it in "K drugu," "the torch" of sexual experience with women (and marriage) has "Chased off the last reveries, / and with them the happiness of our days." If in many of the poems of his youth, Rodzianko wavers between homosexual and heterosexual love, in his epistle to Norov he staunchly champions the beauty of homosexual friendship over the passion of heterosexual love. In the postscript, though, he renounces his own youthful fervor and reads both the beauty of friendship and the passion of love in his wife's eyes. As in "K Ligurinusu," Rodzianko affirms that both kinds of affection are essential, even if neither can bring "all the joys of life to humankind":

> Созданья свѣтлыя давно прошедшихъ дней
> Заманчивые сны младой души моей

Въ васъ верилось тогда, премудрая природа
Двухъ обновителей откроетъ смертныхъ рода,
И (пламенный слѣпецъ) чрезъ дружбу мыслилъ я
Дать человѣчеству всѣ блага бытія ...
Минуло двадцать лѣтъ ... холодный и угрюмый
Смотрю, на юности заоблачныя думы ...
Мечты! Мечты! ... шепчу кивая головой –
И горькая слеза взоръ омочаетъ мой,
Безсвязные листы съ досадой пробѣгаю ...
И дружбу, и любовь въ глазахъ жены читаю.[71]

[Light creations of days long past, the alluring dreams of my young soul, I
believed in you then, that wise nature would reveal the two renewers of the
tribe of mortals, and (a fiery blind man) I thought to grant humankind all the
joys of existence through friendship ... Twenty years have passed ... cold
and gloomy, I look upon the otherworldly dreams of my youth ... Dreams!
Dreams! ... I whisper, shaking my head – and a bitter tear moistens my gaze,
I run through the incoherent pages with annoyance ... And I read both friendship and love in the eyes of my wife.]

The homonormativity of his epistle to Norov is, to the forty-five-year-old Rodzianko, thus a flawed and fleeting passion of his youth, for which he sheds bitter
tears. Most importantly, it is this long-past devotion to and belief in the "dreams"
of "friendship" that occasion the only postscript in the RGB collection. Clearly, it
characterized for him the poetry of his youth more than his civic themes but is at
the same time part of his civic streak. For his contemporaries, homonormativity and
sexual banter were also defining characteristics of his poetry. To call his reputation
as "the bard of love and mirth" and "the bard of Socratic Love" an "aberration" or
"legend," as Vatsuro does, is thus an absurdity. His reputation was what it was, and
the sources of it are now clearly documented. The "unauthorized sexuality" of his
writing played no small role in the creation of this reputation.[72] And it was precisely
because of this reputation that he was welcomed into the Green Lamp: his disregard
for social convention was attractive, especially because such forbidden discourses,
such banter aided in the creation and consolidation of domesticity in the group and
they were concomitant with its libertine mode of dissent. Further, as I hope is clear
from the textological, intertextual, and contextual analysis of "K Ligurinusu" presented earlier, Rodzianko tried his best to live up to the expectations his reputation
inspired in his fellow Lampists.

Del'vig's "Fanni" and Del'vig's Shack

A year before the Green Lamp convened, one of its best poets, Anton Del'vig,
wrote a poem called "Moia khizhina" ("My Shack," 1818) in which he dreams of
an egalitarian and Epicurean domesticity. No doubt, Del'vig in part realized this
dream in the Green Lamp, where friends gathered "without ranks" much like the
friends at his shack. There, at his modest country estate, where his "young wife"

lays the table, and even the oxen frolic and "call, moaning, for their girlfriends,"[73]
Del'vig pictures a future gathering of friends. The second stanza reads:

А вы, моих беспечных лет
Товарищи в весельи, в горе,
Когда я просто был поэт
И света не пускался в море –
Хоть на груди теперь иной
Считает ордена от скуки,
Усядьтесь без чинов со мной,
К бокалам протяните руки,
Старинны песни запоем,
Украдем крылья у веселья,
Поговорим о том о сем,
Красноречивые с похмелья![74]

[And you, comrades in the merriment and misfortune of my carefree years,
when I was simply a poet and did not descend into the sea of society – though
some [of you] now count the medals on [your] chests from boredom, take a
seat without ranks with me, reach for a glass, we will strike up the old songs,
we will steal the wings of merriment, eloquent with drink, we will talk about
this and that!]

With its sensualist trappings – love, wine, song, food – Del'vig's shack is a hedonistic reworking of Karamzin's more chaste image of the poet's shack, a pastoral convention. In his essays from the first decade of the nineteenth century, discussed in chapter 1, Karamzin directs the poet to live outside society, and the shack
in Karamzin's poetry is a place where the poet can find the seclusion and social
authenticity necessary to his art. He often evokes the shack as the antithesis to
society and state, which are ruinous for the true poet. In his "K bednomu poetu"
("To a Poor Poet," 1796), for example, he lists the many flights of fancy that a poet
who is not rich and sated, and who does not have access to society, is capable of in
the secluded and cozy shack where he dwells. He concludes the list, "как все то
исчислить, / Что может стихотворец мыслить / В укромной хижинке своей?"[75]
(How to list everything that a versifier might think in his cozy shack?). This authenticity, for Karamzin, is vital not only to true poetry but to love as well. In his
"Poslanie k zhenshchinam" ("Epistle to Women," 1795), he writes: "И хижину с
тобою, / Безвестность, нищету / Чертогам золотым и славе предпочту"[76] (And I
shall prefer obscurity, penury, and a shack with you to golden mansions and fame).

Karamzin's shack is authentic and pure, the abode of the genuine poet, who, in
Karamzin's eyes, must be pure of heart to produce true poetry. It is also a place for
the poet's audience to truly delight in his art. In his "Darovaniia" ("Gifts," 1796),
the poet's shack even becomes a kind of monument to the deceased poet, where
admirers can go to recite his works and celebrate his life:

Потомство скажет: «Здесь на лире,
На сладкой арфе, в сладком мире

Играл любезнейший поэт;
В сей хижине, для нас священной,
Вел жизнь любимец муз почтенный;
Здесь он собою красил свет;
Здесь будем утром наслаждаться,
Здесь будем солнце провожать,
Читать поэта, восхищаться
И дар его благословлять».[77]

[Posterity will say: "Here on a lyre, on a sweet harp, in sweet peace played the gallant poet; In this shack, sacred to us, the venerable Muses' favorite led his life; here he made beautiful the world; here we will take pleasure in the morning, here we will see off the sun, read the poet, take delight and bless his gift."]

These associations reverberated in Russian poetry for the next couple of decades. Even when working from foreign models, for example, Batiushkov takes up Karamzin's image of the shack with its attendant associations of authenticity, purity, poetry, and love. In his poem "K Filise. Podrazhanie Gressetu." ("To Phyllis. An Imitation of Gresset," 1804–5), the shack is a Karamzinian retreat for the poet:

Ты велишь писать, Филиса, мне,
Как живу я в тихой хижине,
Как я строю замки в воздухе,
Как ловлю руками счастие.
. . . .
Что же делать нам? … Бранить людей? …
Нет, найти святое дружество,
Жить спокойно в мирной хижине;[78]

[You bid me write, Phyllis, about how I live in a quiet shack, how I build castles in the air, how I clutch felicity in my hands…. What are we to do? … Abuse people? … No, we must find sacred friendship, live quietly in a peaceful shack;]

Del'vig's shack departs from this conventional image of a solitary, writerly retreat that Karamzin adopted from antiquity. It is not a kind of pastoral *kabinet*. Nor is it as idealized, as distant, or as abstract as Karamzin's shack. Into this monastic, sentimentalist retreat, Del'vig transposes the hedonistic egalitarianism of Derzhavin's Anacreontic poetry.[79] "Moia khizhina" is particularly reminiscent of Derzhavin's "Pikniki" ("Picnics," 1776). "Pikniki" was first published in 1808, and Del'vig doubtless knew the poem. The third stanza reads:

Мы положили меж друзьями
Законы равенства хранить;
Богатством, властью и чинами
Себя отнюдь не возносить.[80]

[We determined to observe the laws of equality among friends; to boast of our wealth, power, and ranks not at all.]

Derzhavin's friendly gathering, though, lacks the local farmyard details of Del'vig's. Unlike Del'vig's shack, Derzhavin's retreats to the country are not at all writerly. Del'vig's shack is pointedly local, specific, Russian – and it is also the inherited domain of the poet. Del'vig's third stanza reads:

Признайтесь, что блажен поэт
В своем родительском владенье!
Хоть на ландкарте не найдет
Под градусами в протяженье
Там свой овин, здесь огород,
В ряду с Афинами иль Спартой;
Зато никто их не возьмет
Счастливо выдернутой картой.

[You must admit that the poet is blessed at his ancestral holdings! Though on a map he won't find the drying barn over there or this garden here on the same latitude as Athens or Sparta; but then again, no one can take them [from him] with a fortuitously laid card.]

By comparison, Derzhavin's picnic is far more universal, focusing on general Epicurean themes like the opposition between martial prowess and the appreciation of sensual pleasure:

У нас не стыдно и герою
Повиноваться красотам;
Всегда одной дышать войною
Прилично варварам, не нам.

[With us even a hero is not ashamed to supplicate himself to beauties; it is fine for barbarians to live and breathe war alone, but not for us.]

Del'vig's shack is more rooted in a particular mise-en-scène. Like the heroine of his so-called Horatian ode, "Fanni" (1814–19), it is local, corporeal, immediate, and sensual – but at the same time thoroughly literary. And it is a domestic scene, a table far removed from the vagaries of society and state, where the assembled guests drink, eat, and sing "without ranks." It is just this sort of domestic audience to which Del'vig addressed the three poems preserved in the Green Lamp archive. The most domestic of the three is "Fanni": it relies on a web of reminiscences and allusions that were available only to a very small circle of Del'vig's friends. Just as Pushkin's quotation of "Fanni" in his "Zhenshchiny" (see chapter 1) served to lay down an impenetrable barrier between those readers who "got" the allusion and those who did not, the exclusivity of Del'vig's referents in "Fanni" served to underscore the social proximity of his readership. One had to be part of Del'vig's circle or close to it in order to understand the poem correctly.

"Fanni" is a prime example of the literary *shalost'*, a poem addressed to a close social circle, the meaning of which was inaccessible to readers it might offend. Like most *shalosti*, it is thoroughly and unapologetically rooted in sensuality. And like most *shalosti*, it was not intended for publication. Del'vig expended a lot of effort on "Fanni" and he thought it a good enough poem to present at the Green

Lamp. Therefore, we can only conclude that he did not make any attempt to publish "Fanni" because it was not possible to publish such a poem at the time. Nonetheless, this domestic, secreted text seeped over the years through the poetry of Pushkin and Boratynskii into the literary mainstream, thus emerging from domesticity – besides the quotation in "Zhenshchiny," we find allusions to "Fanni" in Pushkin's "K Shcherbininu" and Boratynskii's "Eliziiskie polia" ("Elysian Fields," circa 1821).[81] "Fanni" is built on an exceedingly rich set of subtexts and continued to accrue intertextual meaning in the years after Del'vig wrote it. By the late nineteenth century, the name "Fanni" was a semantic touchstone for a complex set of literary and social associations, which originates, in Russian literature, with Del'vig's "Fanni." In the early redactions of Mikhail Saltykov-Shchedrin's cycle *Pompadury i pompadurshi* (1863–74), for example, we find the following passage: "When in [Krotikov's] presence the old *shaluny*, smacking their lips and squinting, would talk about some ancient Aspasia or about the latest Mme. Pompadour, he would never let on that he knew what they were talking about, but would instead feign ignorance and respectfully ask: who is this Aspasia and how does her body compare with Florence's or Fanni's?"[82] Like Saltykov-Shchedrin's Krotikov, Del'vig deflates the ethos of antiquity in his Horatian ode through reference to a Fanni, who was a real-life legend of Petersburg nightlife. As with his image of the poet's shack, Del'vig opts for the local, corporeal, and sensual over the universal, lofty, and abstract. Meanwhile, transplanting such local color into a classical context is, of course, just as much a transgression of contextual boundaries, just as much a *shalost'* as Kologrivov and Golitsyn's cross-dressing cavalcade on the parade grounds described in chapter 1.

There are three extant manuscript texts of "Fanni" (presented in the following excerpt). The first comes from Del'vig's Lyceum notebooks (plain text) and can be dated 1814–17.[83] The second comes from the Green Lamp archive (variants in plain text in brackets).[84] On the reverse of this manuscript we find the date of its presentation: "Meeting of 17 April, 1819. Chairmanship of member Ulybyshev." The third text of "Fanni" (variants in italics in brackets) comes from Del'vig's 1819 notebook, a collection of fair copies, mostly of published works, apparently compiled as the basis for a planned print volume.[85] The chronology of provenance here is very straightforward, so we can see Del'vig's pattern of revision before and after the poem's presentation at the Green Lamp with particular clarity. My translation is of the third redaction.

Фани [Фанни] (Горацианская ода) [→(No subtitle)→*Горацианская ода*]
Мнѣ ль подъ оковами [оковамы] Гимена
Зѣвать от скучнаго одно? [→Все видеть тоже и одно?→*Все видеть то
    же и одно?*]
Мое блаженство – перемѣна,
Я дѣвъ мѣняю, как вино.

Темира, Дафна и Лилета
Давно, какъ сонъ, забыты мной
И ихъ для памяти поэта
Хранитъ лишь стихъ удачный мой.

Чѣмъ дѣвы робкой и стыдливой [→ *Чемъ с дѣвой робкой и стыдливой*]
Неловкость видѣть, слышать стонъ, [→ *Случайно быть наединѣ,*]
Дрожать и страсти мигъ щастливой [→ *Дрожать и мигъ любви*
    щастливой→ *Дрожать и мигъ любви щастливой*]
Ловить въ ее невинный сонъ: [→ *Ловить ея притворной сонъ, –*
    → *Ловить въ ее притворномъ снѣ:*]

Не слаще ль у прелестной Фани [→ Фанни→ *Фани*]
Быть самому ученикомъ, [→ Послушнымъ быть
    ученикомъ,→ *Послушнымъ быть ученикомъ,*]
Платить любви безпѣчно дани
И оживлять восторги сномъ.

[Is it for me to take up the shackles of Hymen and always see one and the
same thing? Bliss for me is variety; I change maidens like I change wine. I
have long ago forgotten Temira, Daphne, and Lileta. For the poet's memory,
they are preserved only in a verse of mine that turned out well. Rather than
be alone by chance with a timid and bashful wench, to tremble and seize a
moment of joyous love in her feigned sleep – Is it not sweeter to be the marvelous Fanni's obedient pupil, to heedlessly pay the tithe to love and [then]
revive the rapture with sleep.]

In addition to these texts, there is one more interesting textological detail of
"Fanni." Del'vig had two pentameter lines that he wrote down on the margin of
the text in the 1819 notebook: "И сорванный насильно поцелуй / С горящих уст
красавицы невинной"[86] (And a kiss torn by force / From the burning lips of an
innocent beauty). For Del'vig, obviously, these lines are linked to "Fanni," but he
could not use them.

   Del'vig performed most the revisions before the poem was presented to the
Green Lamp. Only three variants appeared later: lines one, two, and four of the
third stanza. The motivation for these variants is quite clear. After correcting
the usage error in line four (the directional-accusative "ловить"), the second line
had to be changed to preserve the rhyme ("сон" → "сне"; "стон" → "наедине"),
and the first line had to be changed, in turn, to accommodate the change to the second line. It seems quite probable that these revisions were suggested by Del'vig's
fellow Lampists. The copy of "K mal'chiku" in the archive has a correction made
in Pushkin's hand, most likely at the April 17, 1819, meeting. Many other poems in
the archive bear such corrections: revising and redrafting was apparently one of the
Lampists' chief occupations during meetings.[87]

   Two of the redactions are subtitled "A Horatian Ode," but we would search
in vain for a single Horatian subtext, theme, or trope on which "Fanni" is based.[88]
The term "Horatian ode," rather, was a generic catchall, one that could be applied
to any poem that treats sex and drinking frankly. The only formal characteristic shared by nearly all "Horatian odes" of the period is the iambic tetrameter.
In any case, the "Horatian ode" was one of the Lampists' favored genres. Rodzianko and Del'vig, in particular, were avid, self-professed practitioners. Indeed,
by 1819, Del'vig had cemented a literary reputation as the new, Russian Horace,
just as Pushkin was called the new Juvenal, and Rodzianko – the Piron of the

Ukraine. These were among the masks they donned as poets. According to Pushkin, Del'vig's first schoolboy attempts at versification were imitations of Horace.[89] Soon after the Green Lamp convened in 1819, Boratynskii published an epistle to Del'vig, which opens, "Так, любезный мой Гораций"[90] (So, my dear Horace). The associations this appellation conjured up for Del'vig are spelled out in his response to Boratynskii's epistle:

> За то ль, Евгений, я Гораций,
> Что пьяный, в миртовом венке,
> Пою вино, любовь и граций,
> Как он, от шума вдалеке,
> И что друзей люблю – старинных,
> А жриц Венеры – молодых ...[91]

[Am I Horace, Evgenii, because while drunk, in a myrtle garland, I sing of wine, love, and the Graces, like him, far from the bustle, and because I like my friends old, and my priestesses of Venus young ...]

Del'vig's Horace writes poetry in drunken seclusion about drinking, sex, and art. In this mask, Del'vig prizes only inebriation, art, lasting homosocial relationships, and fleeting heterosexual relationships. Thus, his subtitle for "Fanni" is ultimately less a literary-generic designation than a behavioral-generic designation and a reiteration of his developing literary reputation. In calling it a "Horatian ode," he announces his intended social posture vis-à-vis the reader, who is treated as an equal with whom Del'vig may engage in sexual banter and take up other topics that are not "appropriate" in a nondomestic context. And in this sense, too, the poem is a *shalost'*, for it self-consciously describes itself as an *act*, a set of behaviors – the "Horatian ode" – rather than a set of formal poetic conventions.

Analyzing the onomastics of "Fanni" provides a useful perspective on Del'vig's audience at the Green Lamp. These names aroused in his audience certain expectations and called up certain associations. We can only assume that Del'vig had his own calculations as to which expectations and associations his poem would evoke and that he reckoned the Lampists an audience that was capable of identifying his referents in "Fanni." Therefore, to some extent, the "associative horizon" of the poem, as Igor Pil'shchikov calls it, corresponds to and describes the associative horizon of the Green Lamp as a group and an audience.[92] Names, since they carry so much and such defined and discrete meaning, are a revealing channel for the common cultural experience that Lampists drew on when defining themselves as a group cemented by both social bonds and shared aesthetic experience.

First, of course, is the question of who Fanni herself might have been. Since Pushkin uses the name in a number of his poems, this was certainly not a stone that scrupulous Pushkinists could leave unturned. Modzalevskii came to the conclusion that Fanni was a fairly famous star of the day's nightlife.[93] Later, the Pushkin commentator Tatiana Tsiavlovskaia concluded that she was a prostitute.[94] The commentators left it at that. Their primary source here is a certain Iurii Nikolaevich Shcherbachev. A dilettante, the elderly Shcherbachev wrote a book about his grandfather and his wife's grandfather, one a confirmed Lampist, the other a "suspected" Lampist. His grandfather was the Lampist Mikhail Shcherbinin, to whom the epistle I quoted earlier is addressed; his wife's grandfather was Pavel Kaverin. Shcherbachev is at pains to show how much Pushkin respected and liked his grandfather, and even accuses Pushkin of sycophancy. He writes that Fanni was an entertainer who performed only for the most exclusive elites. She moonlighted as a highly sought-after consort for gentlemen of the highest rank. Shcherbachev adds that Pushkin could hardly have afforded to enjoy her company, and that, by mentioning her in his epistle to Shcherbinin, Pushkin sought to place himself in the small circle of men who could (apparently including Shcherbinin).[95] Needless to say, despite the confidence of Tsiavlovskaia and Modzalevskii in the veracity of Shcherbachev's claims, they should be taken with a grain of salt.

Of the documents that corroborate Shcherbachev's version, one is of particular interest here: an 1823 letter from the poet Vasilii Tumanskii to the poet Vil'gel'm Kiukhel'beker. Tumanskii was a friend of Pushkin and Del'vig, whom he probably met through his long-time friend and Poltava compatriot, Rodzianko. He concludes his letter with a bit of nostalgia: "I often reminisce about the past; illumined by the sun of youth, these memories are only fond. Jerome and Fanni, you and Madame Smith, Limperani and Agnes enliven my solitary daydreams like characters from an engaging novel."[96] Tumanskii's simile of reminiscence to fiction and of Fanni to a fictional character is not merely an empty figure of speech. The name Fanni and Del'vig's ode to her are a telling concatenation of both very earthly pleasure and literary sensualism – Fanni was both a "lady of the evening" and a conventional name in the European literary tradition.

The name Fanni is certainly not the only name in Del'vig's ode with some literary baggage. Before getting to the Fannies of European literature, I should pause on the other names in Del'vig's ode – Daphne, Temira, and Lileta, the three women whom his lyrical subject has long ago forgotten. These are conventional poetic names dating back to the late eighteenth century, and the name Lileta was associated primarily with Karamzin well into the mid-nineteenth century.[97] This association was so strong that it occasioned one of Vissarion Belinskii's more telling errors. Belinskii was notoriously sloppy in his citations, but his slips are sometimes the best portal into the workings of his reader's brain. In his review of Boratynskii's 1835 collection, he criticized Boratynskii harshly as a Karamzinian throwback. Exasperated by Boratynskii's old-fashioned frivolity in the poem "Sluchai" ("An Event," composed 1819, published 1827), in which Boratynskii describes an evening spent drinking in the company of a Lileta, Belinskii exclaims, "How is this sentimental poem any better than 'Triolet Lilete,' written by Karamzin?"[98] Karamzin, who introduced the genre to Russian literature, did indeed write a "Triolet to Aleta" and a "Triolet to Lizeta," but he did not write one to a Lileta.[99] Apparently, the similar-sounding name "Lileta" was stuck in Belinskii's mind from his readings of Boratynskii, Pushkin, and Del'vig, and was for him intractably associated with that part of Karamzin's legacy he deemed frivolous, and this caused the mistake.

The name "Temira" was a bit more exotic, but had also long been familiar to Russian writers. Batiushkov, for example, quotes Temire's lines from Quinault's libretto for *Roland* in an 1812 letter to Viazemskii.[100] Batiushkov gives no explanation of the quotation, which means that he simply assumed Viazemskii was familiar with both the character and the opera. Presumably, many of their contemporaries knew it as well.

More than anything, though, Del'vig employs the names Lileta and Temira in
his ode to Fanni in order to evoke the more chaste love lyrics of his adolescence, his
first publications: "K Lilete" ("To Lileta," published 1814) and "K Temire" ("To
Temira," published 1815).[101] Del'vig's friends swiftly appropriated these names,
which they used as characteronyms for sexually accessible women. Pushkin exalts
Batiushkov's Lileta, "the joy of beautiful days," in his 1815 epistle to the elder poet,
one of his first publications.[102] Boratynskii borrows the name Lileta in the poem
"Sluchai" (the poem that inspired Belinskii's indignation), and in his "Eliziiskie
polia," he uses the other two names, Daphne and Temira, in a clear evocation of
Del'vig:

> И там на шаловливой лире
> Превозносить я буду вновь
> Покойной Дафне и Темире
> Неприхотливую любовь.[103]

[Even there on a mischievous lyre I will again exalt to dead Daphne and
Temira modest love.]

Poets from outside this close circle were also using the name Lileta in similar
contexts. For example, Rodzianko, who did not meet Del'vig until at least 1817,
composed the line "Embrace me, Lileta!" in 1815 for his "Udovol'stviia zhizni."[104]
The name Daphne was at that time still closely linked to its origins in classical mythology. It could be synonymous with the common noun "nymph." For
example, in the textology of Rodzianko's Horatian ode, "K Ligurinusu," the name
Daphne and the word *nimfa* are interchangeable. This is significant because, by
1819, the word *nimfa* often meant, simply, "prostitute" in Pushkin and Del'vig's
milieu. This has to do with various French euphemisms for "prostitute" that entered
the Russian language in the 1790s and stabilized during the Napoleonic wars.
"Filles de joie" was borrowed as *devy radosti, devy veseliia,* or *devy naslazhdenii.*
Another expression, "nymphes de joie," was translated as *nimfy radosti* or simply
nimfy. Karamzin writes of the Paris red-light district: "*Nimfy radosti* [Karamzin's
italics] approached us one after the other, tossed flowers at us, sighed, laughed,
beckoned us to their grottoes, promised us a thousand pleasures, and disappeared
like phantoms of the moonlit night."[105] And Bulgarin uses this euphemism in his
memoir of Riga during the Prussian campaign against Napoleon: "Debauchery
in Riga was then at a peak.... The Riga camps were a real Sodom ... [and] *nimfy
radosti* ... would ride from city to city, wherever the armies gathered or passed
through."[106] Batiushkov used the expression in the same sense in both his correspondence and his poetry. In March 1814, he wrote Gnedich from Paris, "There are
novelties these days. *Nimfy radosti,* whose brazenness exceeds everything. It is not
the officers who run after them, but they who run after the officers."[107] Batiushkov
had used the term as early as 1810 in his poem "Schastlivets" ("A Lucky Man,"
1810): "Счастья шаткого любимец / С нимфами забвенье пьет"[108] (A favorite
of tipsy fortune drinks oblivion with the nymphs). And Iakov Tolstoi later took up
this usage in his "testament" to the Lampists, "Zaveshchanie": "Простите Нимфы
юны, / прелестницы мои!"[109] (Farewell, young Nymphs, my darlings!). Thus, the
name Daphne – oddly enough, given the chastity of Ovid's Daphne! – was likely

read by Del'vig's contemporaries as a conventional name for a prostitute or other sexually available woman from outside society.

"Fanni" was a no less conventional name than Temira, Daphne, and Lileta, but it was new to Russian literature in the mid-1810s. Del'vig was familiar with many of the famous Fannies of European literature, where the name "Fanni" appears to have developed an association with objects of sexual desire, and/or consorts or prostitutes in the late eighteenth and early nineteenth centuries. There can be absolutely no doubt that, besides referring to a real Saint Petersburg resident, Del'vig taps into a well-defined onomastic vein of European literature, which continued to develop in France throughout the nineteenth century.[110] A short list of literary Fannies that Del'vig knew might include the following texts:[111]

- One of the "indiscreet jewels" in Denis Diderot's novel *Les bijoux indiscrets* (1748) belongs to a woman named Fanni.
- Gottlieb Friedrich Klopstock wrote a series of Horatian odes to a Fanni – his cousin Maria Schmidt, with whom he had an unhappy love affair. Del'vig most certainly knew these poems. Recalling Del'vig's "lessons" with Kiukhel'beker at the Lyceum, Pushkin writes: "Del'vig read Klopstock, Schiller and Holty with one of his classmates, a living lexicon and an inspired commentary."[112] Later, one of Del'vig's friends, Filimonov, published translations of Klopstock's Horatian odes.
- A Fanni figures in Claude Joseph Dorat's *Les malheurs de l'inconstance ou Lettres de la marquise de Circe et du comte de Mirbelle* (1772). Del'vig and his fellow Lampists knew Dorat well. In fact, Iakov Tolstoi put a quote from Dorat beneath an engraving of the Green Lamp symbols (the lamp, the lyre, the anchor) on the frontispiece of his 1821 volume of Lampist verse, *Moe prazdnoe vremia*. It reads: "Far from me is the bitterness of a prickly Critic / I speak to friendship, I have the right to say anything / If one must weigh one's words and measure one's play / To remain free and glad, I renounce the art of writing."
- An immoral young woman named Fani corrupts the chaste hero of an Auguste von LaFontaine novel published in Moscow in 1799 as *Priroda i liubov' ili kartiny chelovecheskogo serdtsa* – a book that, according to Apollon Grigor'ev, was a mainstay of Russian pornography during his adolescence.[113]
- Andre Chenier's odes addressed to a "Fanni" (his lover, Madame le Coulteux) were no doubt "read against" Del'vig's Fanni when the first Chenier edition made it to Russia in late 1819.

Diderot's *The Indiscreet Jewels* (1748) bears special consideration here. Del'vig's circle knew the novel well, and Pushkin borrows from it liberally in his "Tsar Nikita i sorok ego docherei" ("Tsar Nikita and His Forty Daughters," composed 1822).[114] *The Indiscreet Jewels* is a novel about a Congolese ruler who comes into possession of a magic ring, which, when pointed at vaginas – or "Jewels" – has the power to make them talk and tell their stories. He uses the ring on the ladies of his court to find out about their sex lives. One of the "jewels" in the novel, as it happens, belongs to a woman named Fanni. Diderot's Fanni, like Del'vig's, is older, experienced, and quite sexually prolific – she has been the consort of twenty men, and has pursued extracurricular activities with great zeal besides.

During its "interview" with the curious sultan, Fanni's jewel reports a recent discourse its mistress had with a certain young philosopher about the merits of forming emotional attachments to lovers. The subject of their debate is whether it is desirable, or even possible, to form emotional attachments to one's lovers. Fanni, who has retired from society in disillusionment, asks the philosopher, "Do you still think that there are any souls who have escaped the corruption of the age, who still know how to love?"[115] Fanni says that she wants to be loved, and at first the philosopher tries to dissuade her by pointing out that a man in love demands exclusive access to the charms of his beloved. Fanni quite readily agrees, at which point the two switch positions: the philosopher argues that "a woman who forms an attachment saves her reputation and assures that she will always be respected by her lover," and Fanni replies: "I do not understand these things at all. You confuse everything: reputation, love, respect, and I know not what else. Do they not say that infidelity brings dishonor? What! I take a man; he is not to my liking. I take another who does not suit me. I exchange him for a third who does not suit me any better."[116] The philosopher counters with an example from his own life: he had been very much in love with a woman, and the sexual gratification fueled by this emotional state was such that he heartily recommends it. Fanni replies: "How foolish! When all is said and done, I conclude that it is better to love as people love today, taking a lover at one's leisure, keeping him as long as he is amusing, leaving him when boredom sets in, or when caprice demands another. Infidelity offers a variety of pleasures unknown to you bashful lovers."[117] She then pretends that the philosopher won the argument, and says, "You are right, my dear Amisadar, you argue wonderfully. But are you presently in love with someone?"[118] Whereupon the groping begins.

Reading Del'vig's Fanni against Diderot's is, I think, a fruitful exercise. Del'vig's lyrical subject, who changes girls like he changes wine, certainly resembles Diderot's Fanni, who leaves her lovers "when boredom sets in, or when caprice demands another," in at least this respect. The theme of fidelity was a fairly widespread one in Del'vig's childhood. In "Fanni," Del'vig even lampoons the syntax of Karamzin's famous poem on the subject, "K nei" ("To Her," 1794), which opens (italics mine): "И *мне* ль непостояннымъ быть? / И *мне* ль бабочкой порхать, въ надежде / Другую более любить?"[119] (And is *for me* to be inconstant? Is it *for me* to flit like a butterfly, in the hope of loving another more?). Del'vig's preference for unsentimental sex also seems to echo the tastes of Diderot's Fanni, which are motivated by a quintessentially libertine point of view: that it is foolishness to confuse "reputation, love, respect, and I know not what else." In other words, sex is a personal matter, and has nothing to do with social standing (reputation, respect). In a word, it is domestic. Furthermore, the spiritual and moral dimension of sex – so important to the Russian sentimentalist verse populated by all those Liletas, Temiras, and Daphnes – is completely out of the picture.

To my mind, the most interesting reading one can make of Del'vig's "Fanni" is a dual one: this is a poem both about sex and about poetry. One of the most mythic occurrences of the mid-1810s, when Del'vig first drafted the poem, was Batiushkov's visit to the Lyceum in 1815. During that visit, according to Andrei Zorin, Batiushkov urged Pushkin to abandon his sensuous juvenilia and take up the serious, militaristic themes that were sweeping the nation after Alexander I liberated Europe.[120] Pushkin's response to these admonitions was his epistle "K Batiushkovu" ("To Batiushkov," 1815), in which he defends sensualism. Two other poets who would later join the Green Lamp, Arkadii Rodzianko and Iakov Tolstoi, were writing similar defenses of sensualism in 1815–16. Rodzianko's poem "Udovol'stviia zhizni" is a good example.

Thus, one can view "Fanni" as Del'vig's contribution to this debate. On the physical level, Del'vig makes a blunt statement – sex with a no-nonsense, experienced prostitute is preferable to bashful sex with her younger colleagues. His use of literary subtexts, primarily in the form of conventional names, is also a statement of preference: the frankness of Diderot, for example, is better than the bashful periphrasis of sentimentalist verse. And this was a fundamentally political statement in Del'vig's time. As I will discuss at length in the next chapter, sensualism was at that time associated primarily with French libertinism, which in turn was viewed as one of the causes of the French Revolution, the specter that lurked behind all Russian cultural politics in the 1810s and 1820s.

The Diderot commentator Aram Vartanian writes, "Although the *Jewels* has always been popular with readers, until the middle of this century it was ignored or condemned by most critics and scholars, who considered its subject to be irredeemably frivolous and licentious. The judgment is doubly unjust. For, in French writing of the eighteenth century, seeming frivolity often masks genuine seriousness."[121] Vartanian concludes that Diderot adopted such a frivolous tone in the novel, which he reads as a roman à clef, in order to get away with some fairly blunt political and social commentary. The political implications of the Lampist version of libertinism are a little more subtle: it is not so much that Del'vig hides a political message in a bawdy poem, as that creating such a poem and reading it aloud was, in and of itself, a rebellious act.

In Del'vig's day, Diderot was viewed as the principal representative of eighteenth-century French libertinism, an erudite freethinker who defied both the crown and the clergy in France, but cozied up to Catherine II and her court. In Pushkin's words, he was perceived as "an admirer of industry, a skeptic, and a heathen [*bezbozhnik*]."[122] Alluding to *The Indiscreet Jewels* and combining a reference to a local Petersburg prostitute with a literary rogues' gallery of sex objects was much like alluding to Barkoviana – Russia's own obscene verse tradition – or cracking a dirty political joke: context was critical. Declaiming such a poem would be willfully inappropriate, and therefore pathological and/or rebellious, in some contexts, but playful in others. The point is – as we saw with Rodzianko's "K Ligurinusu" – that the Green Lamp was precisely the *right context* for this sort of sexual banter. It was for Del'vig that merry table in his cozy shack, where *shalosti* were the order of the day.

❧4

Ruslan and Liudmila

Rudeness and Sexual Banter

It would be difficult to overstate the significance of Pushkin's *Ruslan i Liudmila* (*Ruslan and Liudmila*, 1820; hereafter *RL*) in the history of Russian literature. For nearly 170 years, it has been almost universally recognized as one of the most important works of the Russian Golden Age. It is no coincidence that Pushkin opens his masterwork, *Eugene Onegin*, with an appeal to "the friends of Liudmila and Ruslan!" For him, *RL*, his first great literary success, was the seed from which sprang a literary career that remains a cornerstone of Russian civilization to this day. *RL* is still a philosopher's stone of Russian literary history – the key to Pushkin, an avenue to "lay hold of this Proteus and wrest from him the secret of his power."[1] Oleg Proskurin, for example, opens his book on Pushkin's poetics by marveling at the significance of *RL* in the scholarly tradition: "Pushkin's first published narrative poem, a pubescent prank [*shalost'*], 'a poetic plaything' ... has been the subject of far more numerous and far more contradictory interpretations than all of Pushkin's other narrative poems.... And this is not by chance: the intense scholarly interest in this text, which is quite straightforward as regards form, reflects the entirely valid notion that to 'solve' 'Ruslan and Liudmila' is, in some sense, to get to the very essence of Pushkin's oeuvre."[2]

Upon its publication in 1820, *RL* was greeted by critics as "a marvelous event in our literature" (Izmailov), "a sublime poem, with which Pushkin's masterful quill has enriched our literature" (Perovskii), "one of the best literary works published this year" (Zykov), and so on.[3] Certainly, not all the critics agreed, and Pushkin also came in for a lot of very harsh criticism. Indeed, the critical debate about the poem that broke out in the Russian periodical press was the single most voluminous, spirited, and even vicious literary polemic of the late 1810s and early 1820s.

Whether one liked the poem or not, though, there was no denying the novelty of *Ruslan and Liudmila*. This was something completely new to Russian literature, and it had a huge impact. In 1844, the critic Vissarion Belinskii recalled, "Nothing can compare with the delight and consternation aroused by Pushkin's first *poema*, 'Ruslan i Liudmila.' Too few works of genius have managed to make such a splash as was made by this childish *poema* utterly lacking in genius.... Be that as it may, but one cannot but understand and approve of the [readers'] delight: Russian literature offered nothing like it. Everything was new in this *poema*: the verse, the poetry, the jokes, and the fairy tale, together with the serious pictures."[4]

As Tomashevskii put it, "the defining characteristic of [*RL*] is its novelty."[5] This novelty fueled not only the lightning-quick development of Pushkin's career – for this is the point at which, as Avram Reitblat says, he "joined the ranks of geniuses" – but also important evolutionary shifts in Russian prosody and style, not to mention the institutions of Russian literature.[6] It was the first large-scale literary *shalost'* published in Russia, and its phenomenal success had a lasting impact on the course of Russian literary and cultural history.

The writing of *RL* was an unusually open process. Pushkin most certainly did not follow Karamzin's directive to spend his time in the *kabinet*. To the contrary, by Pushkin's own profession, it was written "amidst the most dissolute life."[7] And he was most certainly not interested in keeping his work to himself. Pushkin read draft excerpts from the poem periodically in various fora while it was still unfinished: at Zhukovskii's soirees, at nonliterary social gatherings where Pushkin sometimes fielded requests to recite his poetry, at Arzamas and the Green Lamp, and even at the theatrical soirees of the Arzamasians' arch-nemesis, Prince Shakhovskoi. This was not typical of the period, when authors usually presented only finished works in public. Of his *poemy*, Pushkin "released" only *RL* in this fashion. True, *RL* itself is somewhat untypical. At over 2,800 lines (depending on what one regards as the definitive text), it is Pushkin's largest verse work after *Eugene Onegin*.

In any case, Pushkin received feedback on the poem as he wrote it, and this feedback shaped the poem. Just as a stage actor or musician can gauge the mood of the audience, he could see how people reacted to the poem, and he adjusted his "performance" accordingly. His fellow writers offered professional suggestions, criticism, and praise, which he could choose to heed or to ignore. What is less obvious is that Pushkin's readings also opened his *kabinet* to the public, involving listeners in the writing process. As Viacheslav Koshelev puts it, "the author brought into public a *poema* that was still 'fresh,' still unfinished. This gave listeners the sensation of 'being in the moment,' that this was a one-off experience – and led to an internal conviction that a literary sensation, once experienced, cannot be repeated."[8] This is a reversal of Zhukovskii's model discussed in chapter 1: instead of bringing his *kabinet* with him out into society, Pushkin brought society into his *kabinet*. This public mode of writing both necessitated that Pushkin take a very clear "stance" or "line" (in Erving Goffman's parlance) vis-à-vis his audience and allowed him to refine it. Thus, the lyrical subjectivity that Pushkin projects for his reader in the text was constructed in real, live interaction with his listeners and is a fundamentally (one might even say viscerally) social construct. Here, in Tynianovian terms, literary *byt* becomes a literary fact, something Tynianov says is typical of the period, and of domestic texts in particular.[9] The "set" (*ustanovka*) of *RL* is, however, multi-faceted, as it includes the salon, the literary soiree, and the secret society, each with a different subset of social types. Of these, many scholars have traditionally laid the most emphasis on the literary societies Pushkin belonged to during 1818–20; first Arzamas, then the Green Lamp. In this chapter, I attempt to define and quantify two lines of sociopragmatic influence in *RL*: the "rudeness" of Arzamas and the sexual banter of the Green Lamp.

The Arzamasians, for the most part, viewed *RL* as their crowning glory, the decisive victory of the new style over the old style.[10] Arzamasians were involved in the creation of the poem in all sorts of ways from the very beginning. Ironically, Aleksandr Voeikov, who would later criticize *RL*, can be credited with originating the whole idea of writing such a *poema* back in 1813.[11] The Arzamasians nursed the poem like they nursed, cursed, coddled, and cajoled young Pushkin himself – as the great white hope of Russian poetry and, by extension, of their modernization project. In one of the beautiful symmetries of literary history, Pushkin first read excerpts from *RL* at a "farewell session" of Arzamas on April 7, 1818, on the eve of Dmitrii Bludov's departure for London.[12] The group effectively dissolved soon thereafter, gathering only a few more times, but the *poema* was well underway. And when Pushkin finished a draft of the last canto in March 1820, he brought the whole poem to Zhukovskii and read it aloud to him. To mark the occasion, Zhukovskii presented Pushkin his portrait with the famous inscription: "To the conquering student from his conquered teacher on that most gala occasion, the day he finished his *poema* 'Ruslan i Liudmila.' March 26. Great Friday."[13] The significance of the date is, of course, obvious: the completion of the poem marks a death that makes one rejoiceful and hopeful for the future. In a more earthly vein, Proskurin describes the presentation of this gift as a coronation of Pushkin as the new king of Arzamasian galimatias.[14] In any case, the timing is certainly at least partly intentional or invented. Two days later, on March 28, Pushkin wrote Viazemskii that he would "finish the last canto any day now." Given how fluid Pushkin's notion of "finished" was at the time, there can be no doubt that he and Zhukovskii picked the date for its symbolic potency.

We do not know exactly when Pushkin wrote the first lines of *RL*. The most intensive work (at a rate of three to four lines per day on average – staggering speed for a poet) fell between the winter of 1818–19 and the spring of 1820. He wrote the epilogue in July 1820 after being expelled from the capital in May. In other words, the writing of *RL* roughly corresponds to Pushkin's so-called Petersburg period, when he set the foundation of his career, as well as a reputation that would haunt him for the rest of his life. During these two years, *RL* was a constant topic of discussion in the letters of the Arzamasians, even as the group disbanded. Viacheslav Koshelev has assembled a survey of this correspondence.[15] The highlights of his survey, supplemented with other texts, make for a nice little epistolary biography of the poem:

- *May 16, 1818.* Vasilii Pushkin to Viazemskii: "My nephew is a complete freak. He is now writing a new *poema* that has Turgenev enraptured."[16]
- *September 1818.* Batiushkov to Turgenev: "What's the Cricket up to? Has he finished his *poema*? He ought to be locked up at Göttingen and fed milk soup and logic for about three years."[17]
- *November 1818.* Batiushkov to Bludov: "The Cricket is beginning the third canto of his *poema*. A talent wondrous and rare! Taste, wit, inventiveness, gaiety. At 19 years old, Ariosto could not have written better. It is with dismay that I see he has given himself over to dissipation, which is harmful to him and to us, people who love beautiful verse."[18]
- *December 3, 1818.* Turgenev to Viazemskii: "Pushkin is already on the fourth canto of his *poema*, which will have six all together. Just about when he hits twenty [he'll be finished]! Hey, old timers, get out of the way!"
- *December 18, 1818.* Turgenev to Viazemskii: "The Cricket is bouncing around the boulevard and the ———. When is he supposed to get around to commenting on other people's verse: he hardly has time to write his own. But despite his dissolute lifestyle, he is finishing the fourth canto of the *poema*. Give him another two or three ———, and it's a done deal. The first ——— illness was also the first benefactress of his *poema*."[19] An uncensored text of this letter has

not been published, but it is easy enough to fill in the blanks left by the editor. Turgenev is talking about prostitutes and venereal disease and would be happy to see Pushkin incapacitated by a second bout of venereal disease because he slows down enough to focus on the poem only when ill.

- *February 12, 1819.* Turgenev to Viazemskii: "Pushkin has taken to his bed: the old came on to the new, and he's had to take up his *poema* again."[20] That is, Turgenev got his wish, and Pushkin contracted venereal disease again.
- *March 1819.* Batiushkov to Turgenev: "Beg Pushkin in the name of Ariosto to send me his *poema* filled with beauties and – hope, if he honors his legacy more than dissipation."[21]
- *February 25, 1820.* Turgenev to Viazemskii: "The nephew [Pushkin] has almost finished his *poema*, and I've heard it twice in the last few days. It's time to get it to press. I'm hoping that its publication will serve another purpose, for him personally: once he's seen himself among published and therefore respected authors, he will start respecting himself and will change his ways a bit. Now he's known only for small poems and large *shalosti*, but once his *poema* is printed, people will look to him, if not as an Academic wig, at least not as a first-class rake."[22]
- *March 28, 1820.* Pushkin to Viazemskii: "My *poema* is coming to an end – I think I'll finish the last canto any day now. I'm tired of it – which is why I'm not sending you excerpts."[23]
- *Mid-April, 1820.* A. Pushkin to Viazemskii: "Petersburg is stifling for a poet. I thirst for foreign lands; perhaps the noon air [i.e., the South] will enliven my soul. I've finished my *poema*. [Pushkin apparently has in mind the fair copy of the poem.] And only the last, that is, the concluding, line bore me true satisfaction. You shall read the excerpts in the journals, but you will receive it once it's printed – I'm so tired of it that I cannot bring myself to copy it piecemeal for you."[24]
- *May 5, 1820.* Turgenev to Viazemskii: "[Before Pushkin is expelled from Petersburg,] We will try to confiscate his poem, we'll read it and give it over to immortality, that is, to the printer."[25]
- *May 17, 1820.* Karamzin to Viazemskii: "For several days, A. Pushkin has been in entirely unpoetic fear because of his poem on Freedom and some epigrams. He gave me his word to knock it off and left without a hitch for about five months in the Crimea. He was given about 1,000 rubles for the road. It seems that he was touched by the magnanimity of His Highness, which really is touching. It would take a long time to describe all the details; but if Pushkin doesn't correct his ways, he will be a devil even before departing for Hell. We shall see what kind of epilogue he writes for his *poemka!*"[26]

Karamzin's letter requires some commentary. He mentions "about five months in Crimea," and he must have thought that this was Pushkin's original "sentence." That is, as Karamzin understood it, Pushkin would be allowed to return in fall 1820 if he could behave himself. He did not, and he spent five years in exile. Karamzin also mentions one thousand rubles. This is separate from the thousand rubles Pushkin received for *RL*, which was later passed through his commanding officer, Ivan Inzov. Pushkin did not write the epilogue Karamzin mentions until July. The text of the epilogue reached Petersburg in time to be published in *Syn otechestva* in

September. The swiftness with which it made it to press is astonishing, especially if one takes into account that it is quite incendiary: in it, Pushkin unapologetically transforms his previously jolly and impertinent lyrical subject into a wistful and somewhat bitter exile.

The Arzamasians' involvement did not stop here. Zhukovskii was the prime mover behind the publication of *RL*. Pavel Katenin recalls that Zhukovskii was Pushkin's plenipotentiary in all matters related to the first edition and, "in the author's absence took care of the publication and success [i.e., reception] of the *poema*."[27] Pushkin had yet to edit the sixth canto and make a fair copy when he was exiled. He left the manuscript in the care of his brother, Lev. Once Lev Pushkin and his friend, Sergei Sobolevskii, finished making the fair copy, Zhukovskii took it upon himself to hustle it through the censorship procedures and enlisted Gnedich to publish the poem.[28] Zhukovskii also handled the financial details of the edition, sending the exiled Pushkin one thousand rubles (at the time, one of the largest literary honoraria ever paid) for the poem in late May 1820.[29] And other Arzamasians certainly played a role as well. It was most likely through Uvarov's connections that the poem made it past the censors so quickly. And Voeikov, who had recently taken the helm at *Syn otechestva*, saw to the publication there of promotional announcements, as well as Pushkin's addenda, which Pushkin sent from exile too late to get them in the first edition of the book publication. Once the critical melee over *RL* got into full swing, Voeikov also wrote and published the single longest (and mostly positive) review – though his professorial arrogance annoyed almost everyone. So, Arzamas was involved with *RL* every step of the way: before and during the writing, the publication, and the reception.

Scholars have also noted the influence of the Green Lamp, its linguistic norms, and its aesthetic values on *RL*. Tomashevskii follows Slonimskii in arguing that Pushkin originally worked out much of the style he would use in *RL* in a cycle of Green Lamp epistles he wrote in 1819 to Shcherbinin, Iur'ev, Kaverin, Engel'gardt, Nikita Vsevolozhskii, and Del'vig.[30] Tomashevskii also asserts that one of the poem's lyrical digressions (from "Но вы, соперники в любви," lines 2.14–20) is addressed to Pushkin's fellow Lampists.[31] Lotman notes the similarities between the language of *RL* and Pushkin's letter to the Lampist Pavel Mansurov discussed earlier.[32]

But what does it mean to say that *RL* is a "Lampist text"? Certainly, the poetry and "verbal culture" of Pushkin's fellow Lampists form an important subtextual substrate in *RL*. Nonetheless, it would be an oversimplification to say that *RL* is addressed to the Green Lamp (as Tomashevskii claims some parts are) or that the language of *RL* is the language of the Green Lamp. It seems likely that *RL* was "a Green Lamp text" in a much more concrete way. There is circumstantial evidence to suggest that Pushkin read the poem at the Green Lamp. As noted in chapter 3, in his reply to the Investigatory Commission on the Decembrist Uprising, Trubetskoi wrote: "Every member [of the Green Lamp] was required to read his writings at a meeting of the society before publishing them."[33] Pushkin first published excerpts from *RL* in April of 1820, at which time the Green Lamp was still meeting. If he observed the bylaws, then he would have read at least those excerpts to his fellow Lampists by April 1820.

We have documentary evidence that at least one Lampist, Fedor Glinka, heard or read *RL* before its publication, quite possibly at a meeting of the Green Lamp.

In the summer of 1820, alongside Pushkin's last additions to *RL* in *Syn otechestva*, Glinka published his epistle "K Pushkinu," with the following footnote: "This poem was written a year ago, after a reading of the first two Cantos of Ruslan and Liudmila."[34] If Pushkin did present *RL* at the Green Lamp, it must have been at some point after June 1819, when Tolstoi wrote an epistle to Pushkin that describes a drunken carriage ride after a summertime Green Lamp session in late June of that year.[35] In the published text of this epistle (from Tolstoi's 1821 collection *Moe prazdnoe vremia*), the only poem Tolstoi mentions is *RL*:

... Чтобъ нѣжность, вкусъ, витійства сила,
Что отъ боговъ тебѣ даны
И коими Русланъ, Людмила
Удачно такъ облечены

....

Когда стихами и Шампанскимъ
Свои разсудки начиня
И дымомъ окурясь Султанскимъ
Едва дошли мы до коня;[36]

[... that the tenderness, taste, and strength of rhetoric, which has been given you from the gods, and with which Ruslan and Liudmila are so successfully vested ... When, having filled our reason with verse and Champagne, and fumigated ourselves with Sultanic smoke, we could hardly make it to the horse;]

But this passage is absent from the text of Tolstoi's epistle preserved in the Green Lamp archive, which makes no mention of *RL*.[37] In other words, Tolstoi was exposed to *RL* at some point between June 1819 and fall 1820. This fact does not, however, preclude either Glinka's dating ("a year ago") or the possibility that Pushkin may have presented the poem at a meeting of the Green Lamp.

If Pushkin brought drafts of *RL* to the Green Lamp, it is certain that he received much of his initial feedback from the Lampists – which means that the group had significant input as the poem took shape. More importantly, however, the Lampists were part of the poem's projected audience. That is to say, the Green Lamp was (in part, at least) the pragmatic context of *RL*. In the poem, this pragmatic context is evinced by a number of features, most importantly sexual banter; evocation of the Lampists' canon; and the projection of the reader as either a sexually desirable young woman, one of the "empresses" of Pushkin's soul, or a male friend, *sobutyl'nik* (drinking buddy), and co-conspirator. As most every scholar writing on *RL* notes, Pushkin strikes an intimate tone in his interaction with the reader. This is "a conversation with friends and pretty girls."[38] For readers who found that their self-image did not correspond to Pushkin's image of his reader, as we shall see, this could be an affront.

Sexual Banter and Eroticism in *Ruslan and Liudmila*

The erotic in *RL* remains little understood. Though many scholars have touched briefly on it, there is only one special study devoted to the subject.[39] To this day,

there remains a fundamental disagreement about the role and importance of eroticism in the poem. Scholars like Leslie O'Bell are convinced that "first of all, this
is an erotic poem."[40] Others reject this characterization. Slonimskii, for example,
writes, "Erotica is not the true pathos of the *poema*. It merely frames the fabula,
which speaks of something entirely different: of pure love and marital fidelity."[41]
Two factors have clouded our picture of eroticism in *RL* and made it impossible to
come to some agreement about it. First, because the erotic is such a subjective and
elusive category, and one that changes so quickly in any given cultural context, it
is difficult (or impossible?) to define in formal terms. As Lotman says, "It is nearly
impossible now to sense the 'indecency' of this work."[42] Thus, our analysis must
focus on subjects, the readers and the author, and their relationship to the text, and
not the text alone. Second, the eroticism of *RL* is tinged with politics. And as with
the Green Lamp, this concatenation of libertinism and liberalism has confounded
scholars. Slonimskii briefly touched on precisely this aspect of the connection
between *RL* and the Green Lamp. "In this context," he wrote, "the erotica of 'Ruslan,' which is fueled by Voltairean materialistic tendencies, acquired a particular
acuteness. In this sense, Pushkin's 'sinful' *poema* is analogical to his poems of the
Green Lamp period, where erotica alternates with liberal attacks on 'the heavenly
king,' and sometimes against the 'earthly' one. The praise of romantic *shalosti*
and merry feasts in Pushkin's 'Lampist' verse was a demonstration against official
sanctimony. Erotica played the same role in 'Ruslan.' "[43]

The eroticism of *RL* certainly does fit in with the portrait of the Green Lamp
painted in the previous chapter. Though *RL* differs from most Lampist texts in that
it was, from the very start, conceived and executed as a poem destined for publication, the function of eroticism is similar. As in the Green Lamp (and in Horace),
the erotic in *RL* is an antipode to the majesty of militarism and the loftiness of
epos. For example, introducing one particularly steamy (literally: there is a sauna
involved) sex scene, Pushkin writes (4.142–49):

Я не Омер: в стихах высоких
Он может воспевать один
Обеды греческих дружин
И звон и пену чаш глубоких.
Милее, по следам Парни,
Мне славить лирою небрежной
И наготу в ночной тени,
И поцелуй любови нежной!

[I am not Homer: He alone can sing in lofty verse of the feasts of the Greek
detachments and the clink and foam of deep chalices. For me, it is nicer, in
the footsteps of Parny, to proclaim with my careless lyre both nakedness in
the shadow of night and the kiss of tender love.]

This preference for the sensual and intimate over the grandiose and public is, of
course, a commonplace of Lampist verse. This passage also calls to mind Rodzianko's pubescent poems like "Rapture" ("Vostorg," composed 1815) discussed
earlier, which scorn martial and civic pride, exalting instead the authenticity of
sensual pleasure. However, we must first identify the erotic in *RL* in order to dis-

cover how it intertwined with the political. And here many tricky questions must be dealt with.

The trickiest questions are these: What should we characterize as "erotic" in *RL*? Did it violate any particular norms? If so, which ones? What, exactly, is "official sanctimony," and how does Pushkin use eroticism to challenge it in *RL*? I will explore these questions (and others) in the framework of a fairly simple argument – that the eroticism of *RL* made some of Pushkin's contemporaries very uncomfortable; that this discomfort is just as much a matter of offended social sensibilities as it was a matter of what Lotman calls "literary propriety"; and, finally, that these two kinds of offense were concomitant.

First, though, I should place my argument within recent developments in this research tradition. In his study of the young Pushkin as a marketing phenom, Reitblat claims that Pushkin was second-guessing market demand when he wrote *RL*. The reading public wanted sensualism, and Pushkin, Reitblat says, gave it to them, thus launching his career with an unprecedented commercial success. He writes:

> The public would have not been able to understand a poem that was written in a fundamentally new way. Pushkin served up the familiar fare that people were used to in a different way. In managing to offer something that already existed as something new and to successfully arrange these familiar motifs, it is as if Pushkin guessed what the public was waiting for and gave it to them.
>
> In many respects, the poem violated the moral norms [that governed] what was allowable in print, and his contemporaries often criticized it for its commonness [*prostonarodnost'*], "ignoble" plot and lexicon, and for "sensualism" and eroticism. As V. A. Koshelev notes, "Pushkin needed a noisy *debut*," and he got what he wanted. The *poema* attracted the public's attention, became the subject of lively debate and numerous items in the press.[44]

Certainly, it is true that Pushkin wanted to make a splash and that he was successful in this. However, as some of Pushkin's defenders observed back in 1820, *RL* did not violate any "moral norms" that had not been violated before by the poets of antiquity.[45] Naked women and "low" language were nothing new to the Russian reading public. As Pushkin later reflected indignantly: "Is there a single passage in 'Ruslan' where the licentiousness of my jokes could be compared with, say, Ariosto's *shalosti* ...? Even the passage I cut [when preparing the second edition] was a very, very chaste reworking of Ariosto."[46]

No doubt, Pushkin had many foreign models of eroticism to work from, but Russian literature – and, let me be clear, *published* Russian literature – was, of course, a different matter. The way in which Pushkin uses sexual imagery, innuendo, and language *was* fundamentally new to Russian literature. In print, there were essentially two kinds of frankly sexual poetry: the so-called elegant erotica of Ippolit Bogdanovich and Konstantin Batiushkov; and the eighteenth-century burlesque of, say, Vasilii Maikov.[47] These literary standards of erotica play an important role in *RL*, but perhaps less so than other kinds. Lotman notes that the reading public of 1820 was familiar with Apuleus, Boccaccio, Juvenal, Ovid's *Art of Love*, Voltaire, and, I would add, Denis Diderot, Évariste de Parny, and Alexis Piron. Nonetheless, he says, it was totally unprepared for a poem like *RL*, which mixes together all different kinds of literary eroticism. The reader was unable "to find in his cultural arsenal any single 'language' [with which to decode] the entire text."[48] Ultimately, Lotman argues, the iconoclastic literary eclecticism of *RL* was more offensive than its sexual frankness. "We should not forget that Pushkin's *poema* came out in an edition subject to the censors' approval and in an epoch when morality was monitored by the state no less than politics. If there really had been anything in the text that offended the day's accepted norms of propriety, the *poema*, inarguably, would have been held up by the censors. The *poema*'s impropriety is of another kind – it is literary impropriety."[49] Lotman goes on to outline the different, conflicting generic codes that conglomerate in *RL*: the Ossianic, the fairy tale or "bogatyr story," the elegant erotic verse of Batiushkov and Bogdanovich, and more direct Voltairean eroticism, concluding that readers objected to the juxtaposition of codes as improper. Proskurin further develops these ideas, filling them in with analyses of how Pushkin manipulates the erotic subtexts of Batiushkov, Zhukovskii, Barkov, and others.[50] Lotman, Reitblat, Proskurin and the many others who have said essentially the same thing are no doubt right, but this is not the whole story. First of all, the argument that the censors would have stopped anything objectionable is not entirely accurate. In fact, Pushkin simply "got lucky" with the censor when publishing the first edition in 1820 (probably due to personal connections), a circumstance I address in some detail later. He worried that the censor's approval would be reversed even two years after it was published. Inquiring about the sales of *RL* in 1822, he asked his brother, "Has not the censor banned [*Ruslan*]?"[51] While preparing the second edition of *RL* in 1828, Pushkin was forced to cut at least three of the more piquant passages precisely because he feared they would anger his censor, Nicholas I.[52] Secondly, the notion that the poem incensed some critics merely because it was too revolutionary amounts to a pretty silly argument: "Pushkin was just too darn clever for the critics, and they got mad at him for it." This does not fully explain the controversy. Thirdly, and most importantly, *RL* really *did* offend some people, and some thought it very dangerous precisely because of its eroticism.

Nowadays, the "erotic" conventionally refers to signs that elicit physical arousal in the subject interpreting them – images (textual or graphic or whatever) of naked people, sexual acts, feet, angora sweaters, and so on, depending on one's tastes. Today, perhaps, it is hard to imagine that *RL* could be the cause of arousal. Yet, physical arousal was certainly a point of concern for Pushkin's critics. The erstwhile Decembrist, Nikolai Kutuzov, for example, feared that young Russians would read *RL*, become physically aroused, and violate moral norms (i.e., have sex), which, in turn, would lead to a descent into political chaos.[53] In his parable/warning about the dangers of works like *RL*, "Apollon s semeistvom" ("Apollo and His Family," 1821), he waxes catastrophic: "Behold: a passionate youth and a young maiden hungrily devour this [poem] … they descend into a sweet reverie; their gazes glimmer with flame … Fire courses through the veins of [the youth]; the maiden's heart starts racing languorously and stops in her breast … Their enflamed fantasy vanquishes the peacefulness of their quiet, placid life and plunges their hearts into a sea of desire, and perhaps into an ocean of woe…. Are not debauchery and unbelief the causes of mankind's woe? Do they not swallow up kingdoms and peoples like raging springs that bring forests and mountains crashing down in their torrents?"[54] For Kutuzov, unauthorized sexual arousal leads directly to the decline of civilization. One must remember that the French Revolution was still very much on Russians' minds in 1820. In the wake of the Napoleonic Wars, this narrative of decline – that moral degradation leads to social collapse – was commonplace in the Russian myth of recent French history, and Kutuzov was not the only critic of *RL* to invoke it. An anonymous critic from *Nevskii zritel'* (*The Neva Viewer*) writes of *RL*, "When works like this began to proliferate in France at the end of the last century in great numbers, there occurred a decline not only of literature, but also of moral-ity itself."[55] So, for Pushkin's contemporaries, the fatuous licentiousness of *RL* was so pronounced that it could be seen as a latter-day manifestation of French liber-tinism, which, in their eyes, had pushed the French population into a moral anarchy that ultimately led to the Terror. Given that *RL* emerged, to some degree, from the Green Lamp, this is a perceptive observation on the critics' part, and not simply "the blind criticism that met Pushkin's first steps."[56] For the Lampists, just as for these critics, libertinism was a very real challenge to "morality" and to regnant power structures, and that was exactly what they were shooting for. As Armando Marchi writes of libertinism in eighteenth-century Italy: "Every other form of lib-erty came to be subsumed under sexual liberty."[57] That the "shamelessness" of *RL* pales in comparison to that of eighteenth-century Italian obscene poetry is merely a question of degree. The element of skeptical protest that defines libertinism is equally present.[58] *RL* raised political eyebrows, in part, because some people were afraid that it would corrupt the young by arousing them.

Pushkin repeatedly emphasizes the erotic as an important part of *RL*. What is more, he clearly defines a lyrical addressee (i.e., a fictive addressee) for the erotic. Pushkin frames *RL* with a "dedication" to girl-readers, whose attention figures in the poem as the narrator's prime motivation. He concludes the dedication with a declaration to the effect that the opinion of his literary colleagues matters less to him than the "tremor of love" he hopes it will produce in these, his ideal readers:

Ничьих не требуя похвал,
Счастлив уж я надеждой сладкой,
Что дева с трепетом любви
Посмотрит, может быть украдкой,
На песни грешные мои.

[Not demanding anyone's praises, I am already content with the sweet hope that a maiden will look, perhaps furtively, with a tremor of love upon my sinful songs.]

This dedication to young girls invites comparison with the unprintable porno-graphic poetry of eighteenth-century Russia, a corpus subsumed under the term "Barkoviana." The manuscript collections of such poetry, titled *Devich'ia igrushka*, which circulated widely in the late eighteenth and early nineteenth centuries, usu-ally contained a dedication called "Prinoshenie Belinde" – a reference to the hero-ine of Alexander Pope's *The Rape of the Lock*. This dedication is addressed to a young, female reader and recommends the book as a kind of primer in sex for young girls, as well as good material for arousing oneself for the purpose of mas-turbation, a reliable means of preserving virginity. In one rendition, we read: "If games make you merry in company, then this toy can amuse you in solitude.... You will have a husband, to whom you came yet a virgin, and you will give thanks for your chastity to this book; later, you will better savor the delights which for a long time were a fantasy, but not a pleasure received."[59]

Throughout *RL*, Pushkin's lyrical subject returns again and again to the girls, the "empresses of his soul," to whom he dedicates the poem. For example, in a lyrical digression at the beginning of the sixth canto, he addresses himself to one such "dear friend" (*milaia podruga*), and says that "love and a hunger for pleasure" distracted him from the writing of the poem, but that the "tender gaze" she casts on him as he recites it prompts him to sit at her feet and take up his lyre again (4.1–33).

Pushkin's contemporaries felt, if you will, the illocutionary force of these declarations to his ideal reader. One anonymous critic characterizes this desire "to please pretty girls" as the entire "purpose of the poem" (the single most important criterion of classicist criticism).[60] And one of the day's most prominent men of letters, Ivan Dmitriev, couched his reaction in precisely these terms. In a letter to Viazemskii, Dmitriev proposed that Pushkin paraphrase a famous line from act 3, scene 7 of the erotic poet Piron's play *Metromanie* – "La mère en prescrira la lecture à sa fille."[61] This became a common phrase in 1810s society for referring to books with some kind of admirable moral didactic.[62] Dmitriev thought that Pushkin should restate the line as "La mère en defendra la lecture à sa fille." This, he says, should be the epigraph at the beginning of *RL*, for, "without this precaution, his poem will fall from a good mother's hands after the fourth page." Pushkin took Dmitriev's advice to heart in his own way. His introduction to the 1828 edition concludes, "Another ... first-class Russian writer crowned with success greeted this first attempt of a young poet with the following monostich: A mother will order her daughter to spit on this tale."[63]

But what kind of language are we talking about here? What was it in *RL* that daughters should spit on? As Lotman says, "It is nearly impossible now to sense the "indecency" of this work."[64] Was it the digressions addressed to pretty girls? The sex scenes? The general attitude toward sex? I would contend that the whole poem, to some extent, is indecent. Nonetheless, we can take our cue here from two markers and perform a kind of triangulation that enables us to home in on particular passages: (1) Pushkin cut a passage from the second edition for censorship reasons, (2) a passage was noted by critics as immoral or indecent in 1820. When these two markers coincide, we can triangulate indecency, that is, features that violated proprietary norms. Only two passages meet these criteria: the scene of Chernomor's attempted rape of the sleeping Liudmila, and a brief digression on the virtues of nakedness. I discuss each in turn later.

The second edition of *RL* had been in the works since 1822. His finances in ruin, Pushkin was at odds with the Saint Petersburg book dealers in the summer of that year. They had done well on *RL* by holding back part of the print run and boosting demand. An article in *Severnaia pchela* (*Northern Bee*) recalls that "the first edition of Ruslan and Liudmila ... sold out very quickly. Two years later one could get copies only with much effort and for a high price."[65] In 1822, Turgenev and Viazemskii were already discussing the possibility of publishing a second edition.[66] A year later, in 1823, Gnedich proposed publishing a second edition, but Pushkin decided against it. In May 1823, he wrote to Gnedich: "If we can set about publishing a second edition of Ruslan and the Captive, then it would be most expedient for me to rely on your friendship, experience, and care; but your proposals give me pause for a number of reasons. 1) Are you certain that the censor's bureau, which had no choice but to let Ruslan through the first time, will not now come to its senses and block his second coming? I have not the strength to rewrite it to appease the censors, and I do not intend to."[67]

In 1823, Pushkin was still in exile, a marked man, a "dangerous element," and the censors were very wary about approving his material for fear that it would get them in trouble.[68] After his return from exile in 1826, Pushkin's personal censor was the tsar. Paradoxically, this gave him a lot more freedom vis-à-vis censorship: the tsar was a much less demanding and much less scrupulous censor because he had no one to fear. Thus, in 1828 Pushkin was able to publish a second edition of *RL*. Even so, he had to make some cuts in order to publish this second edition.[69]

He cut one of the passages from the fourth canto, when the tranquilized Liudmila is at the mercy of her captor, Chernomor the wizard. Chernomor wants to rape her, but is unable to because he is impotent:

О страшный вид! Волшебник хилый
Ласкает сморщенной рукой
Младые прелести Людмилы;
К ее пленительным устам
Прильнув увядшими устами,
Он, вопреки своим годам,
Уж мыслит хладными трудами
Сорвать сей нежный, тайный цвет,
Храним ый Лелем для другого;
Уже ... но бремя поздних лет
Тягчит бесстыдника седого –
Стоная, дряхлый чародей,
В бессильной дерзости своей,
Пред сонной девой упадает;
В нем сердце ноет, плачет он,...[70]

[O, a terrible sight! The feeble wizard caresses with his wrinkled hand Liudmila's youthful delights; having pressed his withered lips to her captivating lips, he is already thinking, despite his years, of picking with cold labors this tender, secret flower, which Lel' was preserving for another man; and he is already ... but the burden of old age lies heavy on this gray-haired scoundrel – moaning, the decrepit warlock, in his weak audacity falls before the sleeping maiden; his heart breaks, he weeps ...]

At the outset of the *RL* polemic in 1820, an anonymous critic from *Nevskii zritel'* deemed this passage (among others) indecent and unfit for the eyes of young female readers.[71] Voeikov, too, found it objectionable and alluded to it in the end of his review, where he took Pushkin to task for the indecency of *RL*. Concluding his review, Voeikov writes, "Pushkin is right to call his verses *sinful*." And they are "sinful," purely due to eroticism. Voeikov continues, "He is prone to *indiscretion, to speak in double entendres, to hint at things* when he is not allowed to say something, and to use epithets (both appropriately and inappropriately) such as: *naked, half-naked, in only a shift,* even his *hills* are *naked,* and his *swords* are *naked.* He is constantly languishing with desires and with voluptuous fantasies, and in dreams and awake he is always caressing the young delights of maidens, savoring raptures, etc."[72] Voeikov echoes Pushkin's phrase "caressing the young delights [*laskaet mladye prelesti*]," which actually occurs only once in *RL*, thus alluding to the passage in question. Note, however, that Voeikov has Pushkin doing the "caressing" here, not Chernomor. This is significant: in writing like this about sex, Pushkin himself becomes the protagonist of amorous misadventures in the eyes of readers like Voeikov.

Voeikov's transposition calls to mind Clement Greenberg's famous condemnation of Socialist realism (and Repin, as well) as kitsch.[73] One of Greenberg's main arguments is that the Soviet citizen is trained to apprehend any visual representation not in terms of its use of media, its transformation of tradition, and so on, but in a direct way, as a "simulacrum." "In Repin's picture," Greenberg argues, "the peasant recognizes and sees things in the way in which he recognizes and sees things outside of pictures – there is no discontinuity between art and life, no need to accept a convention and say to oneself, that icon represents Jesus because it intends to represent Jesus, even if it does not remind me very much of a man."[74] In verbal art, the inability to separate the writer from what he writes was (and is) a perennial problem for Russian authors. Recall, for example, Gogol's refusal to name a department in the beginning of his "Shinel'" ("The Overcoat," 1842): "There's nothing more irritable than any kind of department."[75] Writing on the very same phenomenon (not among peasants, but among the educated elite) over one hundred years before Greenberg and some twenty years after *RL*, Lermontov says in the introduction to *Geroi nashego vremeni* (*A Hero of Our Time*, 1840): "Some were terribly offended that they were offered as a role model such an immoral man as the Hero of Our Time; and others very cleverly noted that the writer had painted his own portrait and the portraits of his friends ... A joke old and pathetic! But, I suppose, Rus' was created in such a way that everything repeats itself, aside from such nonsense. In Russia, the most fantastic of fantastic fairy tales could hardly avoid accusations of slander!"[76] Among these "fantastic fairy tales" Lermontov might have listed *RL*. Voeikov and others certainly reacted to the sensuous episodes of the poem as though Pushkin himself were perpetrating these acts on their sisters and daughters.

All the nakedness in *RL* apparently troubled not only Voeikov. The other passage in *RL* that meets both our criteria (censorship and critical ire) is a small digression on the subject:

Вы знаете, что наша дева
Была одета в эту ночь,
По обстоятельствам, точь-в-точь
Как наша прабабушка Ева.
Наряд невинный и простой!
Наряд Амура и природы!
Как жаль, что вышел он из моды![77]

[You know that our maiden [i.e., Liudmila] was dressed that night, as it were, just like our great-grandma Eve. A costume innocent and simple! The costume of Amour and nature! What a pity that it's gone out of fashion.]

The anonymous critic from *Nevskii zritel'* italicized the third and fourth lines when he quoted this digression as an example of something that girls should not be exposed to.[78] Apparently, the flippant biblical reference troubled him. The general sentiment here – that there is nothing wrong with being naked – is typical of Pushkin's "naturist" take on sex in *RL*. According to Leslie O'Bell's reading of *RL*, "the theme of *Ruslan and Liudmila* could be defined as 'doing what comes naturally.' "[79] Another passage that drew the ire of Pushkin's contemporaries, and that Pushkin himself later regretted, hinges on this attitude: the famous parody of Zhukovskii's "Vadim" in the fourth canto (4.1–185). In his review, Voeikov suggests that Pushkin should "change this when he publishes the second edition, substituting it with something not so lowly and crude."[80] This parody has been the subject of countless interpretations, the most satisfactory being Proskurin's: "By combining the refrains of Derzhavin's verse with the refrains of Zhukovskii and carefully preserving the lexical and stylistic nuances of his subtexts, while simultaneously *inverting them axiologically*, Pushkin achieved a stunning effect: he freed the theme of erotic hedonism from its negative connotations and made verse about 'vice' sound 'positive.' "[81] Returning again to Barkoviana, this kind of sexual apologetics is part and parcel of the "unprintable" Russian erotic tradition. In "Prinoshenie Belinde" we read that "to be ashamed of what is natural is nothing but hypocrisy."[82]

In a sense, then, as Lotman puts it, this is a kind of "literary impropriety" – the displacement of a set of literary conventions from its traditional environment to one in which it is inappropriate. At the same time, though, it is also a flagrant violation of behavioral norms. Just as it was a *shalost'* to tell a frankly sexual anecdote in front of women or girls (or, indeed, in the presence of most men), it was a *shalost'* to print excessively sexual poetry not only in a format where they might read it, but with a slew of digressions addressed precisely to this audience.[83] Trotting out the sequestered sexual discourse of Barkoviana and the Green Lamp in a published work was highly improper, and many readers were offended.

"Blush, You Wretch!": Rudeness in *Ruslan and Liudmila* and Its Impact on Youth Culture

The preceding section begs the question: What exactly does it mean to say that the erotic passages of Pushkin's *Ruslan and Liudmila offended* many readers? Clearly, they were outraged, but it remains unclear how we should interpret this outrage in the broader frameworks of response theory. This moment of offense is a crucial one because it marks the moment when Pushkin did something that could not be expected; therefore, it often also marks the introduction of formal innovations. Furthermore, coming to grips with the offensive gives us a vantage point on the norms and conventions from which Pushkin departed. This is certainly not a new idea. The critic Jonathan Culler writes, "Since the system of classification depends on exclusion, one looks at what is apparently marginal to the system in order to understand the system.... One must consider ungrammatical sentences in order to work out the grammar of the language, or look at what is 'unthinkable' in a particular milieu in order to discover its deepest assumptions, or at what is unfashionable in order to reconstruct the code of fashion."[84] Erving Goffman recommends situational improprieties as a special domain of sociology for this same reason.[85] To conclude my study of *RL*, I would like to pursue precisely this "angle" on Pushkin's contemporaries' reaction to it.

The rudeness of *RL* is evident in the critical reaction to the poem, which sometimes explicitly decries it. It was a concern, for example, for Voeikov, who characterizes it in his inflammatory review of *RL* as a lack of respect *and* a violation of generic convention. "The epic poet should not for a moment lose sight of his readers, before whom he is obliged to conduct himself politely and respectfully. The [crude] jokes of the market square are offensive to the enlightened public."[86] On the one hand, Voeikov's evocation of the market square is representative of a sentiment widespread among Russian litterateurs, many of whom felt that turning to the Russian folk tradition for literary inspiration or subtexts was "a sign of ignorance and a lack of cultivation."[87] But, Nikolai Mordovchenko points out, the critics of *RL* were less perturbed by the folk motifs in *RL* than by the fact that "in 'Ruslan and Liudmila,' folksiness is dressed up as high poesy."[88]

Voeikov was also troubled by a more direct kind of rudeness. He reacted sternly, for example, to a lyrical digression at the beginning of the third canto of *RL* (3.1–29). Here, Pushkin's lyrical subject addresses a "Zoilus," a nitpicking critic who dares to ask him why he calls Liudmila both "princess" (*kniazhna*) and a "maiden" (*deva*) as if to spite Ruslan, for both words imply that she is yet an unmarried virgin. Pushkin's lyrical subject replies:

> Красней, несчастный, бог с тобою!
> Красней, я спорить не хочу;
> Довольный тем, что прав душою,
> В смиренной кротости молчу.
> Но ты поймешь меня, Климена,
> Потупишь томные глаза,
> Ты, жертва скучного Гимена …
> Я вижу: тайная слеза
> Падет на стих мой, сердцу внятный;
> Ты покраснела, взор погас;
> Вздохнула молча … вздох понятный!
> Ревнивец: бойся, близок час;
> Амур с досадой своенравной
> Вступили в смелый заговор,
> И для главы твоей бесславной
> Готов уж мстительный убор.

[Blush, you wretch, fare thee well! Blush, I don't want to argue; satisfied that I am right in my soul, I am silent in humble meekness. But you will understand me, Climene, you will drop your languorous eyes, you, the victim of dull Hymen … I can see: a furtive tear drops on my verses; you blushed, your gaze grew feeble; you sighed silently … an understandable sigh! Jealous man: be afraid, your hour is nigh; Amour and a capricious fury have entered a bold pact, and for your inglorious head the vengeful haberdashery is already prepared.]

This passage, a *shalost'* in every sense, requires a bit of decoding. "Climene" understands why Liudmila is still a "maiden" and a "princess" because she too, though married, remains a virgin. This same "dull Hymen," the older husband who either repulses his young wife or cannot perform, also figures in Pushkin's "Platonicheskaia liubov'" ("Platonic Love," 1819), a poem that Pushkin probably read at the Green Lamp.[89] In that poem, the lack of sex engenders a love for the "lonely arts" and the heroine becomes an avid masturbator.[90] In *RL*, Climene cries because she does not want to be a virgin, and the poem so arouses her that her husband should fear the cuckold's horns. This passage gained extremely personal overtones after the critical melee of 1820, in which Aleksei Perovskii alluded to Voeikov's virginity (at the age of forty-one) as a polemical jab in one of his articles on *RL*.[91] It is perfectly plausible that just such an ad hominem attack was implicit even in the first edition of *RL*. In any case, Voeikov reacted with indignation. "*The address to Zoilus in the third canto is lacking the cleverness with which the author wanted to season it by feigning ingenuousness. In all seriousness, one might turn his own line back on him: Blush, you wretch, fare thee well! Blush for having forgotten the respect due your readers.*"[92] Meanwhile, Pushkin knew perfectly well what he was up to and freely admitted that his tone here is "impolite." For example, in December of 1820, he jokingly inquired in a letter to Gnedich about the author of Voeikov's review, which was signed with only his initial: "Who is this V., who praises my chastity, scolds me for shamelessness, and tells me: *blush*, you wretch (which, by the way, is very rude)?"[93]

Many other passages in *RL* similarly angered critics, who objected to the impudence and bald rudeness. But where does this rudeness come from? Scholars often characterize the *RL* controversy as a struggle between literary camps.[94] While it is an anachronism to cast this as a battle between "liberal Romanticism" and "conservative classicism" (as many critics have), there were, no doubt, some stable factions involved. Aleksei Perovskii stepped forward to defend Pushkin on behalf of the Karamzinian-Arzamasian crowd; Dmitrii Zykov as the Katenin camp's critic; Andrei Glagolev for the Moscow University camp; and so on. Nonetheless, the fact is that *RL* did not fit neatly into the day's literary-ideological landscape because it represented an emerging stance. With the publication of *RL*, Pushkin effectively came out as the representative of his own camp. Pushkin's rudeness was part of a larger trend, but one that is difficult to put a finger on. Denunciations (*donosy*), a peculiar genre of the period's official culture, provide an excellent picture of this trend.

A week after Pushkin finished *RL*, the minister of the interior, Kochubei, received a denunciation of recent Lyceum graduates, especially Pushkin. Its author was Vasilii Karazin, the founder of Kharkov University, who would later struggle with Del'vig in the Free Society of Amateurs of Russian Literature.[95] Karazin's denunciations of 1819–20 played a role in Alexander I's decision to exile Pushkin in May 1820. In his denunciation of April 2, 1820, he writes that the Lyceum is a hotbed of antigovernment sentiment and cites Pushkin as an example of the rabble-rousers produced there: "But nearly every one of the charges [of the Lyceum], more or less, is a Pushkin, and they have all banded together in some sort of suspicious union."[96] This perception of Pushkin and his Lyceum schoolmates as a sort of group or united front became entrenched in the social and literary landscape of the late Alexandrine

period, and their reputation for insolence, debauchery, and rabble-rousing spread
to other members of their social circle as well. Vladimir Panaev, a poet who, along
with Pushkin's closest literary friends, was a fixture of Sofia Dmitrievna Ponomareva's salon, discerned a behavioral mode, a social pose that they adopted: arrogant, impudent, opinionated, and badly behaved. Panaev recalls in his memoirs that
he denied his good graces to Del'vig, Kiukhel'beker, and Boratynskii because "I
didn't like that they were so cocksure, nor the firm tone in which they gave their
opinions, nor their biases and rather unpraiseworthy behavior: my standards would
not allow me to traffic with such young men."[97] As Pushkin and company published
more and more over the early 1820s, they accrued more prestige. Pushkin, for example, went from five publications in 1818 to twelve in both 1820 and 1821, including
a full-length book (*RL*), and in 1823, he published another long poem (*Kavkazskii
plennik* [*Prisoner of the Caucasus*]) along with seventeen shorter works. Subsequent years saw still more publications. In short, his professional career blossomed
between 1820 and 1823, even as he lived the nomadic life of a political exile.[98] As
Turgenev says in the letter I quoted in the previous chapter, publication was a key
to gaining respect: "published, and therefore respected, authors."[99] It is therefore
natural that these poets found eager epigones among the youth.

According to one important informant, the term "Lyceum spirit" (*litseiskii
dukh*) came to refer to this pose as it became more popular. In 1826, as the Investigatory Commission began to wrap up its task, the writer and publisher Tadeusz
Bulgarin submitted a report on "Lyceum spirit" to the secret police. A former officer in Napoleon's army and a close associate of many of the Decembrist conspirators, Bulgarin had been cooperating with the secret police for years, and assisted
the Commission in 1826 with the particular assiduousness born of fear.[100] Later,
he exploited his connections in the Third Section (the chancellery that grew out
of the Commission) to gain the upper hand in literary disputes both critical and
commercial. His report on "Lyceum spirit" was one of his first and most compre-
hensive after the Decembrist Uprising, which indicates that he thought it an important engine of political unrest, or at least significant enough to go on record about
right away. Bulgarin arrived in Petersburg only in 1819 and, being a poor foreigner
of unremarkable origins, he was certainly not privy to goings-on in the rarified
aristocratic atmosphere of, for example, the Green Lamp. In a word, the notion of
"Lyceum spirit" must have been pretty widespread if Bulgarin knew about it. Here
is what he wrote in the report he filed with the Commission on July 13, 1826 (I have
done my best to accurately render Bulgarin's "exophonic" Russian, which was still
quite rough in 1826):

> 1. *What "Lyceum spirit" means.* In society, it is called *Lyceum spirit* when
> a young man does not respect his elders, is familiar with the bosses, arrogant
> with equals, and contemptuous of inferiors, except for those cases when he
> wants to seem an admirer of *equality*. A young man for this is supposed to
> sarcastically deride all the actions of any person of significant station, all
> the measures of the government; he must either be himself a composer of
> or know by heart all blameworthy Russian epigrams, lampoons, and songs;
> and he must know in French all the most brazen and seditious poems and
> the strongest passages from revolutionary works. Besides all that, he must
> opine about constitutions, legislative chambers, parliaments; he must seem

to doubt Christian dogma, and, above all, present himself as a philanthropist and a Russian patriot. He also possesses an obligation to deride military bearing and training, and to that end the word *shagistika* [the science of marching] has been invented. Prophesying the future, criticism of all measures, or contemptuous silence when anything is praised – these are the defining characteristics of these gentlemen in society. To call someone *a loyal subject* [*blagonamerennyi*] is an insult in their language, to call one *a European* and *a liberal* – honorable appellations. A kind of derisive melancholy always clouds the brow of these boys, and it clears only in hours of wild merriment.

This is the model of young men and even not young men, of whom we have a sufficient number. In the graduates of the Lyceum, their friends, and allies, this character is called in society: *The Lyceum spirit.* For grown men a different name has been selected: Mepris souverain pour le genre humain (mepris for short); for the third category, i.e., real loudmouths – they are called, simply, *liberal*. For example: "What do you think of so-and-so?" "He's all right, but he's got a little Lyceum spirit in him," or: "He's all right, but he's a mepris," or just "A liberal."[101]

Bulgarin also provides his version of the lineage of the Lyceum spirit, which he thinks derives from the Masonic circles of the late eighteenth century. By direct inheritance, the liberalism of these Masonic "Martinists" passed to their sons, who formed subversive groups. In particular, he points to the Arzamasians, who "made ready the gunpowder that subsequently was touched off by the wild flame of the Secret Society."[102] The liberalism of these groups subsequently began to "swirl" in the atmosphere of "mental fermentation" that characterized the Hussar Regiment stationed in Tsarskoe Selo when the first class of the Lyceum reached adolescence. Since no one was looking after the "moral education" of the Lyceum's charges, and since they were given free rein to associate with freethinking officers, debauchees, prostitutes, and other undesirables, it is no surprise that they turned out poorly, biting the hand that fed them.

Most interestingly, though, Bulgarin describes the "effect and influence of Lyceum spirit on society." He writes that with the support of Arzamas and the secret societies, antigovernment lampoons and epigrams brought Pushkin and his comrades respect and fame in the "infected" spheres of high society. As their status increased, their impudence, liberalism, and loose morals also gained status. Much as young people today copy the mode of dress of movie stars or rappers, fashionable teenagers of early 1820s Petersburg society, according to Bulgarin, copied the behavioral modes of Pushkin and his comrades. "They ran around with officers of the Guard, with young aristocrats, they received protection and patronage from the Arzamasians and members of the Secret Society, they capered [*shalili*] with impunity, were poor workers and, because they enjoyed rewards and respect in society for their bad deeds, they set a disastrous course for other young men, who did not heed their parents at home, derided them as *loyal subjects* and considered themselves reformers, the children of a new age, a new generation born to take pleasure in the blessings of their age. It was useless to counsel them. They considered themselves above everyone else."[103] For Bulgarin, these trends – which he thought led to the disastrous Decembrist Uprising – were very much connected to literature. He, like most of his contemporaries, viewed literature as an important engine of "public opinion" (a relatively new concept he invariably harps on in his communiqués to government agents). He writes, for example, that the most important thing in education is "using literature to effect the *cultivation* of minds and to direct them toward a beneficial goal."[104] Though the importance of literature for shaping young minds may be overstated here (Bulgarin, after all, was a commercial publisher), it was certainly something that the state devoted a lot of resources to in the form of censorship, bans, and the harassment of writers.

Returning to 1820, we might characterize *RL* as an important event in the process of popularizing the Lyceum spirit, a process Bulgarin depicts as a done deed in 1826. *RL* was the first major literary success of Pushkin's circle. The demand for the book, perhaps artificially boosted by the book dealers, was such that some enthusiastic readers were forced to copy by hand all 2,800 plus lines of *RL*. Just before the publication of the second edition of *RL* in 1828, one contemporary wrote, "'Ruslan i Liudmila' ... came out in 1820. It sold out right away, and there have long been no copies of it for sale. Fans were paying 25 rubles a copy and were forced to copy it by hand."[105] This success brought further currency to a world view, tenor, and social pose that – in the eyes of their contemporaries, at least – Pushkin and his circle held in common. In particular, though, *RL* and the controversy it inspired cemented Pushkin's reputation as a fatuous and defiant upstart.[106] As Karazin implies in the denunciation quoted previously, Pushkin was already the prime model in 1820 for politically unreliable and potentially dangerous youth, already a common noun: "But nearly every one of them ... is a Pushkin." And, as Pushkin's friend Nikolai Markevich later recalled, "by 1820, Pushkin had become a celebrity for good."[107] Interestingly, as I noted earlier, Pushkin published little before 1820. As such, his initial fame was due less to his publications than to his behavior. As Turgenev said of him in February 1820, "At present he's known only for small poems and large *shalosti*."[108] Contrary to Turgenev's hopes, the publication of *RL*, in combination with exile, brought Pushkin fame as the author of even larger *shalosti*. And he was supported by a broad section of the public. Criticizing Voeikov's review, Archbishop Eugene, for example, wrote to a friend, "Not just Pushkin's adherents [*pushkintsy*], but all the youth are up in arms against the reviewer."[109] By 1822, Pushkin already regretted the unpleasant consequences of this public image.[110] This "social reputation," as Vatsuro calls it, influenced the way that Pushkin's contemporaries read *RL*; and, given his very public writing practice, it also bore on the way Pushkin wrote the poem in 1818–20.

The lyrical digressions of *RL*, again, are a good example. The accepted view has long been that the digressions serve a narratological purpose: to create an ironic bifurcation of the lyrical subject.[111] This idea is worth pausing on because irony is what makes *RL* possible. There is near universal agreement that *RL* is a metafictional work – a *poema*, first and foremost, about poetry. Metafictional texts invariably both "systematically flaunt [their] own condition of artifice"[112] and "criticize previous literary conventions."[113] To do this, metafiction requires the *overt* presence of a reflexive subject in the text. The reflexive subject presupposes a split subjectivity (in the sense of Schlegel): one part of the subject must operate independently of the other in order to comment upon it. Postulating a now standard argument, Tomashevskii says that the subjectivity introduced and maintained in the lyrical digressions "infects" the entire poem. Moreover, he says, this was a major innovation. "That is why ... the entire poem in all its parts is, in a sense, a chat between the author and the reader, the very opposite of the old epic *poema*, in which the author did not reveal himself as an individual in the *poema*'s verse, and the word was dislocated from its speaker, becoming abstract and monosemantic."[114] So, in rhetorical terms, the lyrical digressions of *RL* are the source of its ethos. Pushkin's claim to the reader's attention – his ethos – rubbed many readers the wrong way, and the omnipresence of Pushkin's lyrical subject(s) displeased a number of his critics. In part, this is a question of literary convention. As Tomashevskii says, readers were not used to narrative strategies centered on the subjectivity of the narrator. But Pushkin's contemporaries did not see it purely as a matter of literary aesthetics. It was as if the poet constantly barges in just as the reader is getting to the good parts – an unforgivably rude intrusion. The *Nevskii zritel'* reviewer, for example, wrote, "The poet likes to talk about himself quite a lot and [always seems to be] addressing himself to pretty girls, to preceptors, to actors, and the like – that is what holds up the progress of the action and hinders unity. I would like to be charmed, to forget myself – but, instead, the poet brings my delight to a halt, and instead of Ancient Rus', I see today's world around me: the incongruity becomes plain, and, what's more, all this distracts the reader's attention and belittles the importance of the [poet's] subject."[115]

The expectations that this reviewer has of poets are extremely telling. He wants to "be charmed, to forget himself." In other words, he wants to be entertained and delighted. And the poet should not hinder this with a lot of asides and jokes; paradoxically enough, the poet should keep out of the way and let the reader enjoy himself. The poet here is a kind of a servant to the reader, one who, as Voeikov says, "should not for a moment lose sight of his readers, before whom he is obliged to conduct himself politely and respectfully." Pushkin's lack of respect for his reader, as evinced by the intrusiveness of his narrator, was one of the central themes in the critical polemic of 1820–21. Clearly, he asserted himself more than was customary and, in Goffman's terms, took a "line" that was not in keeping with the expectations of the readership. His lyrical subject, like the obnoxious young man Bulgarin describes, "does not respect his elders, is familiar with his superiors, and arrogant with his equals." As such, we have here an ineluctable intertwining of two sets of conventions: literary and behavioral. Not only did the lyrical digressions that lie at the heart of the poem's pragmatic structure run against literary convention, they were fundamentally rude. It is impossible to separate the two.

This complaint about Pushkin's intrusiveness was voiced at the very outset of the critical debate. Andrei Glagolev's letter to the editor of *Vestnik Evropy* (*The Herald of Europe*), which was the very first critique of *RL* published in 1820, lambastes Pushkin for being outrageously and impudently intrusive.[116] In many respects, Glagolev's letter, a broad programmatic attack on Zhukovskii's epigones (among whom he counts Pushkin), set the terms for the ensuing polemic. At the end of the letter, he lists a few folk motifs in *RL* and makes the following analogy:

> But allow me to dispense with the details and to ask: were a bearded guest in a peasant's coat and *lapti* [bast sandals] somehow to burst into the Moscow Assembly of the Nobility (I am presuming the impossible possible) and screech: *howdy, fellas!* Would such a prankster really be admired? For God's sakes, allow me, an old man, to tell the reading public, by means of your journal, to screw up their eyes at the sight of such strange things. Why should

the flat jokes of old be allowed to crop up among us anew! A crude joke disallowed by enlightened taste is revolting, and not the least bit funny or amusing.[117]

Glagolev's image of the peasant in the Moscow Assembly of the Nobility subsequently became a famous one, and Pushkin (with great pride, it would seem) quotes this passage in his introduction to the second edition of *RL*. Glagolev's central idea here, of course, is that Pushkin has done something completely inappropriate, something, as Jonathan Culler says, "'unthinkable' in a particular milieu."[118] Literary historians have often taken an allegorical approach to Glagolev's image, interpreting it as an intrusion of the national and the Romantic into the exclusive sanctum of classicist aesthetics.[119] Clearly, though, there is something else at stake here: Glagolev is genuinely offended. This, the very first published response to *RL*, introduces the tone of outrage that characterizes the subsequent polemic.

To understand what is really going on here, I would like to return to Brown and Levinson's *Politeness*. In their classification of various kinds of face-threatening acts (FTAs), they list "irreverence, [and] mention of taboo topics, including those that are inappropriate in the context."[120] I should hope I have already made the case that, throughout *RL*, Pushkin is irreverent, that he makes mention of taboo topics, and – especially according to Glagolev – that they were inappropriate in the context. In terms of politeness, this sort of thing threatens the positive face of the addressee because it shows that the addresser "doesn't care about (or is indifferent to)"[121] the self-image or personality claimed by readers like Glagolev. Note that Glagolev, Voeikov, and the reviewer from *Nevskii zritel'* (among others) repeatedly emphasize the notion of "enlightened taste" or "the enlightened public," of which they count themselves members. Their complaint, at root, is that Pushkin does not sufficiently attend to this self-image. He does not ratify the construction of self they want to project and, in failing to do so, he quite baldly calls it into question.

At the same time, it is not as though Pushkin sought to offend *all* his readers. Indeed, by employing the in-group language of the groups from which *RL*, in part, emerged – Arzamas and the Green Lamp – he in fact rigorously attends to the face wants of that small portion of his readership, even as he offends "outsiders." Thus *RL*, this *shalost'*, selects among the readership. By casting his reader as his intimate, Pushkin simultaneously offends those who are not (and who do not wish to be) and pays a compliment to those who are (or who wish to be). And that, in my estimation, is the real reason that *RL* created such a stir.

Epilogue

Pushkin the Pornographer, Two Hundred Years Later

The ballad *Ten' Barkova* (*The Shade of Barkov*, composed circa 1815, hereafter *TB*) has stirred more controversy in the past decade than any other issue in Pushkin studies. This is mostly due to its single most remarkable feature: its lexicon, roughly 30 percent of which is obscene (*mat*). Otherwise, *TB* is a narrative poem that consists of twenty-four twelve-line stanzas and that is unremarkable in every respect expect that it provides an exceptionally unique perspective on Pushkin's early development. Over the course of these 288 lines winds the simple tale of a defrocked priest with the speaking name Ebakov ("Fuckman"). The narrative opens in a Petersburg bordello, where Ebakov finds himself suddenly impotent, an unprecedented disruption. The ghost of the famed eighteenth-century scholar, poet, and vulgarian Ivan Semenovich Barkov appears to help him and swiftly returns Ebakov to good health. As the price for this rescue, Barkov's ghost commands the priest to compose verse devoted wholly to singing the praises of the Great Barkov. Ebakov complies, becoming as a result a celebrated bard himself. His exploits in this capacity eventually lead him to a convent, where he finds himself locked in a cell at the mercy of an elderly abbess who declares she will castrate Ebakov the instant he is no longer able to service her. Eventually, his strength fails him, and the mother superior locks him up in the latrine to await execution of his sentence. But Barkov's ghost again appears to help him out of his difficulty, and when the mother superior returns to make good on her threat, she is greeted by the sight of Barkov's pantless ghost and the full evidence of the priest's renewed vigor. She drops dead of fright on the spot, and Ebakov goes free. As in *Ruslan i Liudmila*, narrative here serves a secondary function, as the supporting structure for a rich tapestry of parodic intertext. The main object of parody is Zhukovskii. His ballad "Gromoboi" ("Gromoboi," 1811) provides the narrative structure, and his diction lurks just beneath the surface of much of the ballad.

The case for attributing *TB* to Pushkin has been accumulating since 1863, and was until recently firmly entrenched. For almost all of the twentieth century, this attribution was an accepted fact of literary history. Leading late Imperial and Soviet Pushkinists – Pavel Shchegolev, Nikolai Lerner, Iurii Tynianov, Dmitrii Blagoi, Sergei Bondi, Boris Tomashevskii, Mstislav Tsiavlovskii, Nikolai Izmailov, Ilya Feinberg, Aleksandr Slonimskii, Iurii Lotman, Vadim Vatsuro, and many others – all believed *TB* was the work of Pushkin. Indeed, the ballad was to be included in the 1937 jubilee edition of Pushkin's collected works. Yet *TB*, not surprisingly, never was published in the Soviet Union.

If a literary work can be said to have a biography, *TB* has one of the oddest in

Russian literature. This biography and the recent controversy tell us little about Pushkin himself, but a lot about the role of the Pushkin myth and the Pushkin industry in contemporary Russian society. I interpret the discomfort *TB* causes primarily as a continuation of the resistance to crossing contextual lines. *"Domesticity cannot be allowed in public work,"* we read in Ushakov's dictionary from the 1930s. Even after the near disintegration of Soviet cultural practice, the Pushkin industry remains "public work." The polemic surrounding *TB* is but another episode in the long history of forcing Pushkin to don his Kammerjunker's uniform, to take his proper place in the contexts of state and society, and to comport himself as befits the occasion.

TB was a popular fixture of the notebook manuscript collections of "unprintable" verse that were compiled, passed around, and copied by young men throughout the nineteenth century. One commentator aptly deems it "pimply samizdat." Were it not for this collective effort, this poem (and many others, many still unknown) would not have been preserved. No less than eight texts of the poem from such collections are known today; if researchers are ever given proper access to the vast Smirnov-Sokolovskii collection of these notebooks at the Russian State Library, many more texts of the poem will no doubt surface.

TB was not written for publication, and its "natural habitat" was precisely this "pimply samizdat." It was thus little known for the first fifty years of its existence. Viktor Gaevskii was the first to mention the ballad in print.[1] For an 1863 article in *Sovremennik*, Gaevskii interviewed surviving members of the 1817 Lyceum class, who said that Pushkin was the author of *TB*. Gaevskii excerpted fifty-three lines of the poem in his article, which was the first time *TB* had ever been in print. The next attempt to publish the poem was by Petr Efremov in his famous 1880 edition of Pushkin's works. Efremov had painstakingly redacted Gaevskii's excerpts of the poem, substituting euphemisms for all the obscene words (no mean feat!). But at the last minute, on the "suggestion" of the censor that *TB* could not be the work of Pushkin, Efremov ordered the poem literally *cut* from the edition's contents. This suggestion must have come after the book was printed and bound, for *TB* remained in the table of contents, and pages 56–57 have been physically excised from almost all the known copies. On several occasions, Efremov defended this action, but his version of the episode varies widely between tellings.[2]

As a result of Efremov's decision, *TB* languished in obscurity for another four decades. Interest in the ballad was renewed in 1928, when an autograph of Pushkin's narrative poem "Monakh" ("The Monk," 1814) was discovered. Gaevskii had described this unknown poem in his 1863 article, and it turned out that he was right: Pushkin had written such a poem, just as his classmates said.[3] Since *TB* and "Monakh" were thought to be of a piece, scholars turned their attention to *TB*. By 1929, two of the day's most prominent old-guard Pushkinists, Pavel Shchegolev and Nikolai Lerner, had publicly expressed certainty that *TB* was indeed written by Pushkin and advocated its publication. And in 1931, Vladimir Orlov published an excerpt from the ballad with an attribution to Pushkin.[4] That same year, Mstislav Tsiavlovskii – then the world's foremost expert on Pushkin's Lyceum-period verse – completed his textological work on *TB* and assembled a remarkable commentary. This proved an auspicious moment. The 1937 "Big Academy" or "jubilee" edition of Pushkin was already in the works, and Tsiavlovskii was charged with preparing the first volume of it, dedicated to Pushkin's Lyceum period. It was decided by the illustrious editorial board of the edition, the single most authoritative group of Pushkinists ever assembled, that *TB* should be included in this volume. In 1936, Tsiavlovskii returned to his *TB* commentary and finished it, but this work was to see light only sixty years later.

The conditions under which the project was completed and the subsequent fate of Tsiavlovskii's text and commentary are straight out of Il'f and Petrov's satires. First, Glavlit (the Main Administration for Literary and Publishing Affairs) determined that, though *TB* was clearly a work indispensable to specialists, the general public could not be exposed to it. Thus, it could not be included in the 1937 jubilee edition. Instead, *TB* and Tsiavlovskii's commentary were to be published separately in a limited edition of three hundred numbered copies exclusively "for internal use" by authorized Pushkinists.

Everyone involved went to great lengths to keep *TB* under wraps. Correspondence regarding the project was stamped "confidential" (*ne podlezhit oglasheniiu*). Tsiavlovskii was forbidden to let any female typist (*mashinistka* – an exclusively female occupation in the Soviet era) see it and spent weeks trying to find a male typist (*mashinist*), but to no avail. Lev Kamenev, who was then director of the editorial staff for the jubilee edition, managed to pull some strings and find a suitable typist. In fact, two typists were found: a deaf-mute husband and wife team who were the only typists in the NKVD's in-house publishing unit. Thus, Tsiavlovskii's text and commentary were typed and formatted by perhaps the two most trusted typographic workers in the nation, in the basement of the NKVD headquarters, and doubtless under heavy guard.

The female half of this team was perhaps the only woman officially allowed to see Tsiavlovskii's text as it wended its way through the various offices and committees of the Academy and Glavlit. Female colleagues were barred from attending editorial meetings where *TB* was to be discussed. Academician Natalia Mikhailova recalled in a recent interview that Tsiavlovskii's wife, Tatiana Tsiavlovskaia, who was by then a full-fledged member of the editorial staff, once donned a wig and men's clothing in order to sneak into one of these meetings; she was caught by Sergei Bondi, who, recognizing her legs (!?), ejected her.[5]

In spite of all the secrecy and all the difficulties with preparing the text, Tsiavlovskii's final draft was approved by the editorial board, and his manuscript was submitted to the Publishing House of the Academy of Sciences in 1936. He signed off on the last set of page proofs in April 1937, and the project was given the green light. It was to be printed at the same NKVD print shop where the deaf-mute couple had done the typing, in the same format as the jubilee edition, and on the same paper – the same in every respect, but secret.

Soon after the page proofs had been signed over, news came that a fire had broken out in the NKVD print shop. All Tsiavlovskii's work on *TB* was presumed lost. He had retained only part of his early handwritten manuscripts. This information comes to us from an interview the lawyer Evgenii Shal'man conducted with Tatiana Tsiavlovskaia in 1961, which he recounts in the foreword to his 1996 publication of Tsiavlovskii's text and commentary.[6] I have not been able to confirm that this fire actually took place; it seems extremely unlikely that it did, for reasons that will soon become apparent. Perhaps an invented fire was thought a less painful way of informing Tsiavlovskii that the project had been cut at the last moment? Perhaps, even twenty-three years later, Tsiavlovskaia herself was not anxious to recount the actual circumstances surrounding the repression of her husband's work? No doubt, it must have been a terrifying time for them both.[7]

Whether or not the fire actually took place, the page proofs survived, as did part of the typed manuscript. Shal'man documents Tatiana Tsiavlovskaia's astounding account of their subsequent fate. The page proofs surfaced in 1939 or 1940, when an unknown individual brought a bound copy to the book dealer Aleksandr Fadeev. The asking price of five hundred rubles seemed reasonable. Fadeev asked a consultant, David Aizenshtadt, to have a look. As it happened, Aizenshtadt was a friend of the Tsiavlovskiis and knew the history of the proofs. He immediately called Tsiavlovskii and summoned him to Fadeev's shop. Before he arrived, however, the book collector Vera Bogdanova, who was present when Fadeev purchased the proofs, demanded that they be sold to her. She was able to raise enough of a scandal that a special session of the board of the Writers' Union was convened to decide the matter. They found in favor of Tsiavlovskii: he was awarded the proofs, and Fadeev was paid five hundred rubles from the Union's fund.

Parts of Tsiavlovskii's typed manuscript surfaced three years later under even stranger circumstances. Shal'man's account of this episode is so vivid and amusing that I cannot resist quoting it in full.

In 1943 a humbly dressed woman knocked at the door of Mstislav Aleksandrovich and Tatiana Grigor'evna's apartment in Koniushennyi Street: "Does Tsiavlovskii live here?" Mstislav Aleksandrovich was ill, and Tatiana Grigor'evna did not want to disturb him. "I'm here on an important matter, I must speak with him! ..." Once in the bedroom, the woman became embarrassed: "I feel awkward speaking of it ... I have obtained a manuscript – it has your name on it." "Manuscript?! How did you get it?" – the expansive Mstislav Aleksandrovich sat up abruptly on the bed. And the woman told her story ... She was a schoolteacher, and had been mobilized at the beginning of the war, assigned to a timber camp next to a military installation. At night, she would hear "the forest groaning with laughter, both male and female." When she investigated "why the trees were groaning," she discovered that some soldiers were educating her young female pupils with recitations of "The Shade of Barkov." Our heroine demanded that they give her the manuscript, but they didn't want to part with their treasure. Then "she made a huge sacrifice." She collected all her vodka ration tickets and traded them for the manuscript. When she returned to Moscow, she "kept the manuscript under her mattress" ("I've got a sixteen-year-old son."). She did not know who Tsiavlovskii was, but, once, she saw his name in the newspaper and was able to find out his address. How to thank this woman? All the money in the house was gathered up ("And Mstislav Aleksandrovich never had money!"). They were able to scrape together 200 rubles and convinced the woman to take them.[8]

The NKVD secret typography, a fire, a remote timber camp, a matter before the Writers' Union – this remarkable journey ended in 1943, and Tsiavlovskii's text and commentary lay quietly in this same apartment on Koniushennyi Street until shortly after the death of his widow in 1978. For three decades after his death, she guarded these documents vigilantly, but would sometimes allow scholars to view them. William Todd was able to arrange such a viewing while a graduate student at Leningrad State University in 1970–71. Unfortunately, Pushkin House staff got wind of the meeting, and it had to be called off.[9]

Tatiana Tsiavlovskaia bequeathed her husband's work on *TB*, along with his other major unpublished works, to Pushkin House. After Tsiavlovskaia's executor signed over the *TB* manuscripts and proofs to Vadim Vatsuro in 1978, access to them became even more difficult. Even eminent scholars like Iurii Lotman were refused access during the 1980s. Lotman complained in a 1983 letter to his friend and colleague Vladimir Toporov, "For me, to go there (Pushkin House) is now the same as to go down to the cesspool (excuse this unappetizing comparison!). In spring I needed a manuscript of Pushkin's *Ten'Barkova* ... They did not give it to me! And even gave me a lecture about how high one has to hold the honor of our classics and so on and so forth."[10] After censorship loosened in the early 1990s and it became possible for obscene words to appear in print, Pushkin House declined to publish *TB* despite great public interest. This decision was and is of no small consequence because Pushkin House was and is the host institution for the Russian Academy's publications of Pushkin – in essence and in fact, Pushkin House continues to form and safeguard the official version of Pushkin.

As publications of *TB* began to proliferate in the 1990s, along with the first significant publications of Barkoviana and other previously "hidden" literature, the traditional attribution of *TB* was called into question for the first time in decades. One might speculate that, as more and more people finally got a chance to read these works, a certain amount of collective, shocked disbelief set in. When the editorial board of the new jubilee edition (in production at Pushkin House since the early 1990s) publicly called the traditional attribution into doubt in 1999, some Pushkinists rushed to get on record as like-minded skeptics, even though some of these scholars had previously attributed *TB* to Pushkin in print without equivocation on a number of occasions.

Things came to a head in 2002, when the founders of the journal *Philologica*, Maksim Shapir and Igor Pil'shchikov, published a scholarly edition of *TB*.[11] At the heart of the book is their textological reconstruction of the ballad and a 300-page scholarly apparatus. The publication of this book – devoted in part to demonstrating beyond any reasonable doubt that, Yes, Virginia, Pushkin wrote *TB* – sparked the most voluminous, impassioned, and often vicious Pushkinistic polemic in recent memory. The main topic in this polemic was, of course, the attribution of *TB*. Throughout 2003 and 2004, Pushkin House staff, the "Moscow Pushkinists," and the journal *Novoe literaturnoe obozrenie* (*New Literary Review*) heaped abuse on Shapir and Pil'shchikov, who – it must be said – gave as good as they got. They published several energetic defenses of the attribution and their own textological practice, as well as scathing exposés of their opponents' polemical misdeeds. They delivered lectures and defended themselves before the Academy. Though there are still some rumbles now and again, the storm more or less subsided in 2005, when *The Annals of the Russian Academy of Sciences, Literature and Language Series* published Shapir and Pil'shchikov's succinct roundup of the attribution arguments and evidence.[12]

Today, despite all the hubbub, it seems the traditional attribution of *TB* is still dominant in that small corner of the Russian popular consciousness occupied by literature: of one hundred Internet publications I surveyed in August 2007 (out of roughly four hundred), ninety-six name Pushkin as the author. Pushkin is named as the author on TV talk shows, in the weekend edition of *Moskovskii komsomolets* (*Moscow Komsomolets*), and in university term papers for sale on the Internet.

Reading through the *TB* attribution polemic, with all its many reversals and inconsistencies, it became apparent to me that the issue of attribution was, in fact, merely the surface manifestation of deeper political, cultural, and ethical questions. In order to uncover some of these issues, I decided to survey the main players in the controversy, as well as a host of other scholars with some behind-the-scenes knowledge of it. I sent out thirty requests for participation in the survey; I got eleven responses. Of the responders, five wish to remain anonymous. The other six were: Pushkin House scholars Ekaterina Larionova and Vadim Rak, Igor Pil'shchikov, Oleg Proskurin, Andrei Zorin, and William Todd.

To get at the heart of the matter, I have looked at a single issue – one that, admittedly, might already be in some respects completely irrelevant: whether or not *TB* ought to be included in the new jubilee edition. Including it would of course constitute an official, state-sponsored acknowledgment of the work as a literary fact, which must then enter into the all-encompassing picture of Pushkin that the Academy Pushkinists insist it is their job to preserve and present.[13] Certainly, with only two volumes to show for the last fifteen years, the jubilee edition carries less and less cultural significance with each passing day. Nonetheless, it seems to me that this particular debate crystallizes the collision of values that sparked such an unlikely scandal.

There are several camps involved in this polemic. They might best be grouped into the following categories: (1) those who profess a belief that Pushkin was not the author of *TB*, and object to including it in the jubilee edition for philological reasons; (2) those who believe Pushkin may have been the author, or one of the authors, but do not want it to become part of the "Academy Pushkin"; and (3) those who believe Pushkin wrote it and that it should be included in the jubilee edition.

In the first camp – those who reject the Pushkin attribution – there is, first and foremost, the editorial board for the new jubilee edition at Pushkin House. Ekaterina Larionova, the current *zamglavredaktor* (de facto editor in chief), who has been on the board for over fifteen years, and who has published extensively on *TB* since 2002, was one of my survey respondents. She writes plainly enough, "I do not think Pushkin was the author of *TB*."[14] She came to this conclusion primarily because of the "low literary level" of the poem, which, she says, is so bad that Pushkin could not have possibly written it. I think it is safe to say that this is now the official position of Pushkin House, at least to the extent one exists (and I should note that Larionova strenuously objects to the idea that one does). Among other things, a recently defended Pushkin House dissertation on "pseudopushkiniana" includes a chapter on *TB*.[15]

The position of the editorial board, however, was not always so unequivocal. The first editor of the new jubilee edition, Vadim Vatsuro, initially held to the traditional attribution. In the 1994 *probnyi tom* (prototype volume) of Pushkin's Lyceum poems, Vatsuro's team attributed *TB* to Pushkin.[16] But because, as one long-time member of the board, Vadim Rak, told me in his survey response, Vatsuro was categorically opposed to including *TB* in the edition proper, they published it as a separate booklet "for internal use only" in a small print run of numbered copies. Five years later, the editorial board had changed its mind. In the first volume of the new jubilee edition, which is basically a reproduction of the *probnyi tom* with some very minor adjustments, Larionova and her colleagues, under the direction of Sergei Fomichev and, nominally, the ailing Vatsuro, found it impossible to attribute the poem to Pushkin (though they forgot to remove the affirmations of that attribution that appear in the commentary a few pages later!). When this volume came out in 1999, many readers were surprised to find that the first sentence of the commentary reads: "This volume contains all the Lyceum-period poems of Pushkin, excluding the obscene poema/ballad 'TB,' which, due to textological and attribution difficulties, will be included in one of the volumes to follow – most likely together with other dubia."[17] I would hardly be the first to point out that difficulties of attribution and textology are hardly an argument for relegating *TB* to dubia. And I am also not the first to note the lack of clarity here: if it is one of Pushkin's poems ("all ... poems of Pushkin ... excluding the obscene poema/ballad"), then why should it be counted dubia?

When, in 2002, Shapir and Pil'shchikov essentially did the editorial board's work for them – marshaling the arguments and evidence, working through the textology, compiling a truly massive scholarly apparatus – Larionova and her Pushkin House colleague, Vadim Rak, had a strange reaction: they savaged Shapir and Pil'shchikov in a *Novaia russkaia kniga* (*New Russian Book*) review of the edition.[18] Rather surprisingly, Larionova confesses in this review that she actually thinks *TB should* have been included in the first volume of the new jubilee edition. Further, she writes that it was excluded not for scholarly reasons, but "for completely understandable ethical considerations." She even says, "The editorial board rightly deserves to be criticized for its fear of stating this openly and for the *intentional* lack of clarity of its statements with regard to TB."[19] It seems pretty clear that she is laying the blame here at the doorstep of her senior colleague, Sergei Fomichev, who was replaced as the head of the Pushkin section at Pushkin House not long after.[20]

But five years later, in 2007, Larionova was of a different mind. In her responses to my survey questions, she stated that she has no doubt that *TB* should not be included in the new jubilee edition, and said that her position is purely a scholarly one – because she does not believe that Pushkin could have written something that bad. One anonymous survey respondent offers the following explanation for this change of heart: Larionova and her colleagues were simply "stuck" with decisions made on the basis of nonscholarly "ethical considerations" and have been doing their best in a difficult position by denying the Pushkin attribution in increasingly categorical forms. Thus, what was originally a completely nonphilological position is now dressed up as a scholarly one, and purely for what this anonymous respondent terms "administrative reasons." Furthermore, as Vadim Rak wrote in his survey responses, "The arguments of those who believe Pushkin to be the author [of *TB*] do not seem convincing enough to me, and the more such arguments are brought forth, the less convincing becomes their growing sum."

In some respects, the predicament of the Pushkin House staff is encapsulated in an anecdote that Oleg Proskurin related to me in his survey responses. In 1996, at a Pushkin conference in Madison, Wisconsin, he asked Sergei Fomichev (then the de facto editor of the new jubilee edition) how his team planned to print obscene works in the new edition. Fomichev replied that, naturally, Pushkin's expletives would be replaced with dashes – the time-honored Soviet tradition of the literary "bleep" – because he felt that the new edition ought to be very distinct from the "heaps of obscenity" (*matershchina*) and "pornography" to be found at the book kiosks and tables in those days. Then Proskurin asked whether they planned to include *TB*, to which question Fomichev replied in the affirmative. Proskurin remarked that since they would have to "bleep out" most of the text, perhaps it would be most expedient to simply bleep out the whole poem and leave only the title and the date.[21] And true enough, printing *TB* with Soviet-style expurgations would have been a huge editorial headache and a mostly pointless exercise. How to make an exception to the "no cussing" rule in this case? The accepted practice was to publish *TB* as a separate, restricted volume, but Fomichev opted for a simpler expedient: simply do nothing for now and see what happens down the road. And now the current editorial board is stuck with this decision.

The second camp in the *TB* polemic is comprised of those who believe Pushkin probably did write the ballad, but abhor the publication of it. Unlike Rak and Larionova, people in this camp are very clear that their stance is primarily an ideological one. Whether Pushkin wrote *TB* or not is mostly a moot point to them: either way, it should not be published. The most prominent voice in this group is Valentin Nepomniashchii, the chair of the Pushkin Commission at the Academy's Institute of World Literature in Moscow. Nepomniashchii has on a number of occasions affirmed the Pushkin attribution in print and in interviews, but now rails against the publication of *TB*.[22] A distant second is Viktor Esipov, who published an article attacking Shapir and Pil'shchikov's attribution arguments in the Pushkin Commission's organ, *Moskovskii pushkinist* (*Moscow Pushkinist*), in 2005, presumably with Nepomniashchii's blessing.[23]

The mindset of this camp was nicely summed up by Nepomniashchii in one sentence from a recent interview titled, piquantly but accurately, "Pushkin as a Matter of National Security": "The publication of such works is simply unthinkable to a person of the Orthodox culture of Russia!"[24] Further, Nepomniashchii considers it the responsibility of the "creative intelligentsia" to regulate the Russian language and to keep its written manifestations free not only of obscenity, but also of all manner of "foreign trash." Lastly, as a product of "Russian Orthodox culture" himself, he considers it imperative to maintain an impenetrable boundary between the spoken word and the written word. To borrow the metaphor Nepomniashchii employs in this interview, the peasants in the village where he vacations (something he is fond of talking about in interviews) know the difference between the *zalo* (main room) in their cottages and the *otkhozhee mesto* (literally: the place to which one walks away to relieve oneself). "And they don't mix them up!" he tells us. Nepomniashchii's frequent references to common folk are, in a way, very fitting. Polling data suggest that a sizable majority of Russians are in favor of broad censorship controls; no doubt, this constituency would prefer not to see the Sun of Russian Poetry besmirched by his own youthful indiscretions.[25]

Obviously, the Nepomniashchii camp's take on *TB* is based in linguistic and aesthetic ideas of a nineteenth-century vintage. And the "Academy Pushkinists" in Saint Petersburg, especially Vadim Rak and Ekaterina Larionova, have long been fighting what seems to be a losing battle against Nepomniashchii's attempts to insist on an approach to Pushkin founded in Orthodox ideology, the anti-Semitic and xenophobic undertones of which are unmistakable.[26] Ironically, however, Nepomniashchii's "Moscow Pushkinists" are in essence reiterating the very same underlying convictions that led the "Academy Pushkinists" under Vatsuro at Pushkin House to publish *TB* as a separate, restricted volume: this "filth" is not fit for print.

Finally, we have the third camp, which believes that Pushkin was the author of *TB* and that it should be included in the jubilee edition. Obviously, Igor Pil'shchikov is the most prominent remaining exponent of these views and has published more on *TB* than anyone, including Tsiavlovskii. But Andrei Nemzer, a philologist turned journalist, sums up this position most succinctly:

> Scholarship [*nauka*] has its rights and obligations. The first of which is to not pull the wool over our eyes [*ne brosat' ten' na pleten'*]. If readers find some sort of abomination in Pushkin's works or, finding out about certain details of his biography and works, turn away from him in disgust – then that's the problem of readers who dreadfully misread and misapprehend [him]. And on whose leash scholars should not be walking.... Prudishness ... and the habit of pronouncing words which neither the speaker nor his addressee believe, as well as hoping for the Russian "*avos'*" (somehow, at some point, we'll figure it out) are characteristics of [Russian] society [and not of scholarship]. Characteristics which are constantly manifested in [Russian] politics, business, and journalism.[27]

For people in this camp, in the end of ends, what is at stake here is the purpose and character of Academy editions. To them, Academy editions are and should be for specialists, who then use them to pass the literary heritage such editions preserve and describe on to non-specialists in the form of popular editions for children and adults, as well as commentaries for schoolteachers and university professors, TV programs, radio shows, websites, and so on. Granted, this idea runs counter to Stalin's directive abolishing the narrative commentary from the 1937 jubilee edition, a directive that supposedly made Pushkin more directly accessible to the average Soviet Ivan Six-Pack (who, doubtless, spent hours poring over *Istoriia Pugacheva*), but that in fact only served to quash the most productive and promising branch of Soviet humanistic scholarship. At least among specialists, however, this seems to be the most widely held opinion of what Academy editions are for: to give the specialists what they need in order to educate the rest of us. And one of the things they need is a complete and full corpus of Pushkin's texts, which includes *TB*.

On the survey questionnaire, I included a question meant to give members of the first and second camps a chance to comment on the third: "How would you describe the motives of scholars who would like to see *TB* included in Academy editions of Pushkin's works?" In his reply to this question, Vadim Rak argues that the enthusiasm for attributing *TB* to Pushkin is part of a larger trend. "This is of a piece with the writers who saturate their language with *mat* and directors who saturate their films and theatrical productions with pornographic scenes. [This enthusiasm for indecency] was initially a manifestation of the intellectual liberation from totalitarian ideology that did not pass when it should have, but held on and grew into a boil on the body of literature ... inevitably including scholarship as well."[28]

Rak is not alone in seeing the scholarly dispute over *TB* as an important episode in the increasingly rapid fluctuation (he would say devolution) of Russian linguistic norms. Most of the popular discourse about *TB* touches on the idea that once Pushkin's foul mouth is officially sanctioned, the flood gates will open – or, at least, will be harder to close! And, as a result, there will be no remedy for the "boil" that Rak laments. Pushkin, surprisingly enough, remains *the* authority on the Russian language. For example, when Deputy Zhirinovskii staged a fairly ridiculous discussion on the status of *mat* in the Duma in 2006 (with predictably nationalistic and anti-intelligentsia overtones), he called upon the music producer Barri Alibasov to read a mildly scabrous passage from Pushkin's letters as proof that this is the "real Russian language."[29] So, Rak's fears are certainly not baseless.

As of this writing, the three camps – the Saint Petersburg Pushkinists, the Moscow Pushkinists, and what we might call the neophilologists – are still at odds over *TB*. Clearly, the positions of all three camps are politically inspired in one way or another, which might explain to some degree the extreme tendentiousness and volatility of the scholarly debate, as well as the unusually broad public interest in this rather arcane philological matter. In some respects, this political tension can be viewed as a natural historical outgrowth of the very same dynamics that made *Ruslan and Liudmila* such a scandalous text: it is an incursion of the "indecent" domestic discourses of sex and profanity into the spheres of society and state. Pushkin doubtless wrote "this filth" partly in order to win the favor and trust of his Lyceum classmates and cement the domestic social bonds between them, thus asserting the primacy of these bonds over those formed according to the rules of state and society. The effort to bring *TB* into the fold of the official canon is therefore a *shalost'* of the first order: it seeks to transpose a work from the domestic periphery to the state center, where it loses much of its meaning. As we have seen in many examples throughout this book, the regimes of Alexander I and Nicholas I greatly feared such crossing of lines and repressed it harshly. It may be that this hysterical and wrathful fear lives on in Russia's powerful today.

What is more clear is that the struggle over *TB* is a chapter in the troubling recent history of free speech in Russia. It is no coincidence that the *TB* controversy should flare up in the first years of the new century. Since the turn of the century, a clamping down on free speech (including, and perhaps even especially, academic free speech) has been underway in Russia. A sense that this is a crucial moment, and that the window of opportunity for publishing works like *TB* may be closing, engendered the urgency with which Pil'shchikov and his allies approach the issue. In Russia, as in any other developed nation, creative works that stretch the boundaries of free speech are vital as precedents to preserve it. In the English-speaking West, for example, we have to thank, in part, writers like William S. Burroughs and Henry Miller, who prevailed in grueling obscenity trials, for our (relative) freedom to use four-letter words in creative works – a freedom that played no small role in the massive shifts of cultural capital and power that characterized the latter half of our twentieth century. As Rak laments, many contemporary Russian authors (and artists, and musicians, and filmmakers, and stage directors) continue to stretch new and different boundaries of "decency" in new and different ways. Many of them have suffered consequences for this exploratory impulse in recent years. Without a doubt, they could work with much more writerly freedom were the organs of state, including Pushkin House, to recognize that Pushkin himself – whose authority even Vladimir Zhirinovskii recognizes – exercised such freedom to the extent and in the form he was able. *TB* is already to some a beacon and bulwark of free speech. If it is finally included in an officially sanctioned Academy edition, it would be more so.

Notes

Introduction

1. I discuss the provenance of this legend – which is now very widespread – in detail later. This story was first put to paper by Aleksandr Herzen in his memoirs, *Byloe i Dumy* (*Past and Thoughts*, 1852). His account is at least partly apocryphal – Herzen, for example, names the minister of popular education as Liven, who didn't take over from Admiral Shishkov until 1828. He also gets the date of the audience wrong. On the whole, though, Herzen's account has been amply corroborated. A. Gertsen, *Byloe i Dumy: Chasti 1–3* (Moscow: Khudozhestvennaia literatura, 1967), 1:157–60.

2. Ronald Hingley, *The Russian Secret Police* (London: Hutchinson, 1970), 30.

3. A. Arkhangel'skii, "Aleksandr Polezhaev," in *Russkie poety: Antologiia russkoi poezii v shesti tomakh*, ed. V. I. Korovin (Moscow: Detskaia literatura, 1996), www .litera.ru/stixiya/articles/631.html.

4. Gertsen, *Byloe i dumy*, 1:158.

5. D. Riabinin, "Aleksandr Polezhaev," *Russkii arkhiv* 1 (1881): 314–65.

6. P. Efremov, *Pamiati A. I. Polezhaeva: 16-ogo ianvaria 1838–1888 gg.; Biograficheskii ocherk po vnov' sobrannym materialam P. A. Efremova* (Moscow: Imperatorskii Moskovskii literaturnyi muzei, 1888).

7. I. Voronin, *A. I. Polezhaev: Zhizn' i tvorchestvo* (Moscow: Khudozhestvennaia literatura, 1954).

8. No doubt, as Vladimir Alexandrov notes, the premium put on the act of debunking and on dubious "interpretive novelty" in recent literary scholarship is counterproductive. See the introduction to his *Limits to Interpretation: The Meanings of "Anna Karenina"* (Madison: University of Wisconsin Press, 2004), 4–9. Accordingly, my goal in this book is not to debunk existing interpretations, but to reveal literary-historical facts long neglected in the scholarly literature for non-scholarly reasons, the "ethical considerations" referred to by one important editor (see E. Larionova's survey responses in my epilogue).

9. B. Eikhenbaum, "Literaturnaia domashnost'," in *Moi vremennik: Slovesnost', nauka, kritika, smes'* (Leningrad: Izdatel'stvo pisatelei v Leningrade, 1929), 82–86.

10. *Tolkovyi slovar' russkogo iazyka*, s. v. "domashnost'," http://feb-web.ru/feb/ushakov/ush-abc/default.asp.

11. See Joseph Peschio and Igor Pil'shchikov, "The Proliferation of Elite Readerships and Circle Poetics in Pushkin and Baratynskii (1820s–1830s)," in *The Space of the Book: Print Culture in the Russian Social Imagination*, ed. Miranda Remnek

(Toronto: University of Toronto Press, 2011), 82–107. See also I. Pil'shchikov, "O 'frantsuzskoi shalosti' Baratynskogo ('Eliziiskie polia': literaturnyi i biograficheskii kontekst)," *Trudy po russkoi i slavianskoi filologii, Literaturovedenie, Novaia seriia* 1 (1994), reprinted in *Tartuskie tetradi*, ed. R. G. Leibov (Moscow: OGI, 2005), 55–81.

12. Witness *Time* magazine's cover just after the World Trade Center attacks: "The Age of Irony Comes to an End" (http://www.time.com/time/covers/1101010924/esroger.html). See also Fred Inglis's take on postmodern pedantry and the death of irony: "A Better Class of Irony," *New Humanist* 118, no. 4 (November 2003), http://newhumanist.org.uk/657/a-better-class-of-irony-fred-inglis-novemberdecember-2003.

13. M. Shapir, "Barkov i Derzhavin: Iz istorii russkogo burleska," in A. S. Pushkin, *Ten' Barkova: Teksty, Kommentarii, Ekskursy*, ed. M. Shapir and I. Pil'shchikov (Moscow: Iazyki slavianskoi kul'tury, 2002), 397–457.

Chapter 1. Roots and Contexts

1. "By the way, dear Pushkin has been sent off to his father in the country for his recent *shalosti*. You know he was assigned to [Mikhail] Vorontsov, well then, the latter gave him an order which required that he depart without fail; he did nothing, and he composed a satire on Vorontsov. How do you like the boy now? I am certain that he will create new poems in his retreat that will be even more piquant." Institute of Russian Literature (Pushkin House), f. 33, op. 2, ed. 35, ll. 23–24, catalog no. 26427. In his Russian translation of this letter, Modzalevskii renders "folies" as "*shalosti*." B. Modzalevskii, "Pushkin, Del'vig i ikh peterburgskie druz'ia v pis'makh S. M. Del'vig," in *Pushkin i ego sovremenniki: Izbrannye trudy*, ed. B. Modzalevskii (St. Petersburg: Iskusstvo-SPB, 1999), 234.

2. A. S. Strudza, "Beseda liubitelei russkogo slova i Arzamas v tsarstvovanie Alekandra I i moi vospominaniia," in *Arzamas: Sbornik v dvukh knigakh*, ed. V. Vatsuro (Moscow: Khudozhestvennaia literatura, 1994), 1:54. In his book *Tvorchestvo Pushkina i problema publichnogo povedeniia poeta* (St. Petersburg: Giperion, 2003), Igor Nemirovskii documents Strudza's observation, arguing that Pushkin was exiled not for political reasons, but because of his erratic and provocative behavior.

3. P. Shchegolev, "Delo o zamechanii, sdelannom Kol. Sek. Al. Pushkinu v neprilichnom postupke v Kamennom teatre," *Byloe* 11 (November 1906): 53–56.

4. O. Proskurin, "Chto skryvalos' pod pantalonami," in *Poeziia Pushkina, ili podvizhnyi palimpsest* (Moscow: OGI, 1999), 306–8.

5. V. Pugachev, "Pushkinskii zamysel tsareubiistva vesnoi 1820 g. i Dekabristy," in *Individual'nyi politicheskii terror v Rossii, XIX–Nachalo XX v.*, ed. B. Ivanov and A. Roginskii (Moscow: Memorial, 1996), 5–16.

6. M. Buturlin, "Zapiski grafa M. D. Buturlina," *Russkii arkhiv* 5 (1897): 30. I quote from the first publication here, but a more recent, though somewhat lacking, publication now exists: *Zapiski grafa M. D. Buturlina: V dvukh tomakh*, ed. M.A. Poliakova (Moscow: Russkaia usad'ba, 2006).

7. Ibid., 29.

8. For example: Polish "szalec" means "to go crazy," szalic – "to drive one crazy." Serbo-Croatian "šaliti se" means "to joke," and "šala" is "a joke."

9. P. Mart'ianov, *Dela i liudi veka: Otryvki iz staroi zapisnoi knizhki, stat'i i zametki* (St. Petersburg: Tip. P. P. Golike, 1893), 1:3.

10. E. Raevskaia, "Vospominaniia Ekateriny Ivanovny Raevskoi," *Istoricheskii vestnik* 11 (1898): 229.

11. Mart'ianov, *Dela i liudi veka*, 1:34.

12. N. Romanov, "Zapiski Nikolaia I," in *Mezhdutsarstvie 1825 goda i vosstanie dekabristov v perepiske i memuarakh chlenov tsarskoi sem'i*, ed. B. E. Syroechkovskii (Moscow-Leningrad: Gos. Izd-vo, 1926), 10–35.

13. Iu. M. Lotman describes some of these episodes in "Bal," in *Besedy o russkoi kul'ture: Byt i traditsii russkogo dvorianstva XVIII–nachalo XIX veka* (St. Petersburg: Iskusstvo-SPB, 2001), 99–100.

14. M. Buturlin, "Zapiski grafa M. D. Buturlina," *Russkii arkhiv* 7 (1897): 354.

15. Ibid., 356.

16. Lotman, "Bal," 100.

17. Buturlin, "Zapiski," *Russkii arkhiv* 7 (1897): 354–55.

18. Ibid., 355.

19. Ibid.

20. Ibid., 356.

21. A. Zorin, "Pokhod v bordel' v Moskve v ianvare 1800 goda (Shiller, gonoreia i pervorodnyi grekh v emotsional'nom mire russkogo dvorianina)," *Novoe literaturnoe obozrenie* 92 (2008): 142–57, http://magazines.russ.ru/nlo/2008/92/.

22. Ibid., 144.

23. David Powelstock, *Becoming Mikhail Lermontov: The Ironies of Romantic Individualism in Nicholas I's Russia* (Evanston, IL: Northwestern University Press, 2005).

24. Powelstock first took up this idea in his "Living into Language: Mikhail Lermontov and the Manufacturing of Intimacy," in *Russian Subjects: Empire, Nation, and the Culture of the Golden Age*, ed. Monika Greenleaf and Stephen Moeller-Sally (Evanston, IL: Northwestern University Press, 1998), 297–324.

25. The political-historical tensions between these two types of freedom, revisited in our era by Berlin, fall outside my purview here. See Isaiah Berlin, "Two Concepts of Liberty," in *Liberty: Incorporating Four Essays on Liberty* (Oxford: Oxford University Press, 2002), 166–217.

26. Erving Goffman, "On Face Work," in *Interaction Ritual: Essays on Face-to-Face Behavior* (Garden City, NY: Doubleday, 1967), 5. I revisit this concept in considerably more detail in chapter 2.

27. Ibid., 12.

28. The Russian noun *privatnost'* is derived from the adjectival calque *privatnyi*, which has no relation to "private" in the primary sense of the English word, but denotes the quality of being "for pay" rather than provided by the state (meaning 2b under "private" in the *Oxford English Dictionary*). The meanings of this word seem to be multiplying in recent years, though they are not yet recorded in dictionaries, and one can now encounter collocations such as *politika privatnosti* (privacy policy).

29. Even the notion of "public opinion" was still a novelty in 1826, such that Faddei Bulgarin was forced to explain the idea at length in his denunciations that year. See chapter 4 for more on these documents.

30. Andreas Schönle, "The Scare of the Self: Sentimentalism, Privacy, and Private Life in Russian Culture, 1780–1820," *Slavic Review* 4 (Winter 1998): 726–27.

31. Ibid., 730.

32. William Mills Todd, *Fiction and Society in the Age of Pushkin: Ideology, Institutions, and Narrative* (Cambridge, MA: Harvard University Press, 1986). Jakobson's

model has, no doubt, been thoroughly misused and overused over the two decades since the publication of Todd's book. Nonetheless, it still works well for the Russian cultural specific. Formalist ideas about the autonomy of poetic language from natural language grow out of a peculiarity of the Russian language (the divide between spoken and written Russian) and can therefore be brushed aside easily enough in the non-Russian context (as in Mary Louise Pratt's *Toward a Speech Act Theory of Literary Discourse* [Bloomington: Indiana University Press, 1977]). Similarly, Jakobson's model of communication, which builds on formalist thought, is specifically Russian. Though neither Jakobsonian construct works very well for many other cultural traditions, they both remain productive frameworks for scholars of Russian literary history. As such, I think it entirely worthwhile to recover Jakobson's model from the doghouse to which recent theoretical fashion has expelled it.

33. Ibid., 6.

34. Eikhenbaum, "Literaturnaia domashnost'," 82–88; Iu. Tynianov, "O literaturnoi evoliutsii," in *Poetika, Istoriia literatury, Kino* (Moscow: Nauka, 1977), 279.

35. For an elegant and penetrating description of these norms and the other ways in which society asserted its independence, see Todd, *Fiction and Society in the Age of Pushkin*, 10–45.

36. Sam Driver, *Puškin: Literature and Social Ideas* (New York: Columbia University Press, 1989), 11.

37. Proskurin, "Chto skryvalos' pod pantalonami," 306–8.

38. Quoted in M. Lemke, *Nikolaevskie zhandarmy i literatura 1826–1855 gg. (Po podlinnym delam tret'ego otdeleniia sobstvennoi E. I. Velichestva kantseliarii)* (St. Petersburg: Tip. S. V. Bunina, 1909), 496. Nicholas refers to a ball at the French embassy in late August of 1830.

39. V. Sollogub, *Vospominaniia* (Moscow: Slovo, 1998), 38–39.

40. Ibid.

41. I. S. Belliustin, *Description of the Clergy in Rural Russia: The Memoir of a Nineteenth-Century Parish Priest*, ed. and trans. Gregory L. Freeze (Ithaca, NY: Cornell University Press, 1985), esp. 126–63.

42. Sollogub, *Vospominaniia*, 40.

43. Ibid., 38.

44. Ibid., 40.

45. Ibid.

46. See Irina Reyfman, *Ritualized Violence Russian Style: The Duel in Russian Culture and Literature* (Stanford: Stanford University Press, 1999), for a fascinating study of the nobility's need for and means of securing self-regulation and physical inviolability. The duel, she finds, was a mechanism for creating and sustaining both the corporate autonomy of society, as well as individual autonomy.

47. Shchegolev, "Delo o zamechanii." Around this same time, Pushkin refers to Gorgoli by name in his "Skazki" ("Fairy Tales," composed December 1818). A. S. Pushkin, *Polnoe sobranie sochinenii v shestnadtsati tomakh*, ed. M. Gor'kii et al. (Moscow: Akademiia nauk SSSR, 1937–1959), 2.2:70, http://feb-web.ru/fob/pushkin/texts/push17/vol02/y11 069 .htm?cmd = 0; hereafter *PSS*.

48. The same can be said of V. A. Nashchokina's memoir of Pushkin: "Rasskazy o Pushkine," in *Pushkin v vospominaniiakh sovremennikov*, ed. V. E. Vatsuro (St. Petersburg: Akademicheskii proekt, 1998), 234–45.

49. Long fingernails were at the time a violation of social propriety. In a section titled "On the Proper Manner of Conducting the Corpus," one etiquette manual

in wide use in the 1810s instructs the reader to trim his nails regularly – just after instructing him not to touch his genitals in public and to avoid blowing his nose while looking at the ceiling. *Pravila uchtivosti* (St. Petersburg: Tip. Mor. shliakhet. kadet. korpusa, 1779), 5. Pushkin's "claws" are often cited by his contemporaries as an example of his disregard for social convention. It was also, of course, a part of the dandy's uniform. On Pushkin and dandyism, see Driver, *Puškin*, 77–102.

50. A. Karatygina, "Moe znakomstvo s Pushkinym," *Russkaia starina* 7 (1880): 567.

51. M. Tsiavlovskii, comp., *Letopis' zhizni i tvorchestva Aleksandra Pushkina v chetyrekh tomakh* (Moscow: Slovo, 1999), 1:148.

52. "Iz rasskazov Kniazia Petra Andreevicha i Kniagini Very Fedorovny Viazem-skikh," *Russkii arkhiv* 2 (1888): 306.

53. This friendly reception did not stop Pushkin, however, from writing a fairly cruel epigram soon after Karatygina's theatrical debut in 1819, in which he ridicules her big feet (*PSS*, 2.1:110, http://feb-web.ru/feb/pushkin/texts/push17/volo2/ y21-110-.htm?cmd = 0). The two had a falling out over the epigram, which Pushkin attempted to ameliorate, in part, with his praise of Kolosova in "K Kateninu" ("To Katenin," composed 1821).

54. E. Baratynskii, *Polnoe sobranie stikhotvorenii v dvukh tomakh* (Leningrad: Sovetskii pisatel', 1936), 1:34–35, http://www.feb-web.ru/feb/common/doc.asp?0&/ feb/boratyn/texts/br1/br12034-.htm.

55. Ibid., 1:266, http://www.feb-web.ru/feb/common/doc.asp?0&/feb/boratyn/ texts/br1/br12266-.htm.

56. Quoted in P. E. Shchegolev, "Liubovnyi byt pushkinskoi epokhi," in *Liubovnyi byt pushkinskoi epokhi*, ed. S. Nikitin and S. T. Ovchinnikova, 2 vols. (Moscow: Vasanta, 1994), 1:194.

57. Quoted in B. Modzalevskii, "Kommentarii," in A. Pushkin, *Pis'ma*, 2 vols. (Moscow-Leningrad: GIZ, 1926–1928), 2:313.

58. Eikhenbaum, "Literaturnaia domashnost'," 83.

59. N. Karamzin, "Mysli ob uedinenii," in *Sochineniia*, 8 vols. (Moscow: Tip. Selivanovskogo, 1803), 7:327–28.

60. N. Karamzin, "Ot chego v Rossii malo avtorskikh talantov," in *Sochineniia*, 7:316.

61. V. A. Zhukovskii, "Pisatel' v obshchestve," in *Sobranie sochinenii: V chetyrekh tomakh* (Leningrad: Gos. izd-vo Khudozhestvennoi lit-ry, 1959–60), 4:400–401.

62. K. N. Batiushkov, "Nechto o poete i poezii," in *Sochineniia* (Moscow: Khudostvennaia literatura, 1955), 375.

63. Jorge Arditi, "Hegemony and Etiquette: An Exploration on the Transformation of Practice and Power in Eighteenth-Century England," *British Journal of Sociology* 45, no. 2 (June 1994): 181.

64. Ibid.

65. Batiushkov, "Nechto o poete i poezii," 374.

66. N. M. Karamzin, "Na grob moego Agatona," in *Sochineniia*, 7:7.

67. Zhukovskii, "Pisatel' v obshchestve," 4:397.

68. William Mills Todd, *The Familiar Letter as a Literary Genre in the Age of Pushkin* (Princeton, NJ: Princeton University Press, 1976), 54.

69. See, for example, Dmitrii Bludov's epigraph to Viazemskii's publication "Literaturnye arzamasskie shalosti": "Let us also recall, not without a smile, our – shall I say it? *literary shalosti*, if for no other reason, then because there was often much liveliness and wit in them." *Russkii arkhiv* 3 (1866): 473.

70. I. Pil'shchikov, "O 'Frantsuzskoi shalosti' Baratynskogo," 85.

71. Zhukovskii, "Pisatel' v obshchestve," 4:400.

72. A. Bestuzhev, "Moe znakomstvo s A. S. Griboedovym," in *A. S. Griboedov v vospominaniiakh sovremennikov*, ed. N. K. Piksanov (Moscow: Federatsiia, 1929), 135, http://feb-web.ru/feb/griboed/critics/vos29/bestu_29.htm?cmd=0.

73. A. Griboedov, *Polnoe sobranie sochinenii*, ed. N. K. Piksanov, 3 vols. (St. Petersburg: Imperatorskaia Akademiia nauk, 1911–1917), 1:211, http://www.feb-web.ru/feb/common/doc.asp?0&/feb/griboed/texts/piks1/proba11.htm.

74. A. Slonimskii, "'Gore ot uma' i komediia epokhi dekabristov (1815–1825)," in *A. S. Griboedov, 1795–1829: Sbornik statei*, ed. I. Klabunovskii (Moscow: Goslitmuzei, 1946), 60.

75. M. Zagoskin, "Molodye suprugi: P'esa A. S. Griboedova," *Severnyi nabliudatel'* 15 (1817): 124–29.

76. Griboedov, *Polnoe sobranie sochinenii*, 3:125, http://www.feb-web.ru/feb/common/doc.asp?0&/feb/griboed/texts/piks3/pi4_v3.htm.

77. See A. Reitblat, "Chtenie vslukh kak kul'turnaia traditsiia," in *Kak Pushkin vyshel v genii: Istoriko-sotsiologicheskie ocherki o knizhnoi kul'ture Pushkinskoi epokhi* (Moscow: Novoe literaturnoe obozrenie, 2001), 30–36.

78. Pil'shchikov, "O 'Frantsuzskoi shalosti' Baratynskogo," 85.

79. Cf. Mary Louise Pratt, *Toward a Speech Act Theory of Literary Discourse* (Bloomington: Indiana University Press, 1977), 109.

80. On the use of domestic poetics to fragment readerships, see Peschio and Pil'shchikov, "The Proliferation of Elite Readerships."

81. Quoted in Pushkin, *Ten' Barkova*, 309. Nabokov and other commentators mistakenly claim that Pushkin was the creator of this pun.

82. A. Pushkin, *Polnoe sobranie sochinenii* (Moscow-Leningrad: Akademiia nauk SSSR, 1937–59), 14:26. Unless otherwise indicated, all quotations of Pushkin are from this edition, with the notation "Pushkin, *PSS*, volume: page(s)."

83. Ibid., 27–29. See M. A. Tsiavlovskii, "Kommentarii," in Pushkin, *Ten' Barkova*, 214.

84. F. Bulgarin, *Vidok Figliarin: Pis'ma i agenturnye zapiski F. V. Bulgarina v III otdelenie*, ed. A. Reitblat (Moscow: Novoe literaturnoe obozrenie, 1998), 105.

85. In an article to which this book owes a great debt, Irina Paperno argues that this pun and others like it can be used to reconstruct the *spoken* language of circles like Arzamas. I. Paperno, "O rekonstruktsii ustnoi rechi iz pis'mennykh istochnikov (kruzhkovaia rech' i domashniaia literatura v pushkinskuiu epokhu)," in *Semantika nominatsii i semiotika ustnoi rechi: Lingvisticheskaia semantika i semiotika I* (Tartu: Tartu Riikliku Ulikooli Toimetised, 1978), 122–34.

86. See, for example, the title of O. Proskurin's chapter, "'Ego pero liubov'iu dyshit' Literaturno-polemicheskii kontekst poeticheskoi shalosti Pushkina," in his *Literaturnye skandaly pushkinskoi epokhi* (Moscow: OGI, 2000), 229–59.

87. The editors of the 1937 edition quite arbitrarily put the third and fourth lines in italics, presumably to underscore even more this performativity.

88. A. Del'vig, *Neizdannye stikhotvoreniia*, ed. M. L. Goffman (Petersburg: Trudy Pushkinskogo doma pri Rossiiskoi Akademii Nauk, 1922), 124. See Iu. M. Lotman, "Tekst i struktura auditorii," in *Izbrannye stat'i, v trekh tomakh* (Tallin: Aleksandra, 1992–93), 1:164.

89. Iu. Shcherbachev, *Priiateli Pushkina M. A. Shcherbinin i P. P. Kaverin* (Moscow: Imperatorskoe obshchestvo istorii i drevnostei rossiiskikh, 1913), 15, 16.

90. See O. Proskurin, "Transformatsiia zhanrov v poezii kontsa 1820-x godov," in Proskurin, *Poeziia Pushkina*, 231–33.

91. John Searle, *Speech Acts: An Essay in the Philosophy of Language* (Cambridge: Cambridge University Press, 1969), chap. 4.

92. Herbert H. Clark and Deanna Wilkes-Gibbs, "Referring as a Collaborative Process," *Cognition* 22 (1986): 1–39.

93. H. Paul Grice, "Logic and Conversation," in *Speech Acts*, Syntax and Semantics 3, ed. Peter Cole and Jerry L. Morgan (New York: Academic Press, 1975), 41–58.

94. Iu. Lotman, "K funktsii ustnoi rechi v kul'turnom bytu pushkinskoi epokhi," in Lotman, *Izbrannye stat'i*, 3:438.

Chapter 2. Arzamas

1. In English, see Todd, *The Familiar Letter as a Literary Genre*, esp. 38–64. For a roundup of English-language biographical entries on all the members of Arzamas, see 198–203. An extraordinary recent addition to this research tradition is Mariia Maiofis's *Vozzvanie k Evrope: Literaturnoe obshchestvo "Arzamas" i rossiiskii modernizatsionnyi proekt, 1815–1818 gg.* (Moscow: Novoe literaturnoe obozrenie, 2008), a remarkable book that has revolutionized our understanding of Arzamas. The most succinct history of Arzamas is V. Vatsuro, "V preddverii pushkinskoi epokhi," in Vatsuro, *Arzamas*, 1:5–27. The classic works on the subject are M. Gillel'son, *Molodoi Pushkin i arzamasskoe bratstvo* (Leningrad: Nauka, 1974); M. Gillel'son, *Ot arzamasskogo bratstva k pushkinskomu krugu pisatelei* (Leningrad: Nauka, 1977); Iu. Tynianov, *Arkhaisty i novatory* (Munich: Wilhelm Fink Verlag, 1967), 87–227. The preeminent Arzamas scholar of the 1990s, Oleg Proskurin, has published a great deal of seminal work on Arzamas. Much of it is to be found in his *Literaturnye skandaly*. His other publications on Arzamas include "Novyi Arzamas – Novyi Ierusalim," *Novoe literaturnoe obozrenie* 19 (1996): 78–129; "*Arzamas*, ili apologiia galimat'i," *Znanie – Sila* (February 1993): 55–62. A great quantity of primary materials is collected and annotated in Vatsuro's *Arzamas: Sbornik v dvukh knigakh*, first cited in chapter 1.

2. Proskurin has revised the dating of the last meeting of Arzamas to April 7, 1818, not September 1817. O. Proskurin, "Kogda zhe Pushkin vstupil v Arzamasskoe obshchestvo," *Toronto Slavic Quarterly* 14 (Fall 2005), http://www.utoronto.ca/tsq/14/proskurin14.shtml.

3. Bulgarin, *Vidok Figliarin*, 113.

4. Ibid., 54. On the ban, see E. Kholodov, ed., *Istoriia russkogo dramaticheskogo teatra v semi tomakh* (Moscow: Iskusstvo, 1977–1987), 2:239–40.

5. Quoted in Lotman, "K funktsii ustnoi rechi," 3:432.

6. V. Pushkin, "Opasnyi sosed" ("A Dangerous Neighbor," 1811), in Vatsuro, *Arzamas*, 2:137. In its original context, this exclamation refers to prostitutes and other bordello riff-raff who proclaim admiration for the play "Novyi Stern" ("The New Sterne," 1805), in which the author, Shakhovskoi, ridicules Karamzin. Some scholars have taken this parodic appropriation from Vasilii Pushkin's poetry as evidence of a rift between these "elder" Arzamasians and their junior compatriots. This is quite wrongheaded, however. In fact, parody was often a way to pay homage to one's literary friends and allies. To cite just one particularly self-evident example, Batiushkov's poem "Pevets vo stane slaveno-variagov" ("A Minstrel in the Camp of the Slaveno-Varangians," 1813), transposes the high diction of Zhukovskii's famous victory hymn

"Pevets vo stane russkikh voinov" ("A Minstrel in the Camp of the Russian Warriors," 1812) into the context of the low fiction of a Beseda meeting. In the high-versus-low dynamics of parody, then almost solely rooted in the neoclassicist distinction between mock-heroic and burlesque, appropriating Zhukovskii's diction serves to put him on a pedestal, and not to attack him.

7. For a stylistic treatment of galimatias, see O. Roninson, "O 'grammatike' arzamasskoi 'galimat'i': Funktsionirovanie russkoi literatury v raznye istoricheskie periody," *Trudy po russkoi i slavianskoi filologii, Literaturovedcheskie* 822 (1988): 4–17.

8. Vatsuro, *Arzamas*, 2:78. See also Gillel'son, *Molodoi Pushkin*, 56–59.

9. Proskurin, *"Arzamas*, ili apologiia galimat'i," 56.

10. See Proskurin, *"Arzamas*, ili apologiia galimat'i," and "Novyi Arzamas – Novyi Ierusalim."

11. Vatsuro, *Arzamas*, 1:107.

12. F. F. Vigel', *Zapiski*, 2 vols. (Moscow: Krug, 1928), 1:360–61.

13. Vatsuro, *Arzamas*, 2:7–10. In a letter to Aleksandr Turgenev, Viazemskii hints at the existence of an "Arzamas Table of Ranks." Vatsuro, *Arzamas*, 2:370.

14. This form became something of a tradition that was periodically updated. Some seventy-five years later, for example, Chekhov composed his "Literaturnaia tabel' o rangakh." A. Chekhov, "Literaturnaia tabel' o rangakh," in *Polnoe sobranie sochinenii i pisem*, 30 vols. (Moscow: Nauka, 1974–1983), 5:143.

15. Vatsuro, *Arzamas*, 1:438.

16. Ruth Amossy, "Ethos at the Crossroads of Disciplines: Rhetoric, Pragmatics, Sociology," *Poetics Today* 22, no. 1 (2001): 2. I draw extensively on Amossy's ideas about institutionally derived ethos in literary works.

17. P. A. Viazemskii, *Ostaf'evskii arkhiv Kniazei Viazemskikh* (St. Petersburg: Izdatel'stvo grafa S. D. Sheremeteva, 1899), 1:54.

18. Quoted in Gillel'son, *Molodoi Pushkin*, 41. On Olenin's circle and Arzamas, see Maiofis, *Vozzvanie k Evrope*, 103–6.

19. On this episode, see Maiofis, *Vozzvanie k Evrope*, 167–75. St. Petersburg State University has posted a marvelous site with the VOLSNKh protocols and other materials: http://www.lib.pu.ru/rus/Volsnx/. For a history of the group from its beginnings, see V. Orlov, *Russkie prosvetiteli 1790–1810-kh godov* (Moscow: Khudozhestvennaia literatura, 1950). For episodes from the rise to power of the Free Society's pro-Shishkov branch, see Proskurin, *Literaturnye skandaly*, 47–81 and 116–28.

20. On the various VOLSNKh-related journals and almanacs, see N. Mordovchenko, "Zhurnalistika nachala XIX veka," in *Istoriia russkoi literatury*, 10 vols. (Moscow: Akademiia nauk SSSR, 1941–56), 5:1:47–50.

21. See his letter to Viazemskii of December 20, 1811, in Vatsuro, *Arzamas*, 1:175.

22. Dashkov wrote a damning review of Shishkov's translations from La Harpe and his accompanying essay on language. The review appeared in the VOLSNKh journal *Tsvetnik* in 1810 (Vatsuro, *Arzamas*, 2:11–43). It is a broad-ranging critique of Shishkov's language politics, and quite salty.

23. For the text of the speech, see Vatsuro, *Arzamas*, 1:183–86.

24. Gillel'son, *Molodoi Pushkin*, 55–56.

25. Maiofis, *Vozzvanie k Evrope*, 166–67.

26. Vatsuro, "V preddverii pushkinskoi epokhi," in Vatsuro, *Arzamas*, 1:16.

27. See Severin's letter to Viazemskii of December 29, 1811, in Vatsuro, *Arzamas*, 1:176. See also Vasilii Pushkin's letter to same of December 20, 1811, ibid., 1:175–76.

28. Vatsuro, *Arzamas*, 1:186. Interestingly, it appears that three of Dashkov's allies

in VOLSNKh, who would later join Arzamas – Batiushkov, Severin, Zhikharev – actually voted in favor of his expulsion before leaving themselves.

29. K. Batiushkov, *Sochineniia v trekh tomakh*, ed. L. M. Maikov and V. I. Saitov (St. Petersburg: Tip. B. S. Balasheva, 1885–1887), 3:185, http://feb-web.ru/feb/batyush/default.asp?/feb/batyush/texts/pso/ps3/ps3.html.

30. Viazemskii's letter to Turgenev of April 4, 1812. Viazemskii, *Ostaf'evskii arkhiv*, 1:3.

31. Vatsuro, *Arzamas*, 1:189.

32. Ibid., 2:181–94.

33. Ibid., 1:175.

34. Ibid., 1:181. First publication: *Tsvetnik* 7 (1810): 92. Second publication: V. A. Zhukovskii, ed., *Sobranie russkikh stikhotvorenii, vziatykh iz sochinenii luchshikh stikhotvortsev rossiiskikh i iz mnogikh russkikh zhurnalov*, 5 vols. (Moscow: Universitetskaia tipogragiia, 1810–1811), 5:221. Like many epigrams of the period, this is an adaptation of a French epigram. See Vatsuro, *Arzamas*, 2:501. On the Western sources of Russian epigrams, see A. Dobritsyn, "Russkie epigrammy XVIII–XIX vekov i ikh zapadnoevropeiskie obraztsy," *Philologica* 7 (2001–2): 9–82.

35. "Literaturnye arzamasskie shalosti," *Russkii arkhiv* 3 (1866): 483.

36. On this episode and these epigrams, see Proskurin, *Literaturnye skandaly*, 84–104. See also Dobritsyn, "Russkie epigrammy," 52–53; and I. Pil'shchikov, "Viazemskii i Fontenel'," *Philologica* 7 (2001–2): 85–87.

37. M. Aronson and S. Reiser, *Literaturnye kruzhki i salony* (St. Petersburg: Akademicheskii proekt, 2001), 53.

38. Vatsuro, *Arzamas*, 1:368. Pushkin, however, did publish a significantly altered version a few years later. Vasilii Pushkin, "K ***," in *Stikhotvoreniia Vasiliia Pushkina* (St. Petersburg: Tip. departamenta narodnogo prosveshcheniia, 1822), 24–26.

39. Vigel', *Zapiski*, 2:62.

40. Gillel'son, *Molodoi Pushkin*, 43.

41. For a discussion of the British analogues to Arzamas, see Shearer West, "Libertinism and the Ideology of Male Friendship in the Portraits of the Society of Dilletanti," *Eighteenth-Century Life* 16, no. 2 (May 1992): 76–104.

42. See Lina Bernstein, "Women on the Verge of a New Language: Russian Salon Hostesses in the First Half of the Nineteenth Century," in *Russia, Women, Culture*, ed. Helena Goscilo and Beth Holmgren (Bloomington: Indiana University Press, 1996), 209–24.

43. See Vadim Vatsuro's study of this group, which was called "The Order of Friends of Enlightenment": V. Vatsuro, *S. D. P.: Iz istorii literaturnogo byta pushkinskoi pory* (Moscow: Kniga, 1989).

44. Todd's *The Familiar Letter as a Literary Genre* is the classic work on the subject. Since its publication, there has been no published work devoted specifically to the Arzamasian letters, a corpus that Todd estimates at over ten thousand texts. Over the last thirty-four years the epistolary style of individual Arzamasians has been the focus of only a handful of specialized works. Igor Pil'shchikov has published the following major contributions on Batiushkov's letters: "Ital'ianskie temy v pis'makh Batiushkova (1807–1820)," in *Batiushkov i literatura Italii: Filologicheskie razyskaniia* (Moscow: Iazyki slavianskoi kul'tury, 2003), 90–116; "Literaturnye tsitaty i alliuzii v pis'makh Batiushkova (Kommentarii k akademicheskomu kommentariiu 1–2)," *Philologica* 1 (1994): 191–201; "Literaturnye tsitaty i alliuzii v pis'makh Batiushkova (Kommentarii k akademicheskomu kommentariiu 3–4)," *Philologica* 2 (1995): 219–58.

R. Lazarchuk, who wrote extensively on familiar letters in the 1970s, has published a small article on Pushkin's letters: "Pis'ma A. S. Pushkina (K probleme genezisa prozaicheskogo stilia)," in *Materialy mezhdunarodnoi Pushkinskoi konferentsii: 1–4 oktiabria 1996 g.*, ed. N. L. Vershinina and L. A. Kapitanova (Pskov: Pskovskii gos. pedagogicheskii instituta,1996), 189–94.

45. Todd, *The Familiar Letter as a Literary Genre*, 11–12. See also his stylistic analysis of this letter on 136.

46. I quote the Shaw translation that Todd uses in his book, from *The Letters of Alexander Pushkin*, trans. J. Thomas Shaw (Madison: University of Wisconsin Press, 1967), 246.

47. Todd, *The Familiar Letter as a Literary Genre*, 135.

48. "The set (*Einstellung*) toward the MESSAGE ... is the POETIC function of language." Roman Jakobson, "Closing Statement: Linguistics and Poetics," in *Style in Language*, ed. Thomas A. Sebeok (Cambridge: MIT Press, 1960), 356.

49. Penelope Brown and Stephen Levinson, *Politeness: Some Universals in Language Usage* (Cambridge: Cambridge University Press, 1987), 61. I discuss Brown and Levinson's model in more detail later.

50. See Brown and Levinson's chart of strategies for positive politeness: *Politeness*, 102.

51. Ibid., 103.

52. Ibid., 107–12.

53. Todd, in *The Familiar Letter as a Literary Genre*, concludes that it was "simply a desire to play with the resources of the language, to enjoy themselves, and to write for the fun of it" (135) that motivated the Arzamasians' letter-writing behaviors.

54. For Zhukovskii's side of this correspondence, see Zhukovskii, *Sobranie sochinenii*, 4:527–56.

55. N. Gogol, *Sobranie sochinenii v deviati tomakh*, ed. V. A. Voropaev and I. A. Vinogradov (Moscow: Russkaia kniga, 1994), 9:361.

56. Zhukovskii, *Sobranie sochinenii*, 4:543.

57. Gogol, *Sobranie sochinenii*, 9:374–75.

58. Quoted in V. Zhivov, *Iazyk i kul'tura v Rossii XVIII veka* (Moscow: Shkola Iazyki russkoi kul'tury, 1996), 218.

59. Karamzin, "Ego Imperatorskomu Velichestvu, ALEKSANDRU I, Samoderzhtsu Vserossiiskomu, na vosshestvie Ego na prestol," in his *Sochineniia*, 1:260–65. In 1803, for example, the nobleman Nikolai Tolstoi (father of Iakov Tolstoi) uses *ty* in a petition to Alexander. Quoted in P. Cherkasov, *Russkii agent vo Frantsii: Iakov Nikolaevich Tolstoi, 1791–1867* (Moscow: KMK Tovarishchestvo nauchnykh izdanii, 2008), 17.

60. For example, in his "Otvet T-vu" ("Reply to Turgenev," composed 1813) and "Poslanie k T-vu" ("Epistle to Turgenev," 1815). Vatsuro, *Arzamas*, 2:217, 316.

61. Pushkin, *PSS*, 13:72.

62. Another aspect of this epistle bears noting: Pushkin is quite frank about Vigel''s sexual orientation. As with Arkadii Rodzianko, whom he dubbed "the Bard of Socratic Love" (see chapter 3), Pushkin uses this as a point of familiarity with Vigel'. (In fact, toward the end of the letter, he fills Vigel' in on potential sexual conquests in Kishinev.) Joking about sexual – or any other – deviance was a way to underscore the domesticity of the interaction, all the more so in this case because the epistle was clearly not intended for publication.

63. See his "K Dashkovu" ("А ты, мой друг, товарищ мой …"), 1812, in *Sochineniia*, 185; and "Poslanie k Turgenevu" ("О ты, который средь обедов …"), 1815, ibid., 254. Compare his letters to Dashkov (1817) and Turgenev (1819): Vatsuro, *Arzamas*, 2:361, 367.

64. That is, the twenty Arzamasians could potentially have corresponded with nineteen of their comrades. A "correspondence" here is defined as one or more letter between Arzamasians. Depending on the year it was written, even one letter can be sufficient to determine pronoun usage.

65. On the use of informal second-person pronouns to claim solidarity in T/V languages, see Roger Brown and Albert F. Gilman, "The Pronouns of Power and Solidarity," in Sebeok, *Style in Language*, 253–76. Clearly, Arzamas eschewed this means of building solidarity.

66. See N. Stepanov, "Druzheskoe pis'mo nachala XIX v.," in *Russkaia proza*, ed. B. Eikhenbaum and Iu. Tynianov (The Hague: Mouton, 1963), 74–101.

67. Todd, *The Familiar Letter as a Literary Genre*, 15. This cliché is the topic of Todd's chapter "Style and the Illusion of Conversational Speech," 134–56.

68. See Susan M. Fitzmaurice, *The Familiar Letter in Early Modern English: A Pragmatic Approach* (Amsterdam: John Benjamins, 2002), and also her "Like Talking on Paper? The Pragmatics of Courtship and the Eighteenth-Century Familiar Letter," *Language Sciences* 22, no. 3 (2000): 359–83; Douglas Biber and Edward Finegan, "Drift and the Evolution of English Styles: A History of Three Genres," *Language: Journal of the Linguistic Society of America* 65, no. 3 (1989): 487–517.

69. Quoted in Fitzmaurice, *The Familiar Letter in Early Modern English*, 17.

70. Quoted in Shtraikh's introduction to Vigel', *Zapiski*, 1:34.

71. K. N. Batiushkov, "Rech' o vliianii legkoi poezii na iazyk, chitannaia pri vstuplenii v 'Obshchestvo liubitelei russkoi slovesnosti' v Moskve. Iiulia … 1816," in *Opyty v stikhakh i proze*, ed. I. M. Semenko (Moscow: Nauka, 1977), 11, http://feb-web.ru/feb/batyush/texts/bop/bop-0082.htm.

72. B. Uspenskii, *Iz istorii russkogo literaturnogo iazyka XVIII–nachala XIX veka: Iazykovaia programma Karamzina i ee istoricheskie korni* (Moscow: Izd-vo Moskovskogo universiteta, 1985), 18.

73. Cynthia Lowenthal, *Lady Mary Wortley Montagu and the Eighteenth-Century Familiar Letter* (Athens: University of Georgia Press, 1994), 29.

74. Todd, *The Familiar Letter as a Literary Genre*, 146–52.

75. J. L. Austin, *How to Do Things with Words* (Cambridge, MA: Harvard University Press, 1962), 22. Jacques Derrida homes in on this statement in his attack on Austin's follower, John Searle. Jacques Derrida, *Limited Inc.* (Evanston, IL: Northwestern University Press, 1988). For Searle's reply to Derrida's initial deconstructions of speech act theory, see John Searle, "The Word Turned Upside Down," *New York Review of Books*, October 27, 1983, 78–80. This debate and associated issues receive an astute treatment in J. Hillis Miller, *Speech Acts in Literature* (Stanford: Stanford University Press, 2001).

76. Searle, *Speech Acts*.

77. Pratt, *Toward a Speech Act Theory of Literary Discourse*.

78. Todd, *The Familiar Letter as a Literary Genre*, 177.

79. Batiushkov, *Sochineniia*, 3:13. The translation is Todd's, *The Familiar Letter as a Literary Genre*, 180.

80. Viazemskii, *Ostaf'evskii arkhiv*, 1:55.

81. Ibid., 1:15.

82. Vatsuro, *Arzamas*, 2:349–50.

83. Ibid., 2:375.

84. Ibid., 2:376.

85. Ibid., 2:350.

86. Geoffrey Leech, *Principles of Pragmatics* (New York: Longman, 1983), 142–45.

87. Jonathan Culpepper, "Towards an Anatomy of Impoliteness," *Journal of Pragmatics* 25, no. 3 (1996): 352.

88. Ibid., 354.

89. Ibid., 352–53.

90. Vatsuro, *Arzamas*, 2:349.

91. Renate Rathmayr, "Métadiscours et réalité linguistique: L'exemple de la politesse russe," *Pragmatics* 9, no. 1 (1999): 75–95. Whether and to what extent these findings can also be applied to the contemporaries of Pushkin is, of course, another question altogether.

92. Richard J. Watts, *Politeness* (Cambridge: Cambridge University Press, 2003), 15.

93. In his *Politeness*, Watts calls into question the fundamental assumptions underlying Brown and Levinson's model, which he views as excessively "idealized." Brown and Levinson also come in for sharp and wide-ranging criticism in Gino Eelen, *A Critique of Politeness Theories* (Manchester, UK: St. Jerome Publishers, 2001).

94. Brown and Levinson, *Politeness*, 61.

95. Ibid., 66–68.

96. Ibid., 74–82.

97. Ibid., 69.

98. Ibid., 81.

99. Ibid., 228–30.

100. Ibid., 229.

101. Irina Reyfman describes Uvarov's fury at Odoevskii's obituary of Pushkin, where he coined the appelation "the Sun of Russian Poetry," in her article "Pushkin the Titular Counselor," in *Taboo Pushkin: Texts, Topics, Interpretations*, ed. Alyssa Gillespie (Madison: University of Wisconsin Press, 2012), 41–59.

102. On this scandalous episode, see N. V. Pertsov and I. A. Pil'shchikov, "'Bessmertnoe ponoshenie' (Ob odnom iz poslednikh burlesknykh opytov Pushkina)," *Philologica: Bilingual Journal of Russian and Theoretical Philology* 8, nos. 19–20 (2003–5): 57–90.

103. Vatsuro, *Arzamas*, 2:351.

104. S. Pereselenkov, "Materialy dlia istorii otnoshenii tsenzury k Pushkinu," *Pushkin i ego sovremenniki* 6 (1908): 8–18.

105. Zhukovskii, *Sobranie sochinenii*, 4:657.

106. Vatsuro, *Arzamas*, 2:559.

107. See Roninson, "O 'grammatike' arzamasskoi 'galimat'i.'"

108. Brown and Levinson, *Politeness*, 70.

109. Ibid., 60. Brown and Levinson list positive politeness as a super-strategy that people use when the "estimation of risk of face loss" is low. Of the ways to do an FTA, only "without redressive action, baldly" presupposes less risk.

110. Ibid., 70.

111. For a discussion of social distance, power asymmetry, and imposition as variables that can be manipulated independently, see ibid., 80–81.

112. Ia. A. Komenskii, *Pravila Blagopristoinosti:Dlia prepodavaniia obuchaiush-chemusia iunoshestvu* (St. Petersburg: Imperatorskaia tipografiia, 1792), 24.

113. Bulgarin, *Vidok Figliarin*, 113.

114. Zhukovskii, *Sobranie sochinenii*, 4:567.

115. Ibid., 569.

116. Ibid., 570.

117. Ibid., 569. Gnedich was the first Russian to translate the *Iliad* in hexameters, per Bludov's advice.

118. Viazemskii, *Ostaf'evskii arkhiv*.

119. I counted only "requests" that were on record. I also distinguished "rhetorical" imperatives (e.g., "Forgive me!" "Farewell!") from "actual" ones (e.g., "Deliver the enclosed letter to Pushkin." "Send me the copies." "Say hello to Batiushkov.") – actual requests being ones with a concrete, perceivable result; in other words, speech acts with a measurable perlocutionary act. I measured frequency by page rather than letter because the letters vary dramatically in length. As such, the expression of frequency is "requests per page" (on average, about 350 words).

120. Viazemskii, *Ostaf'evskii arkhiv*, 1:1–19.

121. Ibid., 1:36–66.

122. Ibid., 1:45.

123. Vatsuro, *Arzamas*, 1:270.

124. Ibid., 1:314.

125. Ibid., 1:316. Zhukovskii refers to Viazemskii's "Pis'mo s lipetskikh vod" ("A Letter from the Lipetsk Springs," 1815), a polemical counterattack on Shakhovskoi. Vatsuro, *Arzamas*, 1:248–52.

126. Ibid., 1:364.

127. Todd, *The Familiar Letter as a Literary Genre*, 113.

Chapter 3. The Green Lamp

1. F. Lialikov, "Studencheskie vospominaniia, 1818–1822," *Russkii arkhiv* 3 (1875): 385.

2. Quoted in B. Tomashevskii, *Pushkin*, 2 vols. (Moscow: Khudozhestvennaia literatura, 1990), 1:179.

3. "Vsepoddanneishee pis'mo Ia. N. Tolstogo ot 26 iiulia 1826 goda," published by Pavel Shchegolev in the appendix of his article "Zelenaia lampa," *Pushkin i ego sovremenniki* 7 (1908): 19–50.

4. "Zapiska Benkendorfa o tainykh obshchestvakh," appendix 1 in Lemke, *Niko-laevskie zhandarmy i literatura*, 576.

5. What some have described as Pushkin's "Green Lamp cycle" includes the poems "Stansy Tolstomu," "Iur'evu," "Shcherbininu," "Engel'gardtu," "Vsevolozhskomu."

6. There are three fundamental scholarly treatments of the Green Lamp: Shchegolev's "Zelenaia lampa"; Boris Modzalevskii's description of the Green Lamp archive, "K istorii 'Zelenoi lampy,'" in *Pushkin i ego sovremenniki*, 9–67; and Boris Tomashevskii's chapter in his *Pushkin*, 1:173–209. Two publications of texts from the Green Lamp archive – compiled, edited, and with commentary by Joe Peschio and Igor Pil'shchikov – are forthcoming in the journal *Pushkin Review* and the Fundamental Digital Library of Russian Literature and Folklore (feb-web.ru). These publications will make the entirety of the archive available.

7. A. Shebunin, "Pushkin i dekabristy: Obzor literatury za 1917–1936 gg.,"

Vremennik pushkinskoi komissii 3 (1937): 458. For a refuation of Soviet politicization of the Green Lamp, see Joe Peschio, "Lighting the Green Lamp: Unpublished and Unknown Poems," in Gillespie, *Taboo Pushkin*, 84–111. In it, I also survey poems from the Green Lamp archive by Pushkin, Tolstoi, Glinka, Rodzianko, Del'vig, Tokarev, and Dolgorukii. The sections on Rodzianko and Del'vig later in this chapter expand on some of the findings in this article.

8. Quoted in I. Nemirovsky, "Why Pushkin Did Not Become a Decembrist," in Gillespie, *Taboo Pushkin*, 61.

9. See historian Petr Cherkasov's fascinating new study, *Russkii agent*.

10. For the text of this letter and other relevant documents, see Shchegolev, "Zelenaia Lampa." In "K istorii 'Zelenoi lampy,'" Modzalevskii asserts that Pavel Kaverin, Mikhail Shcherbinin, Aleksandr Iakubovich, and Vasilii Engel'gardt were among these "suspected" members (10). Earlier Pushkinists also included Ivan Iakushkin.

11. M. Longinov, "Neskol'ko zametok o literaturnom obshchestve "Zelenaia lampa" i uchastii v nem Pushkina (1818–1820)," *Sovremennik* 4 (1857): 264–67.

12. *Arakcheevshchina* was the name critics of the authoritarian and often brutal army leader Aleksei Arakcheev gave the general air of oppression that characterized the late Alexandrine period.

13. Lotman, "K funktsii ustnoi rechi," 438.

14. Ia. Tolstoi, "K Emel'ianovke," in *Moe prazdnoe vremia, ili sobranie nekotorykh stikhotvorenii Ia. N. Tolstogo* (St. Petersburg: Tip. Karla Kraiia, 1821), 63–65; Ia. Tolstoi, "K Emel'ianovke," Pushkin House, f. 244, op. 36, ed. 33.

15. Iu. Lotman, *Pushkin* (St. Petersburg: Iskusstvo-SPB, 1995), 50.

16. O. Przhetslavskii, "Vospominaniia O. A. Przhetslavskogo (1818–1821)," *Russkaia starina* 11 (1874): 466.

17. Alexander's letter of August 1, 1822, published in Cherkasov, *Russkii agent*, 43–44. Before Alexander made it the law of the land, the practice of requiring suspected conspirators to sign such pledges had already been in force for a couple of years, and some Lampists had signed these pledges while the Green Lamp was still in existence. For example, in a letter of supplication to Nicholas I soon after the Decembrist Uprising, Iakov Tolstoi claims that he declined an invitation to join the Northern Society in 1821, "for I had signed a pledge to the government that I would not join any Masonic or secret societies." Quoted in Shchegolev, "Zelenaia lampa," 44.

18. Even Kiukhel'beker, a close childhood friend of two Lampists, Pushkin and Del'vig, knew little about the group. During interrogations after his arrest in 1826, Kiukhel'beker recalled, "I sometimes heard about the society of the Green Lamp, which existed in Saint Petersburg. As I recall, I was even invited to join it, which, however, I did not want to do because of the immoderate use of drink that supposedly reigned there." "Pokazanie Kiukhel'bekera v Varshave 19 ianvaria 1826 g.," *Russkaia starina* 7 (1873): 471.

19. See Tomashevskii, *Pushkin*, 1:175–76; and Lotman, "K funktsii ustnoi rechi."

20. This translates the text in the 1937 edition (*PSS*, 13:11), with the censored obscenities restored according to the text in the 1908 Saitov edition and cross-checked with the autograph (my thanks to Igor Pil'shchikov for his help with this). *Khuerik* (chancre) has been incorrectly restored by recent scholars as "tripper" (gonorrhea), thus masking the consistent repetition of *khui* (cock) throughout. From Shaw's translation of this letter, I have appropriated his rendition of the problematic *nizhnii prokhod* as "lower duct." For an interesting recent analysis of this letter, see Mikhail

Gronas, "Pushkin and the Art of the Letter," in *The Cambridge Companion to Push-kin*, ed. Andrew Kahn (Cambridge: Cambridge University Press, 2006), 132–35.

21. *PSS*, 13:15.

22. Publishing articles on the productions of Imperial theaters was banned from 1815 until new censorship regulations came into force in 1828. On the ban, see Kholodov, *Istoriia russkogo dramaticheskogo teatra*, 2:239–40.

23. Paperno, "O rekonstruktsii ustnoi rechi," 122–23.

24. Thomas Kavanagh, "The Libertine Moment," *Yale French Studies* 94 (1998): 79.

25. Leech, *Principles of Pragmatics*, 142–45.

26. Brown and Levinson, *Politeness*, 66–67.

27. This section, in part, builds on findings described in Joe Peschio, "Once More about Arkadii Rodzianko and Pushkin," *Pushkin Review* 8–9 (2005–6): 77–92.

28. For a bibliography of his publications, see B. Modzalevskii, "Rodzianko," in *Russkii biograficheskii slovar'*, ed. A. A. Polovtsov et al., 25 vols. (St. Petersburg: Imperatorskoe Russkoe Istoricheskoe Obshchestvo, 1896–1913), 14:295–97.

29. "RGB" stands for "Rossiiskaia gosudarstvennaia biblioteka," the Russian State Library, where this manuscript collection is housed. Arkadii Rodzianko, *Stikhotvoreniia, 1812–1840*, Manuscript Division, Russian State Library, f. 201, ed. 7.

30. A. Bestuzhev, "Vzgliad na staruiu i novuiu slovesnost' v Rossii," *Poliarnaia zvezda na 1823 god* (1823): 29.

31. F. Glinka, "K Pushkinu," in *Izbrannye proizvedeniia* (Leningrad: Sovetskii pisatel', 1957), 201–2.

32. Pushkin, *PSS*, 2.1:404; *PSS*, 13:128.

33. Pushkin, *PSS*, 10:52.

34. Modzalevskii, "Kommentarii," 1:274.

35. This entry reads, in part: "The love of boys was so common in Rome that it was impossible to punish this turpitude, into which almost everyone was rushing headlong. Octavius Augustus, that debauched murderer and coward who exiled Ovid, thought it fitting that Vergil sing the charms of Alexis; Horace, his other favorite, created small odes to Ligurine. Horace, who praised Augustus for reforming morals, speaks in his satires of boys and girls in the same way." Voltaire, *Dictionnaire philosophique, Portatif* (London, 1764), 21.

36. See, for example, N. Lerner, "Pushkin i Rodzianko," *Russkii arkhiv* 3 (1900): 145–48; A. Gruzinskii, *Russkaia mysl'* 11 (1908): 230–35; N. Somtsov, "A. S. Pushkin i A. G. Rodzianko," in *Khar'kovskii universitetskii sbornik v pamiat' A. S. Pushkina* (Khar'kov: Pechatnoe delo, 1900), 327–30.

37. V. Vatsuro, "Pushkin i Arkadii Rodzianka (iz istorii grazhdanskoi poezii 1820-kh gg.)," in *Vremennik Pushkinskoi komissii 1969* (Leningrad: Akademia nauk SSSR, 1971), 43–68.

38. Maiofis, *Vozzvanie k Evrope*, 32.

39. L. Ginzburg, ed., *Poety 1820–1830-kh godov*, 2 vols. (Leningrad: Sovetskii pisatel', 1972), 1:164.

40. RGB, 348.

41. RGB, 319.

42. This particular poem is reminiscent of Horace, *Odes* 1.6 and 1.9.

43. "Vstuplenie na prestol Imperatora Nikolaia I v zapiskakh gen.-leit. Mikhailovskogo-Danilevskogo," *Russkaia starina* 68, no. 11 (1890): 505–6.

44. "Aleksandru Ivanovichu Mikhailovskomu-Danilevskomu," in Ginzburg,

Poety 1820–1830 godov, 1:166–67. Judging from their correspondence, housed at Push-kin House, the two often socialized in the mid-1820s, borrowing books from one another, and so on.

45. Vatsuro, "Pushkin i Arkadii Rodzianka," 47.

46. Ibid., 48.

47. For more on this institution of Petersburg literary life in the 1810s and 1820s, see chapter 2. Saint Petersburg State University has posted a marvelous website devoted to the Free Society: http://www.lib.pu.ru/rus/Volsnx/istoria.html. The protocol from the August 8, 1818, meeting is to be found at http://www.lib.pu.ru/rus/Volsnx/prot/prot18.html.

48. See Peschio, "Once More about Arkadii Rodzianko and Pushkin," where this epistle was first published.

49. See Peschio, "Lighting the Green Lamp."

50. "Derzhavin," *Blagonamerennyi* 5 (1819): 201–8; "Poslanie k A. S. Norovu." *Blagonamerennyi* 13 (1819): 3–12.

51. P. Shchebal'skii, "Literator starogo vremeni," *Russkii vestnik* 11 (1871): 300–301.

52. Rodzianko, *Stikhotvoreniia 1812–1840*, Manuscript Division, Russian State Library, f. 201, ed. 7; *Bumagi obshchestva "Zelenaia lampa,"* Pushkin House, f. 244, op. 36, ed. 40.

53. Modzalevskii, "K istorii 'Zelenoi lampy,'" 41.

54. Vatsuro, "Pushkin i Arkadii Rodzianka," 48. There are, of course, only four books in *Odes*. This crude mistake, which Vatsuro repeated in a reprint of the article, and which is so out of character for this famously scrupulous scholar, makes me suspect he was purposely calling attention to this poem, which he could ill-afford to give a serious treatment given the political climate in which he was working and the Soviet taboo on homosexuality.

55. Pushkin, "Rifma," *PSS*, 3.1:240.

56. The history of homosexuality in Russia is a massively understudied subject and a huge can of worms that I can hardly treat in any detail here. Suffice it to say that sex among men was a capital offense in Russia and later the Soviet Union until 1993; de jure, it is still grounds for dismissal from posts in the government of the Russian Federation. Homosexuality only recently became a subject that can even be discussed in public in Russia. On homosociality and homosexuality in British familiar societies, see West, "Libertinism and the Ideology of Male Friendship," 76–104.

57. *PSS*, 3.1:388, http://feb-web.ru/feb/pushkin/texts/push17/vol03/y03-388-.htm. See chapter 2 for more on the context of this epigram.

58. On this family, see Sof'ia Vasil'evna Kapnist-Skalon, "Vospominaniia," in *Zapiski i vospominaniia russkikh zhenshchin XVIII–pervoi poloviny XIX veka*, ed. I. Moiseeva (Moscow: Sovremennik, 1990), 308–11. On the "cult of Troshchinskii" in the Kapnist circle and the impact it may have had on Rodzianko's political biography, see Vatsuro, "Pushkin i Arkadii Rodzianka," 45.

59. RGB, 398 and 88–90.

60. *Horace's Odes and Epodes*, trans. David Mulroy (Ann Arbor: University of Michigan Press, 1994), 188.

61. Ibid., 172.

62. I. Semenko treats the subject in her *Poety pushkinskoi pory* (Moscow: Khu-dozhestvennaia literatura, 1970), 143–56.

63. P. Viazemskii, *Stikhotvoreniia*, ed. L. Ginzburg (Leningrad: Sovetskii pisatel',

1958), 146. A similar trope figures in Pushkin's "Telega zhizni," in Pushkin, *PSS*, 2.1:306.

64. In its Green Lamp version: Modzalevskii, "K istorii 'Zelenoi lampy,'" 34; cf. A. A. Del'vig, *Polnoe sobranie stikhotvorenii* (Leningrad: Sovetskii pisatel', 1959), 101.

65. Pushkin, *PSS*, 2.1:87–88, http://feb-web.ru/feb/common/doc.asp?o&/feb/pushkin/texts/push10/vo1/do1-317.htm.

66. RGB, 42.

67. RGB, 104–7. It is possible that this poem was presented at VOLSNKh on December 19, 1818. According to the minutes, Rodzianko's friend Avram Norov read Rodzianko's poem titled "Poslanie k drugu." However, it is not possible to say for certain whether this is the same poem for, given the society's looseness with titles in the minutes, this title could have been given other poems as well, including the epistle to Norov discussed later.

68. RGB, 132–40. A. Rodzianko, "Poslanie k A. S. Norovu," *Blagonamerennyi* 13 (1819): 3–12. Over half the poem was cut to make it suitable for publication. Vatsuro interprets this epistle as a denunciation of erotic and humorous poetry. "In 1818 this erotic poet writes 'Epistle to A. S. Norov,' where, in total contradiction to his poetic reputation, he declaratively rejects hedonistic poetry and love in the name of wisdom, duty and friendship.... Rodzianko here presages the critical part of the Decembrists' literary programs." Vatsuro, "Pushkin i Arkadii Rozianka," 51–52. This is patently absurd, for, as Vatsuro knew perfectly well, Rodzianko continued writing "hedonistic" poetry for another two decades.

69. RGB, 133.

70. Ibid., 134.

71. Ibid., 140.

72. This is a central concept elaborated in Robert P. Maccubbin, ed., *'Tis Nature's Fault: Unauthorized Sexuality during the Enlightenment* (Cambridge: Cambridge University Press, 1987).

73. This trope was later echoed in Pushkin's *Ruslan i Liudmila* in a lyrical digression on the love life of chickens (Pushkin, *PSS*, 4:27–28.)

74. Del'vig, *Polnoe sobranie stikhotvorenii*, 122–23.

75. N. Karamzin, *Polnoe sobranie stikhotvorenii* (Moscow-Leningrad: Sovetskii pisatel', 1966), 195, http://imwerden.de/pdf/karamzin_polnoe_sobranie_stixotvoreny.pdf.

76. Ibid., 110.

77. Ibid., 150.

78. K. Batiushkov, *Polnoe sobranie stikhotvorenii* (Moscow-Leningrad: Sovetskii pisatel', 1964), 66, http://feb-web.ru/feb/batyush/texts/bat/bat-065-.htm.

79. On Derzhavin's Anacreontic poetry, see G. Makogonenko, "Anakreontika Derzhavina i ee mesto v poezii nachala XIX v.," in *Anakreonticheskie pesni*, by G. Derzhavin (Moscow: Nauka, 1986), 251–95.

80. G. Derzhavin, *Stikhotvoreniia* (Leningrad: Biblioteka poeta, 1957), 1:79–80, http://www.rvb.ru/18vek/derzhavin/toc.htm.

81. On these allusions, see Peschio and Pil'shchikov, "The Proliferation of Elite Readerships."

82. M. Saltykov-Shchedrin, *Pompadury i pompadurshi*, vol. 8 of *Sobranie sochinenii* (Moscow: Khudozhestvennaia literatura, 1965–77), 440.

83. A. Del'vig, *Neizdannye stikhotvoreniia*, ed. M. Hofmann (Petersburg: Gos. tip. Izmailovsk, 1922), 125.

84. Pushkin House, f. 244, op. 1, ed. 763, l. 1 [Previously cataloged as f. 244, op. 36, no. 14, l. 1].

85. Del'vig, *Neizdannye stikhotvoreniia*, 50; cf. A. Del'vig, *Polnoe sobranie stikhotvorenii* (Leningrad: Sovetskii pisatel', 1959), 100–101. For a description of the 1819 notebook, see Del'vig, *Polnoe sobranie stikhotvorenii*, 262.

86. Del'vig, *Polnoe sobranie stikhotvorenii*, 283.

87. See Peschio's "Lighting the Green Lamp" on this editing work.

88. It is slightly reminiscent of Horace's "bashful prostitute Lyde" from *Odes* 2.11, but the connection is tenuous and diffuse.

89. Pushkin, "Del'vig," *PSS*, 11:274, http://feb-web.ru/feb/pushkin/texts/push17/vol11/y11-273-.htm.

90. Evgenii Baratynskii, "Del'vigu," *Polnoe sobranie stikhotvorenii v dvukh tomakh*, 100–101, http://feb-web.ru/feb/boratyn/texts/br1/br12100-.htm?cmd=0.

91. Del'vig, "K Evgeniiu," in *Polnoe sobranie stikhotvorenii*, 129.

92. Pil'shchikov, "O 'Frantsuzskoi shalosti' Baratynskogo," 85.

93. Modzalevskii, "K istorii 'Zelenoi lampy,'" 33.

94. See Tsiavlovskaia's commentary to "K Shcherbininu," in *Sobranie sochinenii A. S. Pushkina v desiati tomakh* (Moscow: Khudozhestvennaia literatura, 1959–62), 1:568.

95. Shcherbachev, *Priiateli Pushkina*, 15, 16, 182.

96. This letter has a note from Pushkin and is now included in Pushkin editions. Puskin, *PSS*, 13:82, http://feb-web.ru/feb/common/doc.asp?o&/feb/pushkin/texts/push17/vol13/y132081-.htm. For a discussion of this letter, see Iu. N. Tynianov, "Pushkin i Kiukhel'beker," *Literaturnoe nasledstvo* 16–18 (1934): 351–55, http://feb-web.ru/feb/pushkin/critics/lit/lit-321-.htm?cmd=0. Tynianov writes: "The names Gerome, Fanni, Limperani remain unexplicated and are apparently connected with personages they encountered while traveling together in Western Europe" (355). However, he presents no evidence to support this proposition.

97. See, for example, his poem "K Lile," in *Sochineniia*, 1:204–6.

98. V. G. Belinskii, "O stikhotvoreniiakh g. Baratynskogo," in his *Vzgliad na russkuiu literaturu* (Moscow: Sovremennik, 1988), 170; E. Baratynskii, *Polnoe sobranie sochinenii* (St. Petersburg: Izd. Razriada iziashchnoi slovesnosti Imp. akad. nauk, 1914–15), 91, http://feb-web.ru/feb/boratyn/texts/bo1/bo120912.htm?cmd=0.

99. Karamzin, *Polnoe sobranie sochinenii*, 111 and 139, http://imwerden.de/pdf/karamzin_polnoe_sobranie_stixotvoreny.pdf.

100. Pil'shchikov, *Batiushkov i literatura Italii*, 105.

101. Del'vig, *Polnoe sobranie stikhotvorenii*, 69 and 102–3.

102. "K Batiushkovu," *PSS*, 1:72, http://feb-web.ru/feb/pushkin/texts/push17/vol01/y012072-.htm?cmd=0.

103. Baratynskii, *Polnoe sobranie stikhotvorenii v 2 tomakh*, 1:31. On this allusion, see Peschio and Pil'shchikov, "The Proliferation of Elite Readerships."

104. RGB, 42. The poem's first publication is earlier in this chapter.

105. N. Karamzin, *Pis'ma russkogo puteshestvennika* (Leningrad: Nauka, 1984), 216. Thanks to the anonymous reviewer for the University of Wisconsin Press for pointing out this usage.

106. F. Bulgarin, *Vospominaniia* (Moscow: Zakharov, 2001), 276.

107. K. N. Batiushkov, *Sochineniia v dvukh tomakh* (Moscow: Khudozhestvennaia literatura, 1989), 2:273.

108. K. N. Batiushkov, *Sochineniia* (Moscow: Khudozhestvennaia literatura, 1955), 124.

109. Pushkin House, f. 244, op. 36, ed. 15, l. 1 v.

110. A prostitute named Fanni, for example, is mentioned in Alphonse Karr's *Sous les tilleuls* (1832), one of Pushkin's favorite novels. And Ernest Feydeau's novel *Fanni* (1858) is about the corrupt morals of the midcentury French bourgeoisie.

111. An extensive search by myself and colleagues has revealed no evidence that Del'vig or his contemporaries knew of John Cleland's novel *Fanny Hill*, hence its absence from this list.

112. Pushkin, "Del'vig," *PSS*, 11:274, http://feb-web.ru/feb/pushkin/texts/push17/vol11/y11-273-.htm.

113. A. Lafontaine, *Priroda i liubov' ili kartiny chelovecheskogo serdtsa. S nemetskogo perevel I. Timkovskii* (Moscow: Moskovskaia universitetskaia tipografiia u Ridigera i Klaudiia, 1799). A copy of this extraordinarily rare book is housed at the Museum of the Book at the Russian State Library. See A. Grigor'ev, *Vospominaniia* (Leningrad: Nauka, 1980), 40.

114. J. Douglas Clayton and Natalia Vesselova analyze the connection, known to scholars since the early 1990s, in "Resexing Literature: Tsar Nikita and his Forty Daughters," in Gillespie, *Taboo Pushkin*, 224–38.

115. Denis Diderot, *The Indiscreet Jewels*, trans. Sophie Hawkes (New York: Marsilio, 1993), 191.

116. Ibid., 192.

117. Ibid., 194.

118. Ibid., 195.

119. Karamzin, *Sochineniia*, 1:98.

120. A. Zorin, "Batiushkov v 1814–1815 gg.," *Izvestiia AN SSSR: Seriia literatury i iazyka* 4 (1988): 376–77. Batiushkov was urging others to do the same. See his letter to Viazemskii in Vatsuro, *Arzamas*, 1:296.

121. Diderot, *Indiscreet Jewels*, ix.

122. "K vel'mozhe," *PSS*, 3, 1:218, http://feb-web.ru/feb/pushkin/texts/push17/vol03/y03-217-.htm?cmd=0.

Chapter 4. *Ruslan and Liudmila*

1. Leslie O'Bell, "Young Pushkin: *Ruslan and Liudmila* in its Lyrical Context," *Russian Review* 44 (1985): 139.

2. Proskurin, *Poeziia Pushkina*, 15.

3. A. Izmailov, " 'Ruslan i Liudmila' Poema v shesti pesniakh," in *Pushkin v prizhiznennoi kritike, 1820–1827*, ed. V. E. Vatsuro (St. Petersburg: Gos. Pushkinskii teatral'nyi tsentr, 1996), 74; A. Perovskii, "Zamechaniia na razbor poemy 'Ruslan i Liudmila,' napechatannyi v 34, 35, 36 i 37 knizhkakh 'Syna otechestva,' " ibid., 75; D. Zykov, "Pis'mo k sochiniteliu kritiki na poemu 'Ruslan i Liudmila,' " ibid., 82.

4. V. Belinskii, *Polnoe sobranie sochinenii*, 13 vols. (Moscow: Akademiia nauk SSSR, 1953–59), 7:358, 361.

5. Tomashevskii, *Pushkin*, 1:305.

6. On the impact of *RL* on prosodic evolution, see Tomashevksii, *Pushkin*, 1:323–26. On its impact on the Russian literary marketplace, see A. Reitblat, "Kak

Pushkin vyshel v genii (O literaturnoi reputatsii Pushkina)," in Reitblat, *Kak Pushkin vyshel v genii*, 58–60.

7. Pushkin, *PSS*, 4:280.

8. V. Koshelev, *Pervaia kniga Pushkina* (Tomsk: Vodolei, 1997), 8.

9. Tynianov, "O literaturnoi evoliutsii," 279.

10. Recent literary-historical accounts of how the Arzamasians approached the concept of a new national epos include: Koshelev, *Pervaia kniga Pushkina*, 27–34; N. Vetsheva, "Problema poemy v teorii i praktike arzamastsev," *Problemy metoda i zhanra* 10 (1988): 93–103.

11. Tomashevskii, *Pushkin*, 1:299–300.

12. See Vasilii L'vovich Pushkin's letter to Viazemskii of April 17, 1818. V. L. Pushkin, *Stikhi, proza, pis'ma*, ed. N. I. Mikhailova (Moscow: Sovetskaia Rossiia, 1989), 225–26.

13. Quoted in Modzalevskii, "Kommentarii," 1:201, http://feb-web.ru/feb/pushkin/texts/selected/pp1/pp13175-.htm.

14. Proskurin, *Poeziia Pushkina*, 54–55.

15. Koshelev, *Pervaia kniga Pushkina*, 7–12.

16. Ibid., 7.

17. Ibid., 8.

18. Vatsuro, *Arzamas*, 2:366.

19. Viazemskii, *Ostaf'evskii arkhiv*, 1:174.

20. Ibid., 1:191.

21. Quoted in Koshelev, *Pervaia kniga Pushkina*, 10. "Hope" here is a politically tinged word; the "green" of "the Green Lamp" is the color of hope.

22. Viazemskii, *Ostaf'evskii arkhiv*, 2:23–24.

23. Pushkin, *PSS*, 13:12.

24. Ibid., 13:15.

25. Viazemskii, *Ostaf'evskii arkhiv*, 2:37.

26. "Iz rasskazov Kniazia Petra Andreevicha i Kniagini Very Fedorovny Viazemskikh," *Russkii arkhiv* 2 (1888): 306.

27. P. Katenin, "Vospominaniia o Pushkine," in *A. S. Pushkin v vospominaniiakh sovremennikov v dvukh tomakh*, ed. V. Vatsuro (St. Petersburg: Akademicheckii proekt, 1998), 1:183.

28. Koshelev, *Pervaia kniga Pushkina*, 151.

29. Tomashevskii, *Pushkin*, 1:298.

30. Ibid., 1:307. Proskurin concurs that the style of *RL* is the style of the friendly epistle – a genre most closely associated in Pushkin's oeuvre with the Green Lamp in 1818–19. Proskurin, *Poeziia Pushkina*, 22.

31. Except where otherwise indicated, all citations of *RL* are canto and line numbers from the text published in *PSS*, 4:1–88. As an aside, I do not happen to agree with Tomashevskii: the image of the reader here carries none of the specific tropes associated with the Green Lamp.

32. Lotman, *Pushkin*, 52.

33. Quoted in Shchegolev, "Zelenaia lampa," 28.

34. F. Glinka, "K Pushkinu," *Syn otechestva* 38 (1820): 231–33.

35. For the story of this epistle's genesis, see B. Modzalevskii, "Iakov Nikolaevich Tolstoi," *Russkii arkhiv* 9 (1899): 593. For the dating, see Tsiavlovskii, *Letopis' zhizni i tvorchestva*, 1:144.

36. Ia. Tolstoi, "Poslanie k A. S. Pushkinu," in *Moe prazdnoe vremia*, 48–51.

37. Ia. Tolstoi, "K Pushkinu," Pushkin House, f. 244, op. 36, ed. 34.

38. Tomashevskii, *Pushkin*, 1:318.

39. J.-F. Jacquard [Zhakkar], "Mezhdu 'do' i 'posle': Eroticheskii element v poeme Pushkina 'Ruslan i Liudmila,'" *Russian Studies: Ezhekvartal'nik russkoi filologii i kul'tury* 1 (1994): 158–72.

40. O'Bell, "Young Pushkin," 141.

41. A. L. Slonimskii, *Masterstvo Pushkina* (Moscow: Khudozhestvennaia literatura, 1959), 208.

42. Lotman, "Analiz poeticheskogo teksta," in *O poetakh i poezii* (St. Petersburg: Iskusstvo-SPB, 1996), 110.

43. A. Slonimskii, "Pervaia poema Pushkina," *Vremennik Pushkinskoi komissii* 3 (1937): 201, http://feb-web.ru/feb/pushkin/serial/v37/v372183-.htm.

44. Reitblat, "Kak Pushkin vyshel v genii," 58–59.

45. One anonymous critic, for example, put this at the heart of his defense of Pushkin. See "K izdateliu 'Syna otechestva,'" in Vatsuro, *Pushkin v prizhiznennoi kritike*, 28–30.

46. Pushkin, "Oproverzhenie na kritiki," *PSS*, 11:144.

47. Naturally, there was also a huge Russian tradition of literature "not for print," which most educated males knew quite well.

48. Iu. Lotman, "Analiz poeticheskogo teksta," 112.

49. Ibid., 110.

50. Proskurin, *Poeziia Pushkina*, 36–51.

51. Pushkin, *PSS*, 13:42.

52. See L. Shlionskii, "K voprosu o definitivnom tekste poemy 'Ruslan i Liudmila,'" in *Pushkin: Issledovaniia i materialy*, ed. N. V. Izmailov (Leningrad: Akademiia nauk SSSR, 1960), 3:378–401.

53. This is an aspect of Decembrist ethics not commonly discussed in the scholarly literature: a Puritanical strain that was very much fueled by Christian devotion. In the twentieth century, Tomashevskii was the first to publish excerpts from Kutuzov's review, and he carefully skirted the religiosity so unbefitting a revolutionary.

54. N. Kutuzov, "Apollon s semeistvom," in Vatsuro, *Pushkin v prizhiznennoi kritike*, 93.

55. "Zamechaniia na poemu 'Ruslan i Liudmila,' soch. Aleksandra Pushkina," ibid., 73.

56. Tomashevskii, *Pushkin*, 1:302.

57. A. Marchi, "Obscene Literature in Eighteenth-Century Italy," in Maccubbin, *'Tis Nature's Fault*, 246.

58. See Kavanagh, "The Libertine Moment," 79–100.

59. I. Barkov, *Devich'ia igrushka, ili sochineniia gospodina Barkova*, ed. A. L. Zorin and N. Sapov (Moscow: Ladomir, 1992), 39–40. Barkovian subtexts (and, indeed, the eighteenth-century pornographic tradition in general) in nineteenth-century Russian literature is a huge topic, which it has become possible to study only recently. The most significant contribution on the subject to date is M. Shapir and I. Pil'shchikov's commentary in Pushkin, *Ten' Barkova*. On one Barkovian subtext in *RL*, see Proskurin, *Poeziia Pushkina*, 48–52.

60. "Zamechaniia na poemu 'Ruslan i Liudmila,'" 72.

61. This letter is quoted in Gillel'son, *Molodoi Pushkin*, 189. Dmitriev had used this line in his epistle to Mikhail Murav'ev back in 1803.

62. Pushkin noted the irony of this usage: "This verse became a saying. Note that

Piron (aside from his *Metromanie*) was only any good in those poems that one cannot even allude to without offending propriety." Pushkin, *PSS*, 6:272.

63. Pushkin, *PSS*, 4:280. Just who this "first-class" writer was remains unknown. Most likely, it was Pushkin himself. As such, we have three levels of parody: Dmitriev parodies Piron, and Pushkin parodies Dmitriev.

64. Lotman, "Analiz poeticheskogo teksta," 110.

65. Quoted in Koshelev, *Pervaia Kniga Pushkina*, 152. On the commercial history of *RL*, see Koshelev, *Pervaia kniga Pushkina*, 150–54; S. Gessen, *Knigoizdatel' Aleksandr Pushkin: Literaturnye dokhody Pushkina* (Leningrad: Akademiia, 1930), 32–36; N. Smirnov-Sokol'skii, *Rasskazy o prizhiznennykh izdaniiakh Pushkina* (Moscow: Vsesoiuznaia knizhnaia palata, 1962), 51–53.

66. Viazemskii, *Ostaf'evskii arkhiv*, 2:257.

67. Pushkin, *PSS*, 13:62. Point number 2 was not forthcoming. Pushkin expressed similar doubts to Viazemskii; ibid., 13:68–69.

68. Slonimskii, *Masterstvo Pushkina*, 211.

69. See Shlionskii, "K voprosu o definitivnom tekste."

70. This passage was cut from the now standard text of *RL* at 4.325. I quote here from Pushkin, *Polnoe sobranie sochinenii v desiati tomakh* (Moscow: Akademiia nauk SSSR, 1957), 4:503.

71. "Zamechaniia na poemu 'Ruslan i Liudmila,'" 73.

72. A. Voeikov, "Razbor poemy 'Ruslan i Liudmila,'" in Vatsuro, *Pushkin v prizhiznennoi kritike*, 68.

73. Clement Greenberg, "Avant-Garde and Kitsch," *The Partisan Reader* (1946): 378–89. It is in this article that he advanced his famous formula: the avant-garde imitates the processes of art; kitsch imitates the effect of art.

74. Ibid., 386.

75. N. V. Gogol, *Sobranie sochinenii v deviati tomakh*, ed. V. A. Voropaev and I. A. Vinogradov (Moscow: Russkaia kniga, 1994), 3:109.

76. M. Iu. Lermontov, *Geroi nashego vremeni*, ed. V. A. Manuilov and O. V. Miller (St. Petersburg: Akademicheskii proekt, 1996), 49.

77. Pushkin, *Polnoe sobranie sochinenii v desiati tomakh*, 4:501–2. This passage was cut from the second edition at 2.230.

78. "Zamechaniia na poemu 'Ruslan i Liudmila,'" 73.

79. O'Bell, "Young Pushkin," 141.

80. Voeikov, "Razbor poemy 'Ruslan i Liudmila,'" 58.

81. Proskurin, *Poeziia Pushkina*, 41.

82. Barkov, *Devich'ia igrushka*, 40.

83. Recall Sollogub's description of Kologrivov's mischievous jokes from chapter 1.

84. Jonathan Culler, *Framing the Sign: Criticism and Its Institutions* (Oxford: Basil Blackwell, 1988), 168.

85. Erving Goffman, *Behavior in Public Places: Notes on the Social Organization of Gatherings* (New York: Free Press of Glencoe, 1963), 3–4.

86. Voeikov, "Razbor poemy 'Ruslan i Liudmila,'" 58.

87. N. I. Mordovchenko, *Russkaia kritika pervoi chetverti XIX veka* (Moscow: Akademiia nauk SSSR, 1959), 145.

88. Ibid., 159.

89. Pushkin, *PSS*, 2, 1:106–7. Also known as "Platonizm."

90. In 1825, Pushkin decided not to include "Platonicheskaia liubov'" in his first poetry collection, and made a note on the manuscript: "Do not include [this poem],

for I want to be a man of morals." B. Tomashevskii and M. Tsiavlovskii, "Istoriia tetradi Vsevolozhskogo," in *Pushkin*, vol. 1 of *Letopisi gosudarstvennogo literaturnogo muzeia*, ed. M. A. Tsiavlovskii (Moscow: Zhurnal'no-gazetnoe ob"edinenie, 1936), 49.

91. See Vatsuro's commentary in *Pushkin v prizhiznennoi kritike*, 357.

92. Voeikov, "Razbor poemy 'Ruslan i Liudmila,'" 64. Viazemskii was incensed by this passage: "Every line toward the end of his [Voeikov's] review of 'Ruslan' is stupid. How dare he say, and not even *in jest*: 'Blush for having forgotten the respect due your readers.'" See his letter of September 24, 1820, in Vatsuro, *Arzamas*, 2:382.

93. Pushkin, *PSS*, 13:21.

94. Mordovchenko, for example, sees *RL* as part of "the struggle for Romanticism" and its critics as "reactionary Classicists." See his *Russkaia kritika*, 157–65. In this, he follows Tomashevskii. See Tomashevskii, *Pushkin*, 1:302.

95. On this Free Society (not to be confused with VOLSNKh, discussed earlier), see V. G. Bazanov, *Vol'noe obshchestvo liubitelei rossiiskoi slovesnosti* (Petrozavodsk: GIZ Karelo-Finskoi SSR, 1949).

96. V. Karazin, "Zapiska ministru vnutrennykh del Kochubeiu ot 2 aprelia 1820 goda," *Russkaia starina* 5 (1899): 278.

97. "Vospominaniia V. I. Panaeva," *Vestnik evropy* 9 (September 1867): 264. Curiously, Tadeusz Bulgarin used precisely the same language to describe the Arzamasians in his denunciations (discussed later). For example: "Главная характеристическая черта членов Арзамасского общества, по которой и теперь можно отличить их между миллионами людей, есть: чрезвычайно надменный тон, резкость в суждениях, самонадеянность" (The main characteristic trait of the members of the Arzamas Society, which still makes it possible to pick them out among millions of people, is: an extremely arrogant tone, an abruptness of opinion, cocksureness). Quoted in Bulgarin, *Vidok Figliarin*, 113.

98. N. Siniavskii and M. A. Tsiavlovskii, *Pushkin v pechati 1814–1837: Khronologicheskii ukazatel' proizvedenii Pushkina* (Moscow: Sotsial'no-ekonomicheskoe izd-vo, 1938), 12–23.

99. Viazemskii, *Ostaf'evskii arkhiv*, 2:23–24.

100. A common scholarly narrative would have it that Bulgarin did not become an informant until after the Uprising, but this view has been thoroughly debunked by Tat'iana Kuzovkina. See the first chapter of her dissertation, "Fenomen Bulgarina: Problema literaturnoi taktiki" (PhD diss., Tartu University, 2007). Published online by Tartu University, http://dspace.utlib.ee/dspace/bitstream/handle/10062/2911/ tatjana_kuzovkina_uus.pdf.

101. Bulgarin, *Vidok Figliarin*, 105.

102. Ibid., 114.

103. Ibid., 109. See chapter 2. Precisely this sort of rebellious behavior was very fashionable among university students of the early 1820s.

104. Ibid., 107.

105. Quoted in Koshelev, *Pervaia kniga Pushkina*, 152.

106. This is a commonplace of Pushkin scholarship. For example, *RL* is a pivotal moment in Reitblat's analysis of the evolution of Pushkin's reputation in his *Kak Pushkin vyshel v genii*.

107. V. Vatsuro, ed., *A. S. Pushkin v vospominaniiakh sovremennikov v dvukh tomakh* (St. Petersburg: Akademicheskii proekt, 1998), 1:158.

108. Viazmeskii, *Ostaf'evskii arkhiv*, 2:23–24.

109. Quoted in Koshelev, *Pervaia kniga Pushkina*, 161.

110. In an 1822 letter from Kishinev, he advises his younger brother, who was then coming out into society, to keep his mouth shut, avoid familiarity, think the worst of people until proven wrong, to conquer women by feigning disinterest, and so on. He concludes the letter: "Les principes que je vous propose, je les dois a une douloureuse experience.... Ils peuvent vous sauver des jours d'angoisse et de rage" (I owe to painful experience the principles I propose to you.... They can save you from days of anguish and rage). Pushkin, *PSS*, 13:50.

111. Tomashevskii, *Pushkin*, 1:272–74.

112. Robert Alter, *Partial Magic: The Novel as a Self-Conscious Genre* (Berkeley: University of California Press, 1975), x.

113. Susana Onega Jaén and José Angel García Landa, eds., *Narratology: An Introduction* (New York: Longman, 1996), 31.

114. Tomashevskii, *Pushkin*, 1:274.

115. "Zamechaniia na poemu 'Ruslan i Liudmila,'" 69.

116. A. Glagolev, "Eshche kritika (pis'mo k redaktoru)," in Vatsuro, *Pushkin v prizhiznennoi kritike*, 25–27.

117. Ibid., 27.

118. Culler, *Framing the Sign*, 168. Note that this is precisely the language Glagolev uses: "I am presuming the impossible possible."

119. See, for example, Mordovchenko, *Russkaia kritika*, 158; Tomashevskii, *Pushkin*, 1:302.

120. Brown and Levinson, *Politeness*, 67.

121. Ibid., 66.

Epilogue

1. V. Gaevskii, "Pushkin v litsee i litseiskie ego stikhotvoreniia," *Sovremennik* 97, no. 7 (1863): 155–57.

2. For a detailed account of this episode, see M. Tsiavlovskii, "Kommentarii," in Pushkin, *Ten' Barkova*, 169–71.

3. *Krasnyi arkhiv* 31 (1928): 171. See also N. O. Lerner, "Neizvestnaia ballada A. S. Pushkina 'Ten' Barkova,'" *Ogonek* 5, February 3, 1929.

4. V. Orlov, ed., *Epigramma i satira: Iz istorii literaturnoi bor'by XIX veka* (Moscow: Academia, 1931–32), 1:85.

5. "Neproshedshee vremia," *Ekho Moskvy*, June 4, 2006. Transcript available at http://anni-lj.livejournal.com/84471.html?thread=33015 (last accessed April 19, 2012).

6. E. Shal'man, "Vstupitel'naia zametka," *Philologica: A Bilingual Journal of Russian and Theoretical Philology* 3 (1996): 133–35.

7. One as yet uncorroborated version of what actually happened has the ring of truth to it. I. L. Feinberg attributes the disappearance of the page proofs and the manuscripts to the repression of S. B. Ingulov, the head of Glavlit, who was shot soon after accepting them. Everyone was simply too afraid to ask what became of Tsiavlovskii's work. I. L. Feinberg, "Istoriia nesostoiavsheisia publikatsii (Iz vospominanii I. L. Feinberga)," *LG Dos'e* 26, June 1990.

8. Shal'man, "Vstupitel'naia zametka," 134–35.

9. William Todd to the author, e-mail communication, October 5, 2007.

10. Iu. Lotman, *Pis'ma, 1940–1993* (Moscow: Shkola Iazyki russkoi kul'tury, 1997),

686. Quoted in I. Pil'shchikov," If Only Pushkin Had Not Written This Filth: *The Shade of Barkov* and Philological Cover-Ups," in Gillespie, *Taboo Pushkin*, 159–84. The translation is Pil'shchikov's.

11. Pushkin, *Ten'Barkova*.

12. I. A. Pil'shchikov and M. I. Shapir, "Eshche raz ob avtorstve ballady Pushkina 'Ten' Barkova,'" *Izvestiia RAN: Seriia literatury i iazyka* 64, no. 3 (2005): 41–52. It is this work that I would recommend as a starting point for readers interested in the particulars of the debate.

13. Vadim Rak, "O krizise akademicheskogo pushkinovedeniia i podmetakh velikikh pushkinistov," *Neva* 1 (2003), http://magazines.russ.ru/neva/2003/1/pak.html.

14. Unless otherwise noted, the quotations come from responses to the survey I conducted in 2007.

15. A. V. Dubrovskii, "Stikhotvornaia psevdopushkiniana (Issledovanie tekstov, pripisyvaemykh Pushkinu)" (Kand. diss., Institute of Russian Literature, 2007).

16. A. S. Pushkin, *Stikhotvoreniia litseiskikh let, 1813–1817*, ed. M. A. Tsiavlovskii, T. G. Tsiavlovskaia, et al. (St. Petersburg: Nauka, 1994), 511.

17. A. Pushkin, *Polnoe sobranie sochinenii v dvadtsati tomakh*, ed. N. Skatov (St. Petersburg: Nauka, 1999), 1:564.

18. E. Larionova and V. Rak, review of *Ten' Barkova: Teksty, kommentarii, ekskursy*, by A. S. Pushkin, ed. and comp. I. Pil'shchikov and M. Shapir, *Novaia russkaia kniga* 2, no. 13 (2002): 51–56, http://magazines.russ.ru/nrk/2002/2/rak.html.

19. Ibid., 52n3, italics mine.

20. See the official history of Pushkin House, "Otdel pushkinovedeniia," http://pushkinskijdom.ru/Default.aspx?tabid=68&PageContentID=13.

21. Mikhail Gasparov corroborates Proskurin's account in his *Zapisi i vypiski* (Moscow: Novoe literaturnoe obozrenie, 2008), 276.

22. For details on Nepomniashchii's published record, see Pil'shchikov and Shapir, "Eshche raz ob avtorstve ballady Pushkina 'Ten' Barkova,'" 41–42.

23. Viktor Esipov, "Okolo 'Teni Barkova,'" *Moskovskii pushkinist: Ezhegodnyi sbornik* 11 (2005): 22–61.

24. Irina Konaeva, "Pushkin kak vopros natsional'noi bezopasnosti," *Relga* 14, no. 116, September 16, 2005, http://www.relga.ru/Environ/WebObjects/tgu-www.woa/wa/Main?textid=612&level1=main&level2=articles.

25. Richard Pipes, "Flight from Freedom: What Russians Think and Want," *Foreign Affairs* (May–June 2004), http://www.foreignaffairs.com/articles/59887/richard-pipes/flight-from-freedom-what-russians-think-and-want.

26. See especially E. Larionova, review of *Sobranie sochinenii, tom pervyi*, by A. S. Pushkin, ed. V. C. Nepomniashchii, *Novaia russkaia kniga* 2 (2001), http://magazines.russ.ru/nrk/2001/2/larion.html.

27. Andrei Nemzer, "Ten' na pleten'," *Vremia MN*, August 7, 1999, http://www.guelman.ru/culture/reviews/1999-08-07/ten/.

28. He continues, rather pointedly, "As for foreign scholars, I suspect that when they insist on the publication of TB, they do not entirely understand just how dirty this 'work' is because Russian for them is a *learned* language."

29. Zhirinovskii also suggested to the plenum, which included such prominent linguists as Viktor Alekseevich Vinogradov, that the foreign word *tualet* (toilet) should be replaced with the more Russian *srannik* (shitter). For video of the session, see http://www.youtube.com/watch?v=WTZPOdJtzKg.

Index